FOREWORD BY ADRIAN ROGERS

ISLAM RISING

THE NEVER ENDING JIHAD AGAINST CHRISTIANITY

JIM MURK

BOOK ONE

21st CENTURY PRESS
PUBLISHING WITH PURPOSE
WWW.21STCENTURYPRESS.COM

ISLAM RISING: BOOK ONE
THE NEVER ENDING JIHAD AGAINST CHRISTIANITY
By Dr. James M. Murk
Copyright © 2006

Published by 21st Century Press

All rights reserved. No part of this book may be used or reproduced in any manner whatsoever or stored in any database or retrieval system without written permission except in the case of brief quotations used in critical articles and reviews. All Scripture quotations, unless otherwise noted, are from the HOLY BIBLE: NEW INTERNATIONAL VERSION®. NIV®. Copyright © 1973, 1978, 1984 by International Bible Society. Used by permission of Zondervan Publishing House.

Requests for permissions should be addressed to:
21st Century Press
2131 W. Republic Rd.
PMB 41
Springfield, MO 65807

ISBN 0-9766243-9-7

Cover: Lee Fredrickson
Book Design: Terry White

Visit our website at: 21stcenturypress.com

21st Century Press
2131 W. Republic Rd., PMB 41
Springfield, MO 65807

21ST CENTURY
PRESS
PUBLISHING WITH PURPOSE
WWW.21STCENTURYPRESS.COM

DEDICATION

To my dearest wife Donna, treasured companion and faithful partner in ministry— mother of 5, grandmother of 15—our legacy together, all dedicated to the Lord and serving Him.

ACKNOWLEDGMENTS

I am indebted to Dr. Stu Bundy, a dear friend and board member of Murk Family Ministries, Inc. for resolutely suggesting to me to translate my knowledge of Islam into a book. Also Dr. Kenton Beshore urged and prodded me to get it published.

I want to thank three of my granddaughters—Jessica, Brienne, and Brittany—and also my daughter Beverly for helping to proof read some of these chapters. Another friend of many years Professor Hobie Farrell also gave his advice on some chapters. Above all I am deeply grateful for the encouragement of all of my family, and also want to thank all our partners in this ministry for helping make this book possible. And a very special thanks to Bob and Polly Reese without whose prayers and exceptionally generous support this project might have taken a much longer time.

I am also grateful to Dr. James Combs, Provost of Louisiana Baptist University, who mentored me in tying together all my previous academic work in History, Anthropology and Theology enabling me to achieve the Ph.D.

TABLE OF CONTENTS

FOREWORD

I first met Dr. Jim Murk and his musical family team at the Continental Congress on the Family in St. Louis in 1975. They were an example of a Christian family serving the Lord.

My staff and I were impressed with their music, their message, and their dedication as a genuine ministry. They were not merely entertainment. They were not only inspired gospel singers, but each of the children was skilled on violin, viola, or cello. It was most unusual.

They had been serving each year for several years on some mission field sharing the Gospel with music. We decided we should invite them to Bellevue. They ministered with us every year for several years. We were always blessed with their music, and Dr. Murk's messages presenting each song were a wellspring of Godly instruction and exhortation.

Eventually four of the children married and are now all in their own ministries for the Lord sharing the Gospel with music in many parts of the world. Dr. Jim, his wife Donna, and their oldest daughter Beverly continued as a trio team. Beverly is a skilled Gospel concert violinist. She has recorded a worship album of violin with guitar called "Morning by Morning" (Isaiah 50:4), which is ministering all over the world by radio.

As a trio they joined our Bellevue mission to Romania in 1993. They had previously ministered in Latin America, Spain and Portugal and had learned to sing and preach in the languages. They have made several foreign language recordings. It surprised us that not only did they sing everything in Romanian, but Dr. Murk did all his speaking in the language as well.

In an intimate association of several weeks, I found Jim Murk to have a depth of Biblical and theological knowledge, which went beyond his calling as a minister of music. I learned that by the age of 23 he had earned three Master's degrees in history, anthropology, and theology and was a candidate for a Ph.D. at a major American university. Before his gospel ministry in music he had taught several years in Christian colleges.

Dr. Murk had begun to be greatly concerned with the rejection in America of our original Biblical foundation and values. He knew that many Christians were unaware of their heritage. He thus began to incorporate a message with his musical program on teaching about America's Biblical roots and how leftist liberals were seeking to distort and cover up these origins and change America into a completely secular society dominated by secular humanism and materialism. The introduction of new amoral values that perverted the original meaning of our Constitution was a great concern to him. He defended the Biblical or evangelical Christian position in hundreds of articles and letters copies of which he distributed at his concerts and seminars. Some of these are published on his website www.murkfamilyministries.org under "Jim's Articles."

Dr. Murk believed that America had been ordained by God with a special purpose in this world. (1) To show what a nation could become when based on Biblical principles, which were demonstrated in its founding documents and in the faith and vision of most of our Founding Fathers; (2) To send Christian missionaries to the nations which helped lay the foundation for the tremendous growth of

Christianity in the world today; (3) To be used by God to inhibit Satan's ambition to completely dominate all the nations of the Earth.

First of all, America defeated the pagan Hitler in his ambition to rule the world from Germany and destroy all Jews and confessing Christians. Next our nation became the principal bulwark against Communism, which aimed to change every nation into a Communist state with the goal of organizing the world into secular economic units where religion would be eliminated and even the concept of God would be rejected.

Now America has been the first to vigorously oppose radical Islam, which presents a danger to the entire world in its ambition to take over every nation either politically or by force and subject everyone to the will of Allah and shari'ah law. We know now that terrorist activities are much more than criminal acts. We have therefore declared War on Terror. As the last super power, America continues to be the only nation that stands in the way of Satan's effort to take over the world, this time using radical Islam.

In the last four years Dr. Murk has been teaching seminars on "What Christians Need to Know About Islam and Terrorism." He studied Islam in the graduate school of anthropology at the University of Minnesota and then taught Islamic Culture Sphere to students at Wheaton College many of whom were committed to missionary service.

This book covers many topics. Who was Muhammad and what are the core teachings of Islam? How does Islam differ from Christianity? Is Allah the same as the God of the Bible? What is Holy Jihad? Who are the terrorists, and what do they want from us? Is Islam a religion of peace, justice and tolerance as has been claimed? Comparisons are made between Jesus and Muhammad, the Bible and the Qur'an, Allah and the God of the Bible, and other basics in the teachings of Christianity and Islam. Also what is our responsibility as Christians toward our Muslim neighbors? Finally what does the influx of 4 million immigrants from Islamic nations mean for our American society? To what extent are we in danger from terrorism in America? What is being taught in their mosques concerning Israel, Christianity, Western culture and America? What does the Bible say about Islam and the Last Days? What does the revival of Islam mean for America, for Israel, and for the world?

This book is an outgrowth of Dr. Murk's study and teaching over many years. I believe that every concerned Christian should read it. We are, without any doubt, in the end times, and radical Islam may be Satan's final effort to take over the whole world and subject it to his will.

—Dr. Adrian Rogers
Senior Pastor Emeritus
Bellevue Baptist Church
Memphis, Tennessee

In memory of Dr. Adrian Rogers
1931-2005

INTRODUCTION

INTRODUCING THE BOOK—AN OVERVIEW

THE AMBITIONS OF ISLAMISM AS
A WORLD POWER

When historians look back on this day, they will have to conclude that the most empowering, dynamic, and influential happenings have been (1) the surging rise of militant Islam, (2) the incredible resurrection of Israel as a nation, and (3) the escalating expansion of grassroots Christianity all over the world. Israel and Christianity are presently in grave conflict with the rise of Islam, and, as the world looks on, one wonders who will endure.

Since 1914, Nazis, Communists and now Islamic fundamentalists (Islamo-fascists) have been inspired with the goal of world conquest and control. These systems are evil, but they can project a kind of reasonableness, a moral purpose, and even a "form of godliness." Nazis and Communists and Islamists have all claimed the moral high road. They have similarly justified any means to promote and impose their doctrines and social systems on others, seeking to extend their power and influence on the entire world. In the Bible this desire of men for global domination has always been presented as a goal in opposition to God.

All three of these movements have used the same techniques, employed similar practices, and followed many of the same principles: (1) They have practiced mass killing or murder of millions of inconvenient and innocent human beings; (2) They have cultivated the motivating force of hatred as a part of their philosophy and arsenal of weapons; (3) They have used propaganda, a euphemism for the "big lie," to excuse, confuse, persuade, and deceive their followers and their opponents; (4) They are all totalitarian systems seeking to impose their will on the world.

All extremists have a sense that they are the custodians of the moral right with the best answers to human problems. They seek therefore to forcibly impose their values on the rest of us. These include those on the extreme left in the Western world. These "secular fundamentalists" possess a totalitarian spirit. This is certainly true among leftists in America. They are guilty of promoting mass murder in the guise of abortion and euthanasia. They are also unabashed in their use of hatred and flagrant lying to advance their causes. Altogether these groups are part of an "evil cabal," and don't even realize it. They also support each other and have cooperated from time to time in their goals and tactics. (See David Horowitz, *Unholy Alliance: Radical Islam and the American Left*, Regnery Publishing, 2004)

The Bible identifies Satan as a real person, a fallen angel, who is the "ruler of the darkness" of this world. He is also called the "ruler of the kingdom of the air." The Apostle Paul says that it is this satanic spirit that dwells in the "children of disobedience" or in those human beings who choose to go their own way rather than the way of God the Creator. (Letter to the Ephesians 2:1-3) The Creator's will has been revealed to us through the prophets, apostles and Jesus Christ Himself. This was recorded and passed on to us in what we call His Word, the Sacred Scriptures. Later on in this Introduction we will expound further on this worldview and the premise of this book.

Satan's people—"the children of disobedience"—can appear to be rational and even good, but their plans are ultimately exposed in the light of day to be destructive because Satan is a hater, the "father of lies" and not a lover of truth or of mankind. By definition what is "destructive" we call "immoral". That which we call "moral" is what is "constructive." The true Creator God is "constructive" and therefore "good" by definition. He created everything and determines right and wrong with reference to Himself and to His will. Whereas the Creator God is "The Builder," Satan is called "The Destroyer."

Enthusiastic Christians want to evangelize, or win by persuasion, individuals in the world to the lordship of Christ who will someday return to cleanse the Earth and set up His Kingdom. Contrariwise, dedicated Islamists envision a military type takeover of all the nations of world and the restoration of a united Islamic super state called the Caliphate. This would be a theocracy with all men in subjection to Allah and his shari'ah law. It is the primary goal and motivating force behind fundamentalist Islam. Terrorism is just one of the tools they are using to try to achieve this goal.

Islam is a "johnny come lately" to the world of religion. In its infancy in the 7th and 8th centuries--632-732—Muslim armies coming out of Arabia conquered a huge area of the Middle East, swept across all of North Africa and up into Spain and even France. This expansion of Islam was later continued by the Ottoman Turks who defeated the Byzantine or Eastern Roman Empire taking Constantinople in 1453. All of these lands had been predominantly Christian. Four of the Christian patriarchates--Jerusalem, Antioch, Alexandria in Egypt, and Constantinople—came under Muslim control leaving Rome in the West as the only remaining major Christian metropolis.

Islam continued its expansion into Central Asia and Western China, down into India and eventually into

Malaysia and Indonesia as far as the southern Philippine Islands. This was all achieved primarily by military conquest, the forcible conversion of millions, and the slaughter of other millions of resistant pagans. Today Islam is the second largest world religion numbering over 1.3 billion adherents.

Islam, after her initial phenomenal expansion, gradually became dormant losing supremacy and was surpassed in power, world influence, and commercial success by Christian Europe and America. Since the First World War, however, Islam has experienced a significant revival driven by the orthodox or fundamentalist sects such as the Muslim Brotherhood in Egypt, Wahhabism in Saudi Arabia, and the Shiite Ayatollahs of Iran who wish to continue this conquest of all the world's nations begun almost 14 centuries ago. They are encouraged in this by the discovery of the great reservoirs of oil, which they have called Allah's treasure, and the resource for military power that it brings. What does this mean for today's world? How best can we understand it? What do we need to know about Islam and its potential threat for the future?

America and other western nations are in the midst of a worldwide conflict with this militant form of Islam, which claims that it is only being faithful to the truth of the Qur'an and to the teachings of Muhammad. Some are calling this struggle World War IV--the Cold War having been WWIII. This is more than simply a War on Terror. In all honesty, it is a war of Western civilization against a resurgent, militant, orthodox Islam called Islamism, whose followers and sympathizers are found within all the Muslim nations. Can this be true? Many have tried to assure us, including Muslims themselves, that Islam is a peaceful and tolerant religion and that Islamism is an aberration. So-called moderate Muslims, such as King Abdullah of Jordan, decry the outrageous behavior of their militant brothers.

Let us take a journey from the present into the past and then back to the present. Then let us also think about the future. With the availability of weapons of mass destruction, we have entered an age that has before this been pictured only in science fiction. Events portend gloom and doom, but the Bible suggests a happy ending for those who dedicate themselves to the Creator God. It is called "The Blessed Hope." I hope that all of our readers discover it.

What is Going to Happen?

Islam is not just a religion. Islam is a complete political, economic, social, educational and religious network with its own forms of governing, exercising law, teaching the young, and controlling society. Ideally the Islamic *ummah*, or community, encompasses all the Islamic nations together into one empire. It is called a Caliphate and seeks to reproduce the original organization of the Islamic culture sphere. Its leader is called the *Caliph*, meaning "representative" of Muhammad. The goal of Islamist idealists today is to restore this union of Islamic peoples and then extend its power and control over the entire earth.

In order to understand the rise of Islamic fundamentalism today, it is necessary to know the early history of the movement, the exact teachings of the Qur'an, which is the ultimate authority for Islamic belief and practice, and the teachings or sayings and accounts of Muhammad called the *hadith*, which comprise many volumes.

After 9/11 the atmosphere in America changed. It was as if we came out of a deep sleep, at least for a time. Old patriotic values surfaced and were combined with what used to be much more common in America--a religious concern. "God bless America" signs were all over the place. The ACLU seemed to cower in a corner. More than this, we began to look at the world in a new light. News of the Middle East was ever-present on TV, and the Arabs and Islam became a common topic of conversation. An article in *The National Review* said, *"The West realized that it knew little about the Arab world--in fact, dangerously little. Why do they hate us so? It seemed imperative to learn more about the Arabs--to learn, for example, what they were saying to one another. . The Arab world had always been dark this way; it needed to come into the light."* (5/6/2002, p. 33)

Frontline, the PBS TV information show, in June 2002 presented what to me was a very distorted picture of Islam as it relates to America. The most discomforting part about the program was a round table discussion between what seemed to be uninformed Christians and well-prepared Muslims from Chicago's south side. The Muslim leader made the assertion, "After all, we all worship the same god." Nothing, as we shall see, could be further from the truth.

I used to teach ethnology as it related to missions, as part of the Anthropology Department at Wheaton College. One of my courses, which I had drawn up and introduced to the curriculum, was called "The Islamic Culture Sphere." It was a subject I had studied in depth in graduate school when working on a Master's degree in anthropology. Right this minute I am looking at three copies (three different translations) of the Muslim holy book, the Qur'an (Koran) sitting on my desk. Believe me, among many other major differences between Islam and Judeo/Christianity is that Allah of the Qur'an and Jehovah (Yahweh) of the Bible--the God of Abraham, Isaac, and Jacob, the One whom our Lord Jesus called Father--are two very different beings.

This is a complicated story with its roots in centuries of history. The religion of Islam dates by their own reckoning from AD 622, the date of the Hijra—Muhammad's 200-mile flight from the sacred Arab city of Mecca to Yathrib. This town was later renamed Medina, meaning "the city of the prophet." Being persecuted in his hometown, Muhammad was welcomed in Yathrib, where he not only continued to exercise his calling as a prophet, but also became a political leader. From the beginning therefore there has been no separation of church and state in Islamic teaching.

Of the approximately 1.3 billion Muslims in the world probably about 200 hundred million are very serious conservative adherents to the strict teachings of the Qur'an. These literalists are being called fundamentalists or Muslim extremists, and the growing militancy of some of them is a threat to the very existence of Western civilization just as it was 1300 years ago. Millions of Muslims live in Europe where some have become a hub of violence, terrorism, and anti-Jewish activism. France has seen numerous attacks on synagogues and conflict with government edicts. Spain, Holland and Britain have experienced severe terrorists acts by bombings or assassinations.

The events of today are preparing the Middle East for the Great War predicted for the last days by Ezekiel (chapters 38-39) and many other prophets of the Old Testament. We now understand that there will be a confederacy of Muslim and other nations bent on destroying Israel and reconquering Jerusalem, considered Islam's third most sacred city. The only obstacle that might deter another all out Muslim attack upon Israel is the military might of the United States. The ability or commitment of the USA to defend Israel therefore must be neutralized.

I have been teaching this for five years; namely, that the power of America will be compromised in some way. My best guess has been that someday nuclear devices might be detonated in several of our major cities, e.g., New York, Chicago, Los Angeles, Miami, and Washington D.C. Recent credible news on the Internet is claiming that al-Qaeda has the bomb and may have smuggled some smaller nuclear units into our country. Many political, military, and business leaders today including former Secretary of Defense Cohen and financier Warren Buffet have said it is not a matter of if, but only a matter of when a WMD is triggered in this country. The United States is also trying to stockpile small pox vaccine and prepare for other possible biological warfare agents.

Islam has replaced Communism as the #1 enemy of Christian faith in the world. Of the ten nations most vigorously persecuting Christians today, eight are Islamic. This is part of the Muslim effort to Islamicize the world. They have once again become energized in trying to spread their religion. Many countries are open societies and practice freedom of religion which is an asset for Muslim evangelizing. There is minimal tolerance of other religions today, however, in most Muslim societies. No Christian missionaries are allowed in many Muslim nations where evangelism may be punished severely as in Saudi Arabia. In fact, if a Muslim would dare to become a Christian in many Muslim nations, he could very likely be executed or murdered just as Muhammad commanded.

Both atheistic Marxism and Islam are creeds deeply rooted in Satan's efforts to deceive mankind. Although seemingly poles apart in world view, they show some amazing affinities in social and economic philosophy. Their concept of human equality is similar. Much of Islamic economic teaching is also akin to socialism. Note the work of the Islamic philosopher Sayyid Qutb mentioned later on in this chapter.

As much as 30% of the Soviet Union is Islamic especially

in the Caucasus region and in Central Asia. The USSR had close relationships with Iraq and Iran and supported the Arab states against Israel in their major wars, supplying them with most of their arms. Muslims and leftist liberals including Marxists have shown their affinity also in their recent cooperation in demonstrations in Washington D.C. against Israeli treatment of the Palestinians.

The Background of Modern Islamic Fundamentalism

Wahhabism is the primary contemporary Islamic religious sect, which, more than any other movement, has fathered the radical, militant movement we call Islamism. It is named for a Muslim scholar and 18th century Arab teacher Muhammad ibn Abd al-Wahhab (1703-93). At that time Arabia and the rest of the Middle East were a part of the Ottoman Empire. The Ottoman Turks had conquered the eastern Roman or Byzantine Empire and occupied Constantinople in 1453, which they retained as their capital renaming it Istanbul. They controlled Turkey, part of the Balkans, and just about the entire Middle East until they chose the side of the Kaiser in the First World War and lost their empire.

After their defeat of the Ottomans, the Allies dismembered the empire and created the crazy quilt of nations in that area which exists to this day: Turkey, Iraq, Iran, Syria, Lebanon, Palestine, Jordan, Arabia, Kuwait, Qatar, Yemen, and other smaller states in the coastal areas of the Arabian Peninsula. Their boundaries, as in Africa, tended sometimes to be arbitrary divisions splitting tribes and nations. The very large Kurdish population, for example, was not united in a nation, which would have been natural, but was divided among Iraq, Iran and Turkey. This has resulted in continuing tensions and conflict ever since.

Abd al-Wahhab had taught a return to the purity of the Islam as practiced in the first three centuries—from the time of Muhammad to about 950. He was offended by the secularism of the Ottomans and urged the Arab peoples to emulate the Prophet and strictly adhere to the teachings of the Qur'an.

For centuries the Ottomans had been able to contain sectarian movements, such as the Wahhabites in Arabia. With the demise of the Empire, however, these Islamists supported by the Sunni tribe of Saud gained control of most of the territory of the Arabian Peninsula and replaced the Hashemites, descendants of Muhammad, as the protectors of the holy cities of Mecca and Medina.

In 1932 the Kingdom of Saudi Arabia was established by Abdul Aziz bin Saud. The teachings of the Wahhabi sect of Islam became a dominant influence in the new kingdom. This had far reaching implications for the rapid rise of militant Islam throughout the Muslim world.

Today Wahhabism has been exported throughout the world. With the backing of Saudi wealth, thousands of schools called madrassas have been established from the Philippines to America. Here untold numbers of Muslim youth are taught the Qur'an and absorb the harsh values of Islamic fundamentalism. Over 2000 of these Wahhabite schools in Pakistan produced the *talib*, meaning "seeker of truth" or "student." These young men trained in this literalist understanding of Islam were called the Taliban. They fought and gained control over Afghanistan after the defeat of the Soviet Union and provided a haven for Osama bin Laden. As a Wahhabite Saudi Islamist, bin Laden trained his terrorist al-Qaeda gangs in camps throughout that nation not only in the use of arms, but also in his religious philosophy.

After World War I there was a resurgence of militant Islam in several countries besides Arabia. Hassan al-Banna founded the Muslim Brotherhood in Egypt in 1928, a fore-runner of all contemporary militant Islamist organizations. It was initially a reaction to the secularization of Turkey by Kemal Ataturk in 1924. Its influence spread throughout the Islamic world. Both Yasser Arafat and Saddam Hussein were educated in Egypt and were influenced by the Brotherhood, which borrowed many ideas from the Italian fascists and the Nazis. It is no accident that Saddam Hussein modeled his Baath political party after the Nazi party in Germany and copied many of Hitler's ideas.

Out of this Muslim Brotherhood movement came the Islamist ideologist Sayyid Qutb who has been called "the brains behind Osama bin Laden." He was the best contemporary theorist of the new Islamism and has influenced the whole militant Muslim movement. He visited the United States after World War II and came to despise our culture and our country. He saw American liberty and democracy as violating the very heart and soul of Islam. Thinking he might find the best people among the practicing Christians, as the Qur'an actually suggests, he visited a church. He was shocked and disgusted to find that they were sponsoring a dance. This intimate mixing of the sexes enraged his Qur'anic code of morality.

Sayyid Qutb's most important book was *Signposts Along the Road*. He argued for a monolithic Islamic state or Caliphate achieved by however much violence was necessary. He wanted to see all national boundaries among Muslims abolished and the Caliphate resurrected over a new Islamic *ummah* or community of brothers. "The society he envisioned would be classless, one in which the 'selfish individual' of liberal societies would be abolished and the 'exploitation of man by man' would cease." It is amazing how close Sayyid's social and economic philosophy coincides with Marxism. Did they both have the same spiritual origin or author?

ISLAM'S PRESENCE IN THIS WORLD

Numbering about 1.3 billion adherents, Islam is the second largest religion in the world. It has a large majority in fifty-three different nations. Thirty of these are 87% or more Islamic. Most of these nations are found within the 10/40 (N. Latitude) window often pointed to by Christians as the most unevangelized area of the globe, reaching from Morocco in the West, across North Africa, through the Middle East and Central Asia, to Western China.

There is an Islamic population of 130 million in India, a majority of 96% in Pakistan, 85% in Bangladesh, 80% in Indonesia, which is the largest Muslim nation, 58% in Malaysia, and almost 4 million in the southern Philippine Islands. There are as many as twenty-four million Muslims in Europe, including Eastern Europe and the Balkans. There are about 5.9 million in France, three million in Germany, 1.7 million in Great Britain and almost 900,000 in the Netherlands. Each of these populations multiplies every year.

It is said that there are more mosques in England than churches. Paris is 20% Muslim, made up of mostly young people. In southern France there also are more mosques than churches. France is right now reacting against the religious presence of Islam in public life especially in the wearing of headscarves in public schools. Rotterdam in Holland, the home of the reformer Desiderius Erasmus who influenced Martin Luther, has become 40% Muslim. Malmo Sweden is now 50% Muslim, and it looks like the Swedes have lost this city.

Belgium, Sweden, Denmark, and Switzerland have substantial Muslim populations that are over 3% of the population. Muslims have said that of all the European nations, they expect Holland to become the first Islamic state. Hopes for this happening are now slim, however, because recent terrorist acts are causing the Dutch to rethink their extremely tolerant policies. It is estimated that with the disparity in birthrates between Europeans and Muslims, however, 50% of the children in Holland under the age of 18 could be of Muslim descent by the year 2020.

This Islamic presence in Europe has produced an active anti-Jewish sentiment and major demonstrations opposing the war in Iraq. It is very likely that the high percentage of Muslims in France and Germany influenced the foreign policies of those nations with respect to America's war against Saddam Hussein along with the corruption within the "oil for food program" of the United Nations. The recent bombing of trains in Spain certainly influenced a change in government and the pullout of Spanish troops from Iraq.

Finally there may be as many as four million who profess the Islamic faith in the United States or 1.5% of the population. Muslim leaders claim that there are about seven million Muslims in America; however, the most recent accurate statistics from the Religious Congregations and Membership survey of 2000, which came out September 20, 2002, counts 1.6 million practicing Muslims in America. This is based on actual mosque attendance. If this number is at least half of those who claim Islam as their religion, we come up with a more modest estimate of somewhat over three million. This is probably a more realistic figure at least for practicing Muslims.

THE PRESENT CONFLICT
A RENEWAL OF ISLAMIC MILITANCY

Two major developments in the past fifty years have brought Islam into the open as a major player in the modern world.

1. Oil was discovered on Arab lands in the Middle East. This incomparably valuable natural resource was explored by Standard Oil of California after an exclusive contract was granted to them by King Ibn Saud in 1933. A vast field of at least 260 billion barrels of oil and 225 trillion cubic feet of natural gas has made the Saudis spectacularly wealthy. Other major Middle Eastern oil fields were found in Iraq, Iran, Kuwait and smaller nations on the Arabian Peninsula. Some have called it "Allah's treasure," and some regard it as Allah's provision by which Islam can influence the entire world. Faithful Muslims believe that this provides Islam the opportunity and responsibility to continue their destiny of spreading Islam and Islamic law to every nation on earth, which began in the 7th century.

2. In 1948 Israel was declared a new nation on lands in Palestine. The decision of the United Nations to partition Palestine in 1947 had been summarily rejected by the Arabs. When Israel declared its status as an independent state on May 14, 1948, five Arab nations—Egypt, Jordan, Lebanon, Syria, and Iraq—immediately attacked the new Jewish nation with their armies. In what seemed a miraculous deliverance, each Arab army in turn was humiliated by Israel's much smaller forces.

The Arabs' traumatic defeat in the Six Day War in 1967 and their loss of Jerusalem, was the major cause of the reawakening that we now call Islamic fundamentalism. It has spread through the Muslim world like a fire. These militants are labeled by most of the world as extremists or radicals. They are committed to many of the original belligerent views expressed in the Qur'an, which teaches that the whole earth must submit to Allah and his law. To either convert or ultimately destroy the infidel, who will not submit to Allah, is part of this commitment. (See Sura 9:5 and the chapter "Holy Jihad.")

The Ayatollah Khomeini, religious leader of Iran after the revolution against the Shah in 1978, prophesied that it was Islam's destiny to conquer the world. Only the United States stands in the way of this goal. The USA was cast by him in the role of the "Great Satan" and must be neutralized. Israel, he said, is the "Little Satan" and must be obliterated.

The stated goal of militant Islam is to destroy Western civilization, Judaism, Christianity, Hinduism, Buddhism, all other religions and cultures and impose the "shari'ah" or Islamic law on all the nations of the earth. This would make the earth one great "ummah" or Muslim community where all could live in peace and prosperity under the rule of Allah. The peace that is extolled in the Qur'an, however, is a peace that only exists within the Islamic community. Contrary to a lot of current propaganda, Islam does not extend peace in general to the world or to anyone who will not submit his will to Allah. Most of those who live outside the great Islamic *ummah* comprise what is called Dar al-Harb or "The House of the Resistors" commonly called "The House of War."

Militant Islam has replaced Communism as our number one enemy. They both have had visions of world conquest. The Soviet Union and her satellite nations wanted to impose Marxist/Leninist socialism on all the nations of the earth. They believed that only under their kind of regime could the entire world prosper, become peaceful and thus fulfill its destiny. Their belief was based in a philosophy, which acted as a religion with atheistic secular humanism as its foundation. Mankind was the only god and could determine his own future. Instead of submission to the rules of a god like Allah, men must submit to the State, which would be superintended by a dictatorship of the proletariat in a classless society of equals. The details in Islam and Communism are different, but the overall goals and many of the beliefs concerning the organization and values of human society are the same. They are both satanic creeds.

Moderate Muslims are aghast at what is happening. They sincerely believe that Islam teaches a doctrine of peace and tolerance. They interpret the Qur'an as being tolerant of other religions and other cultures. They cite Sura 2:256, *"There shall be no coercion in matters of faith."* They see Islam as a positive good in the world with its emphasis on prayer, fasting, almsgiving and good works. Islamic fundamentalists are condemned as radical abusers of the teachings of Muhammad. Is this true? Which approach to the world is found in the Qur'an? Is Islam a peaceful religion? Can Islam be tolerant of other religions?

Every militant conservative movement in the history of Islam has sought to get back to what they believed were the true teachings of the Qur'an and Muhammad. Ultimately these teachings are very exclusive. They do not allow tolerance of infidels or unbelievers. Originally infidels, including Jews and Christians, were forced either to convert, or were killed, or were sternly supervised in behavior and taxed heavily for the privileges of living within the Islamic community. Pagans and idolaters, on the other hand, were always to be killed if they would not convert.

Jews and Christians are called "people of the book" or "people of an earlier revelation." This refers to the Bible, which Islam teaches is an earlier, incomplete revelation of Allah. The Qur'an says that some of the dedicated Christians are good people. (Sura 5:82) On the other hand, Muslims cannot be allied with them or be friends with them. (Sura 5:51, 56) They were required to pay a special head tax called the *jizya* for the privilege of living among Muslims. (Sura 9:29) Their status was called *dhimmitude*. They were on the level of "second class citizens." If the "people of the book," however, will not conduct their lives according to the *shari'ah* or Islamic law, they should also be killed. The Qur'an sometimes seems to contradict itself, but the preponderance of its teaching is against an unqualified tolerance. This certainly encourages enmity and not peace.

The Four Major Groupings of Muslims

According to a recent report on the BBC drawn from an analysis of the Rand Corporation there are four major groups in the Islamic culture sphere:

1. The Fundamentalists who utterly reject democratic values and western culture and wish to return all Islamic nations to Islamic law or the shari'ah and then to impose it on the rest of the world. The Taliban in Afghanistan are an example as are most of the Wahhabi sect and the militant radicals and terrorists today.

2. The Traditionalists who adhere to the Qur'an and the Hadith in opinion and spirit and are resistant to innovation, change, and modern customs and manners. They tend to reject westernized education and any western ideas, which cannot be easily adapted to their Islamic culture and religion. Along with the Fundamentalists they believe in the unity of the Islamic religion with the state, economics, education, and all aspects of cultural life. One might call them non-militant fundamentalists.

3. The Modernists want Islam to adjust to the modern world and become a part of the global economy to borrow the good ideas and practices from the rest of the world and make their contribution to its culture. This would include most of the political leaders of even Egypt and Pakistan and certainly Morocco and Indonesia and other less radical regimes.

4. The Secularists wish for a complete separation of church and state like Turkey, an Islamic nation where the clerics have been suppressed and a kind of democracy is practiced.

What is the relative strength of these four groups in Islam? It is wishful thinking to believe that the Modernists and Secularists have the edge. In recent years with the advent of the nation of Israel, the war with Russia in Afghanistan, and the intervention by the United States in Muslim nations, the balance of power is leaning toward the Fundamentalists and the Traditionalists although no one could with absolute certainty assess their strength in terms of numbers. To these external irritants one must add the influence of the growing, fervently evangelistic, militant harangues of clerics and mullahs in mosques and schools pushing the ideal of Holy Jihad all over the Muslim world and in other nations where they have immigrated. This is being called "extremism."

How do we define extremism? Is it the same as "literalism," or a firm belief in the truth of the Qur'an and Muhammad's teaching without equivocation or interpretation? According to Irshad Manji, a Canadian Muslim journalist, speaking to the Aspen Institute Conference in Berlin recently, literalism is not just widespread, but it is where most Muslims are in the world today. It is mainstream; it is "basic" Islam. He says,

"The key is to recognize that because literalism is mainstream in Islam today, the thin minority of Muslims who have any intention of engaging in terror are nonetheless protected by the vast majority of moderate Muslims who don't know how to debate and dissent with that proclivity."   (Quoted in Blankley, *The West's Last Chance*, p. 45.)

WHERE WE BEGIN
OUR BIBLICAL WORLD VIEW
PREMISES, AND PRESUPPOSITIONS

All human societies on Earth profess a belief in a spiritual or nonphysical world. Investigations by anthropologists have found that there is a universal spiritual theme in human cultures and have concluded, "Man has a religious need." There is no society existing today that does not have some kind of religion. All of these religions recognize a spiritual dimension, which is believed to be apart from the natural world, which we experience with our physical senses.

In academia today these beliefs are often classed as superstitious or unscientific. We can find, however, little evidence in the history of science and scientists that science or scientific discovery demands an exclusively secular anti-supernaturalistic point of view. This is a myth first promoted by the 18th century Philosophes of the Enlightenment, such as Diderot and Voltaire, that science and religion must always be at odds. Virtually all the famous scientists of the past believed in a Supreme Being and were very religious in outlook. The greatest of them all Sir Isaac Newton spent more time studying the Bible than the universe. Albert Einstein also believed in the world of the spiritual or what has been called the supernatural. Einstein said to the theologian and philosopher Martin

Buber in 1911, "What we physicists strive for is just to draw His lines after Him," and ten years later he said, "I want to know how God created this world. . . I want to know His thoughts, the rest are details."

This is the Judeo/Christian or Biblical worldview. A majority of scientists and scholars even today apparently acknowledge what we might call "the spiritual." A recent survey of 1646 American scientists at 21 research universities found that only one-third of these scientists said they did not believe in God. Also 76% of medical doctors did profess a belief in God and the spiritual. (*The Washington Times Weekly Edition,* August 22-28, 2005, pp. 1, 23)   Most scientists themselves therefore still believe that there is a world, or something out there, beyond our senses or even beyond what our best instruments can probe or measure. For want of a better descriptive word, the term "supernatural" has often been used to describe the vast area that seems hopelessly beyond the realm of our senses and outside the present scope of scientific investigation, but not of our rational thought and imagination.

If we all had the mind and viewpoint of God, however, everything would be natural. To God nothing is supernatural. By definition He is a part of everything and understands everything because He created it.

Man's Quest for the Infinite

Man has always had the capacity to achieve an amazing amount of knowledge and eventually discover the most complicated and remote mathematic and scientific truths when he put his mind to it. The conviction that this is possible actually goes all the way back to Genesis in the Bible where the Godhead says concerning man at the time of the building of the Tower of Babel, *"Nothing they plan to do will be impossible for them"* (Genesis 11:6). As a rational being with a fantastic computer brain, man has not yet probed to the limits of his abilities or potential knowledge.

The Greeks were great thinkers, mathematicians, and experimenters. Who knows how much early civilizations knew? The destruction of the great library of ancient knowledge in Alexandria was a tremendous loss to the world. Just imagine what we might have learned that the ancients had discovered!

An example of the fact that their understanding of scientific knowledge was far beyond anything we had imagined is the Antikythera Mechanism. This gear run machine, a virtual mechanical model of the universe, had been lost to posterity, but was discovered in an ocean wreck off the island of Antikythera at the bottom of the Aegean Sea. It has been dated to about 87 B.C. This very complicated assembly of gears was created by some unknown Greek genius possibly from the island of Rhodes in order to produce accurate measurements of solar, lunar and planetary motions. It has been called the first analog computer predating by over 1900 years Charles Babbage (1791-1871), whose invention of a calculating mechanism called Difference Engine No. 1 gave him the title "father of the computer." Knowledge accumulates and one generation builds on another. How much further would we be ahead today if ancient knowledge had not been lost?

So-called dispassionate secular inquiry, which denies the spiritual realm, does not create any better science or discoveries except in the mind of the secular atheist. The more man has probed and discovered about the nature of matter and the universe, the closer he has come to admitting that there must be dimensions beyond the material and the physical senses, and that behind all that we observe and experience there must exist a super intelligence.

The probability of the universe, the earth and man

being just chance occurrences, while taken for granted by the secular fundamentalist, is an emotional belief not based on objective, dispassionate reason. British astronomer and former atheist Fred Hoyle confirmed this a few years ago in an address to the British Royal Astronomical Society. He claimed that, in light of the current discoveries in biology and astrophysics, to believe that the universe, the earth and man all happened by chance is like suggesting that a monster tornado could go through a huge junkyard and come out the other side with a fully formed 747 airplane. The law of probability suggests that there is only a 1 chance in 10 to the 45th power (10,000,000,000,000,000,000,000,000,000,000,000, 000,000,000,000) that the universe could have come into existence with the necessary timing, structure and composition to allow the development of the Earth and man.

Recent discoveries in cosmogony and cosmology show there must be a super intelligence existing outside the universe that put all this together. In the Biblical revelation He is called the Creator God who exists in all the dimensions He has created. We are immediately aware of only three dimensions—length, breadth, and height—plus time. Theoretical physics has concluded, however, that there must be more dimensions, which we do not experience directly. Their present theories suggest that it took nine of these dimensions to bring the universe into existence. Some physicists suggest that there even may be parallel universes, which we cannot experience but nevertheless exist, coincident with the universe that we know. All we are trying to say is that even modern scientific thought accepts that there is a world out there beyond what we can directly experience. This is what the Bible calls "the spiritual," and what we, from our limited point of view, call "the supernatural."

Judeo/Christianity and Islam and the Supernatural

Judaism, Christianity and Islam all believe in the existence of a spiritual world. There is little we can call Muslim theology, but Muslims believe in the existence of one god, Satan, angels, jinn or spirits both good and evil, a final judgment, and the continuation of a soul-life after death in a Paradise or Hell.

The Biblical worldview teaches us that there is a continuing conflict in the universe—a dualism between good or the better, and evil or the worse. These are personified in God and his angelic hosts on the one hand and Satan and the demonic hosts, or fallen angels, on the other. Satan is pictured as an angel of light, a superior being created by God and in rebellion against Him, seeking to make himself equal to God or even to take the place of God the Creator.

Satan is pictured in the Bible as trying to mess up the Creator's plans from the very beginning—from the Garden of Eden to the temptations of Christ in the Wilderness and in Gethsemane, but God the Creator had a plan called a mystery (*musterion* in the Greek New Testament), which means "a secret." In spite of man's many failures, God gained the victory for all of us over Satan with the crucifixion of Jesus the Christ. Here, Satan in scheming to kill Jesus, was unmasked before the entire universe for the duplicitous, hating, scheming, and lying being that he is.

The Bible teaches that Jesus is the human expression of God the Creator—God in the flesh, or God incarnate. *"Through Him all things were made; without Him nothing was made that has been made."* (John 1:3) Jesus said, *"He that has seen me has seen the Father. . I and my Father are One."* (John 14:9-11 and 10:30) He is the *"I am who I am"*—Jehovah or Yahweh of the Old Testament (Exodus 3:14)--a name that is used over 7,000 times to designate the Creator God who communicates with human beings.

This was all confirmed by God the Father in the resurrection. The resurrection declared Jesus to be the Son of God and assures our personal salvation and the eventual redemption of the entire universe. This also heralded Satan's ultimate defeat and eventual elimination as the enemy of mankind.

I would like to show in this book why, from all my study and observation, I have come to view Islam as Satan's major effort to replace Judeo/Christianity, and why the Qur'an, which denies that Jesus was either crucified or resurrected, is Satan's substitute for the Bible.

Jews and Christians, together and separately, have both become the special object of Satan's wrath. Militant Islamists therefore are demonstrating a malevolent, almost pathological hatred of Jews and Christians and are seeking to destroy them whenever and wherever they can in many parts of the world. Muhammad taught that Jews and Christians were "people of the earlier revelation" of Allah, but that this original revelation of God to man was tarnished or corrupted by them. He was especially antagonized by the Jews because they resisted and scorned his teachings and role as a prophet in Medina. He proclaimed that all Jews must die before the Day of Resurrection could take place. The implications of this teaching for the conflict in the Middle East are titanic.

In this first volume, *Islam Rising, Part 1,* we will examine the history and doctrines of Islam, the life and teachings of Muhammad, the Qur'an, the god Allah, Holy Jihad, and the relationship of Muslims to Christianity. Later, in a second volume *Islam Rising, Part 2,* we will examine the history of Islam and the Jews, including the five Arab/Israeli wars and the grave conflicts called the Intifadas that have arisen over the new State of Israel, and all the attempts for peace. Then what is Islam's relationship to America? What is the impact of the Iraq war and President George W. Bush's vision for the establishment of democracy and freedom in the Middle East? Finally, in Part 2, we shall try to find out if the prophecies of the Bible have anything to say about Islam in the last days. What kind of future does the world have to look forward to in light of the reawakening of this new militant, fundamentalist Islam?

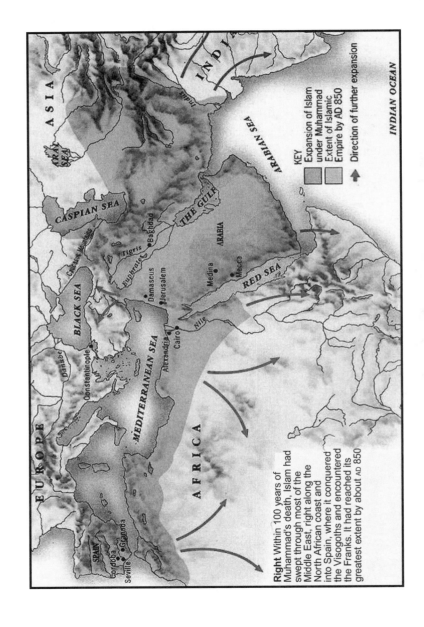

Right Within 100 years of Muhammad's death, Islam had swept through most of the Middle East, right along the North African coast and into Spain, where it conquered the Visogoths and encountered the Franks. It had reached its greatest extent by about AD 850

Chapter 1

MUHAMMAD

WHO WAS MUHAMMAD?

An Historical Outline

570   Born in Mecca\Quraysh tribe\His father is Abdallah\Orphaned\Raised by Uncle Talib\Trained to be Merchant\Camel driver with trade caravans to Syria

595   Married Khadijah\Wealthy widow\Ran her market in the city square\A religious man\Spent time in caves in fasting and meditation

610   Month of Ramadan\Claimed revelation from Gabriel\Called to be a "warner" and prophet\ rejected by the Quraysh in Mecca

619   Khadijah dies\Muhammad in poverty\Preaches one god, judgment, equality, giving to the poor, daily prayer\Begins to take many wives including 9 year old Aisha

622   The Hijra—flight to Yathrib (Medina) with 150 followers. This event is regarded as the beginning of Islam. Muhammad becomes a political leader ruling in Medina ("the city of the prophet")\ Raises several armies to fight the Meccans

622-628 Raids over 50 caravans for booty\Executes over 700 Jews and confiscates their goods, wives and children\ Becomes wealthy\Fights several wars\Declares 10 year truce in 628—called the truce of Hudaybiyyah

630   Muhammad breaks the truce and attacks Mecca
         with 10,000 men forcing all to accept Islam\Destroys
         idols of Ka'aba\Subdues all of Arabia to Islam

610-632 The Qur'an (recitations) are recorded by
         Muhammad's followers

632   Muhammad dies at 62 years of age after returning
         from a pilgrimage (*hajj*) to Mecca.

The Origins of Muhammad's Life and His Religion

Muhammad ibn Abdallah was born in Mecca in the Hijaz or eastern Arabia in 570, five hundred years after the destruction of Jerusalem by the Romans. His father, whose name means "servant of Allah," died before he was born. His mother Amina died when he was six, and his grandfather Abdel Mutaleb took responsibility for his care.

Two years later when his grandfather died, Muhammad was taken into the family of his uncle Abu Talib. His family was part of the most numerous and powerful of the Arab tribes, the Quraysh. Mecca had been a sacred city to the Arabs for generations, and many of the Quraysh had become rich by supplying the needs of pilgrims who came from all over Arabia to visit the shrine of al-Ka'aba.

The Quraysh were custodians of this cube-shaped building, which housed a hallowed black stone, probably a meteorite, which for generations had been held sacred by the Arabs before the time of Muhammad. They were animists and polytheists. Their shrine was also the site of at least 360 idols imaging their many gods that were presided over by their chief god Allah. As a boy Muhammad had a religious upbringing, as various members of his family had been custodians of the Ka'aba.

At thirteen Muhammad began to work for the caravans,

which plied their trade between Mecca and the northeast as far as Damascus, Syria. He drove the camels and even tended sheep and goats, which was considered a lowly occupation. One of his employers was a rich widow Khadijah. She recognized him as a young man of good character from a good family. Even though she was fifteen years his senior, Khadijah proposed marriage to Muhammad in 595 when he was 25 years old. She was 40. They lived faithfully together until Khadijah's death in 619. They had six children—two sons who died in infancy plus four daughters. In later years he always held her up as an example of the ideal wife much to the discomfort of some of his later wives.

Muhammad was a pious man. He had come under the influence of an Ebionite Christian pastor by the name of Waraqa ibn Naufal, a good friend and distant cousin of both his grandfather and his wife Khadijah. He learned to spend much time in meditation, fasting and prayer in caves in the mountains north of Mecca.

It was in the cave of Mt. Hira that he had his first dream or vision in the sacred month of Ramadan in 610 when he was 40 years old. At first he thought it was the visitation of a jinn or evil spirit, but he was dissuaded of this by his wife Khadijah and Waraqa who thought that this was a calling from the true God. Finally Muhammad decided his visitor was an angel, whom he identified as Jibril or Gabriel.

The angel began to teach him about the one true god and compelled him to memorize and recite these teachings. These "recitations" of Muhammad became the Qur'an. Nearly three years elapsed between his first and second visions. During the second visitation he received the call to be a "warner" to his people the Arabs. It caused great excitement in Muhammad's family. Jews and Christians had their prophets and worshiped the Creator, but the Arabs had never had a prophet among them.

It is significant to observe that the teachings of Pastor Waraqa, doctrines of the heretical Judaic Christian sect of the Ebionites, are reflected in the teachings of Muhammad and the Qur'an. The Ebionites were Jews who revered Jesus of Nazareth as a great prophet, born of a virgin, a performer of miracles, and anointed by God to teach the Gospel which was simply defined as a new interpretation of the law. Salvation was achieved through the observance of this law. They did not believe, however, that Jesus was divine, nor that he had been crucified or resurrected to be the Savior of mankind. However, because he was the special Anointed One, or the Messiah, sent by God, he would return to defeat the Antichrist in the last days.

The Ebionites were legalists like the Pharisees or like the Judaizers opposed by the Apostle Paul in his letter to the Galatians. This New Testament book, as we shall see, reads like it could have been written to Muslims. Paul was regarded by the Ebionites as a usurper, a heathen or a heretic. Muslims to this day regard the Apostle Paul as the corrupter of the true Gospel, whereas he is regarded by Christians as its finest expositor and defender.

Ebionites were called Nazara because they followed the teachings of Jesus of Nazareth.They have been variously described as Judaizing Christians or Christianized Jews. The early church considered them one of the many heretical sects. Waraqa himself was perhaps of Jewish descent. Early observers of Islam sometimes regarded it also as either an aberration of Judaism or as another Christian heresy of which there were many. Muslims deny, however, that Muhammad learned his doctrines from any Christians, and this is accurate because Pastor Waraqa could hardly be called a genuine Christian. Waraqa who was an old man of nearly 100 years may have seen in the young Muhammad a confirmation and successor in his own faith and thus encouraged him.

The most important of the Quraysh gods was the Moon god called Al-Ilah or "the god" meaning "the chief god." Muhammad was convinced, considering what he knew of the religion of Jews and Christians, that there was only one Creator god. It is said that he always had refused to worship any of the idols in the Ka'aba even though members of his family had been responsible for some of the supervision of this sacred shrine. He and those who followed him identified the one God of Jews and Christians to be the same as Al-Ilah who was worshiped by the Quraysh and other western Semitic tribes. Al-Ilah was originally the "moon god," and a vestige of that origin is still found in the Islamic symbol of the crescent moon. (See the chapter on Allah.)

Muhammad began to teach his family and intimate friends that there was no other god but one, and that he, Muhammad, had been called by Al-Ilah to warn his people. He declared that Al-Ilah, shortened to *Allah*, was the god who called on all men everywhere to submit to his laws. He would be their judge on the last day. Although the Quraysh tribe were idolaters, they already believed that the high god of their pantheon was the same deity the Jews and Christians called the Creator. It took many years, however, before the Arabs were willing to give up their other gods.

Khadijah, who was literate, encouraged Muhammad in his religious quest and was perhaps the first to write down his utterances, which were supposed to be the very words of Allah himself. She believed that her husband had been called to be a prophet to his people. During a period of 22 years from 610 to 632 A.D. these revelations to Muhammad called "recitations" were recorded, memorized and gathered together by his followers. *Qur'an* is the Arabic word for "recitation."

The Hijra—Muhammad's Flight—Mecca to Medina—Beginning of Islam—Conflicts with Christians and Jews

Because of the prosperity of the Quraysh tribe, there was a great gap in Mecca between the rich and the poor, which Muhammad sought to remedy. He taught that the ideal community, called an "ummah," should be one in which there is equity and justice, peace and compassion. Hence Muhammad taught that the rich must share with the poor and that every man should give part of his income to help others.

Their wealth had made the Quraysh a proud people, which Muhammad tried to counteract by teaching a humbling, submissive position of prayer. This was to be performed five times a day, one of the Five Pillars, a requirement for all practicing Muslims. Since the consumption of alcohol, especially wine, was a problem for the Arab tribes, Muhammad condemned any use of alcoholic beverages as a part of his religion. He also forbade the eating of pork. Without doubt the observance of both dietary commands enhanced the health of his followers.

He gathered around him a few converts who believed in him and his visions. However, after the death of his wife and his uncle in 619, he became poor and was persecuted by the Quraysh in Mecca. In 622 he fled from Mecca for his life with his best friend Abu Bakr. They traveled north over 200 miles to the city of Yathrib where he was joined by 150 of his followers. He had been invited to Yathrib by a few believers who wanted him to arbitrate their disputes and heal their feuds.

The people of Yathrib were predisposed to believe Muhammad's doctrine of the one Supreme Being, because three Jewish clans were prominent there. Besides, they were delighted to have their own prophet and renamed their town Medina, meaning "the city of the prophet." Muhammad wrote a new constitution for them and united the city under his leadership. It was thus in Medina that Muhammad became a political leader as well as a prophet. There is to this day no separation of church and state in Islam. The prophet's flight to Yathrib or Medina marks the beginning of the religion of Islam. It is called the *Hijra*.

All the while Muhammad continued to hear and recite the words of Allah, which were recorded by the faithful. Their numbers continued to grow, but it was to be expected that he would make not just a few enemies. In Mecca the powerful interests of his own tribe had been greatly offended by his insistence that their idols be destroyed and that the rich must share with the poor. They were also put off by Muhammad's constant warnings about the last judgment and hell.

Muhammad and his disciples had provoked the Meccan merchants by raiding their caravans for booty. This is what began the wars between the Muslims and the Meccans in 624. Muhammad raised several armies of from 200 to 10,000 men, and in time conquered his old city of Mecca. Through his many military raids and skirmishes and the sending of missionary emissaries, he gained complete control of Arabia by 630. He made his final pilgrimage to Mecca in 632. This is called the *hajj* and became another of the five major good works or religious practices called "pillars" to be performed by all Muslims. Muhammad actually had simply retained and incorporated into Islam one of the most ancient and important rituals of the Arabian tribes. Soon after his return to Medina, he died unexpectedly in that same year. It was rumored that he had been poisoned, but others say he died of natural causes. He had lived for only 62 years.

In Medina, Muhammad had expected the Jews would become his allies, but they mocked his imperfect knowledge of the Torah, his illiteracy, and some of his heretical ideas, and they organized against him. Muhammad's response was simply to eliminate his opposition in Medina. He exiled two of the three clans of Jews from the city, confiscating some of their property. He then made a final example of the remaining Jewish Qurayzah clan who had sympathized with and supported his enemies in Mecca. Muhammad decided to execute these Jewish men. He had over 700 of them beheaded and buried their bodies in a common trench grave. He then distributed their widows among his followers, and sold their children into slavery. The Muslims seized all the Jews' property and rejoiced in that it was the greatest accumulation of booty they had ever gained. This all helped to finance their later military conquests. With this action of the prophet as their example, many Muslims today look forward to taking an enormous booty when they can appropriate the wealth of a defeated Israel.

Commands to Fight:
The Rapid Early Spread of Islam

To support his new community of believers, Muhammad and his followers raided as many as 22 (some claim over 70) different commercial caravans, stealing the equivalent of many thousands of dollars worth of property. Because of the poverty of the people, this kind of brigandage was not uncommon in Arabia amounting to a forced redistribution of the wealth. There is no accurate record of the numbers who were killed in those early days in the name of Allah and his prophet; nevertheless, Muhammad's revelations from Allah at this time justified these actions.

Sura 22:39-40 reads, *"Permission is granted those (to take up arms) who fight because they were oppressed. Allah is certainly able to give help to those who were driven away from their homes for no other reason than they said-'Our Lord is Allah.'"* This statement referred specifically to the Muslims having been persecuted in Mecca by the Quraysh tribe who had become the avowed enemies of Muhammad and his followers. This could be called the Muslim "right of retaliation."

Other references in the Qur'an which support these tactics include Sura 2:244 —

"Fight in the cause of Allah, knowing that Allah hears and knows everything." Sura 4:95—*"The faithful who sit idle, other than those who are disabled, are not equal to those who fight in the cause of Allah with their wealth and lives. Allah has exalted those in rank who fight for the faith. Those who fight in the cause of Allah and are killed receive the special reward of the blotting out of their sins and reception into "gardens with rippling streams,"* in other words, Paradise. (Sura 3:195)

The Qur'an gives Muslims another direct command to fight in Sura 2:216, 218. *"You are commanded to fight, and you dislike it. But it is possible that you dislike what is good for you. . . Surely those who believe, and those who leave their homes and fight in the cause of Allah, may hope for His benevolence, for Allah is forgiving and kind."* Other passages include Sura 8:38 and 59 and Sura 9:5, 29 and 39. Muslims in these passages are actually commanded to make war for Allah until *"Allah's religion shall reign supreme."* and *"If you do not go to war, he* (Allah) *will punish you sternly."*

In light of these and many other like admonitions from the Qur'an plus the example of Muhammad himself, is it any wonder that the religion of Islam was spread by the sword? Many statements could be cited from the teachings of Muhammad in his sayings (the *hadith*), which support warfare, violence, and militancy. (See chapter on Holy Jihad.) Today Islamic radicals justify their aggressive actions by these teachings and examples.

Muhammad as a military leader set the pace for Islamic practice throughout the first 100 years of the expansion of the religion. No one can deny that Islam was spread by the force of arms across North Africa, through Spain and as far as southern France where the Muslims were turned back by Charles Martel (The Hammer) at the Battle of Tours or Poitiers in 732. Islamic militants moved into all the Christian lands of the Middle East—Iraq and Iran, into the Caucasus mountain regions and eventually into India. They established eastern and western political centers (Caliphates) at Cordoba, Spain and Baghdad and rose to become the most powerful civilization of the world for several centuries. The Caliph (*khalif*) was the political leader meaning the "representative" of Muhammad after his death.

Eventually Turks, who had been converted to Islam, came out of Central Asia and conquered the Eastern Roman or Byzantine Empire, taking Constantinople in 1453 and renaming it Istanbul. The Ottoman Empire continued its rampage through the Balkans to the gates of Vienna in the 16th and 17th centuries (1529 and 1683) where their armies were finally halted. If they had not been repulsed, all of Europe might have been forced to become Islamic just like the Albanians and the Bosnians. Bitter animosities were born in those years that are still being played out by Orthodox Catholic Serbs and Roman Catholic Croats against the Muslim communities, who are the descendants of those who converted to Islam under the Ottomans. It was during this time that the shape of the crescent moon, a Muslim symbol, inspired Viennese bakers to invent the croissant—an interesting piece of historical trivia.

Appraising the Prophet Muhammad

How are we to evaluate Muhammad? There is no need to doubt his visions or his utterances. From the Bible we learn that there is a spiritual world, and that it is composed of those who represent the Creator God and also his adversaries, namely, Satan and his demonic hosts. Were the revelations to Muhammad, however, really from the God of the Bible—the God of Abraham, Isaac and Jacob, who made an eternal covenant with King David? Were they really from the God of Heaven who, according to the prophecies of the Old Testament and the testimony of the New Testament, sent His only Son as a descendant of King David to be the Savior of mankind and the ultimate Ruler of all men? Or was it a false and lying spirit sent by the one whom Jesus called "the father of lies." The testimony of the Bible, or what Muhammad called "the earlier revelation," and the teachings of the Qur'an cannot both be the ultimate authority. They clearly contradict each other. (See Chapter 2: The Qur'an)

There is no doubt that Muhammad finally believed the idea that he had been chosen as a warner and then a prophet to lead his Arab brothers out of idolatry to monotheism and to teach them a basic moral code by which they could live in a community of prosperity and peace. This code of behavior was considered the will of Allah and is called the *shari'ah* or Islamic law. Islam means "submission" or "resignation." A Muslim is one who submits or resigns himself to Allah's will.There is a great simplicity in this teaching, which helps to account for its rapid and wide acceptance.

Among Muslims Muhammad is regarded as the very embodiment of his teachings. He is the great example. As one of his many wives Aisha is reported to have said, *"His way of life is the Qur'an."* There is no other prophet more exalted or venerated among his followers. One may defame Allah even to the extent of being an atheist, but one will take his life in his hands if he shows disrespect for the prophet. There is an old Muslim saying, *"You can deny god, but you cannot deny the prophet."* Muslims show as much or more reverence for Muhammad as Christians show for Jesus. Although he demanded respect and obedience, Muhammad disclaimed perfection; however, it seems that he is often exalted by the faithful almost as if he were divine. Muhammad embodies or personifies both the Qur'an and the faith of Islam. In fact the Qur'an often cites Allah and Muhammad in the same breath, almost as alter egos, e.g., "obedience to Allah and the Apostle," "the gifts of Allah and the Apostle's," and "Allah's pleasure and the Apostle's."   For some detail of this dual application see Sura 9.

Muslims teach that Muhammad's coming was prophesied in the Bible (Sura 26:196). They apply to Muhammad many of the prophecies, which the New Testament ascribes to the coming of Jesus the Messiah. For example, Muhammad is the "servant" foretold by Isaiah in chapter 42. He is the chief cornerstone which the builders rejected in Psalm 118:22. He is the "prophet" foretold to Moses in Deuteronomy 18:18.   Finally he was the Paraclete or Counselor whom Jesus said would come after him to help his disciples.

The immediate problem with this latter claim is that Jesus said that this would happen a few days after He went away at which time the disciples would be baptized by the Holy Spirit (Acts 1:4-5). Also Jesus said that the Counselor would be the "Spirit of truth" who would be with them and live in them. All of this was absolutely impossible for Muhammad who was born over 500 years after the time of the death, burial, resurrection and ascension of Jesus the Messiah. These claims are all fraudulent and show that Islam has a lying spirit.

The record of the life and actions of Muhammad is called the *sunnah*, meaning "The trodden path." His sayings are included in the *hadith* or the written traditions of Muhammad's life and teachings. The sunnah and hadith are not divine revelation as is the Qur'an, but they offer a living commentary on the Qur'an in the person of the prophet—his sayings and accounts of his life and behavior. How Muhammad himself put into practice and submitted himself to the words of Allah in the Qur'an is an important part of the basis for *shari'ah* or Islamic law. He is regarded as the Perfect Model whom all should imitate.

It is not always easy to separate fact from fable, but we can draw a positive picture of the man. Judged by the standards of his time and in comparison to others, he was an essentially decent man although very flawed by Biblical standards or even by the imperfect mores of our own day. He never claimed to be sinless, but his life is regarded by Muslims as the highest ideal, the perfect example, and the living fulfillment of Allah's commands. Conveniently Muhammad was treated as being above the law. He was granted privileges that no other man could have. Muslims would cringe at the thought, but he is treated like a god or at the least superhuman.

We have no image of Muhammad, but he is reported to have been slender and of medium height, broad shouldered with a strong physique, having an oval face, black eyes and hair, a long nose, a patriarchal beard and a commanding presence. Being used to poverty he did everything for himself from mending his own garments to cobbling his shoes. He even helped his wives with the cooking. He laughed and smiled often, had a creative imagination and an apparent genius for poetry. Arab society had its roots in oral traditions, and although there were those who could read and write, capacities for memorization and recitation were cultivated abilities in the culture. There is not much doubt that Muhammad himself was virtually illiterate. He began working full time in his early teens and so there was not much time for an education. Nothing much was written down. Most of what we know of the prophet, in fact, comes from oral traditions, which were not written down until long after his death.

From a human standpoint there is much to admire about Muhammad. There can be no doubt about his sincerity. He wanted to change his Arab society, which he saw steeped in superstitious idolatry and selfishness. At first it seems he believed that he would find support from both Jews and Christians whose God he thought he was following. Perhaps he dreamed of uniting all three religions that claimed Abraham as their father into one inclusive whole. He discovered, however, that the utterances, which were a product of his trances, the direct revelation from the one whom he believed to be the angel Gabriel, contradicted the basic teachings of Christianity. These teachings were also at variance with many of the facts recorded in the Torah—the books of Moses. He soon began to regard Jews and Christians as his enemies in his effort to resurrect what he believed to be the pure, uncorrupted, ancient monotheism. The initially tolerant tone and teaching of the Qur'an changed into an aggressive polemic against the infidels.

Muhammad appealed only to the recitations in the Qur'an as the singular proof of his authenticity. When people asked him to show them a miraculous sign, he simply pointed to the Qur'an. How could he, an illiterate man, have created such beautiful poetry? Later tradition—the *sunnah*—attributes miracles to Muhammad, but none are found recorded in the early

Islamic history or in the text of the Qur'an. Muhammad himself made no claim to be a worker of miracles except for the miracle of the Qur'an itself.

What Muhammad did claim was authority for himself. He had been accepted as the political leader of Medina and had written a constitution or rules for the running of the society in the first two years of his residence there. As the Prophet or spokesman for Allah, Muhammad regarded his own word as virtual law. He had been asked to mediate numbers of disputes, which added to his prestige and dictatorial power.

Revelations from Allah always came at the most convenient times to enforce Muhammad's position. *"Accept what the Apostle gives you, and refrain from what he forbids (abstain from it.)"* (Sura 59:7) Then the Qur'an adds, *"Have fear of Allah. Allah is stern (severe) in retribution."* In other words, you had better obey the prophet, or Allah will punish you severely. The teaching *"He who obeys the Apostle obeys Allah."* gave Muhammad almost unlimited authority. (Sura 4:80) The Qur'an warns further that if anyone has received the message from Muhammad and opposes him, going his own way and taking a different path, his eternal abode shall be hell fire. (4:115) This kind of sanction certainly confirmed and supported the prophet's prestige and power. This theocratic authority led to the Caliphs, or "representatives" of the prophet, having dictatorial control, which is the political culture of the majority of Muslim nations to this day. Liberty, democracy, and freedoms of speech, conscience and religion are all foreign to Islam.

Muhammad and his followers came to believe that he had brought the final revelation, which superseded all other revelations from God. Muhammad as the last prophet had uttered the last words to all men everywhere from the Creator. Islam and the Qur'an therefore are considered to be the final authority on all religious, as well as political, social, and economic, matters in the world.

Muslims claim that where Judaism and Christianity, the other great monotheistic faiths, are at variance with Islam, it is the Judeo-Christian writings and teachings which have become corrupted. The earlier revelations are only true when they coincide with or support the revelations given to Muhammad. Any contradictions must be rejected in favor of the complete and final revelation in the Qur'an. This is Islamic dogma. It is based solely on faith. There is no archeological, historical or linguistic evidence whatsoever which even suggests the tiniest iota of support for these assertions.

Some Serious Criticisms of Muhammad

(1) Muhammad commanded his followers to raid merchant caravans in order to steal supplies to support themselves. He took up arms and led at least three of these raids himself and raised armies to fight his enemies. Islam was born and grew in the midst of conflict and violence. Muhammad was more a prophet of war than of peace.

For years after Muhammad's death, his representatives (Caliphs) were involved in warfare with others and among themselves. Even Aisha, child bride of Muhammad and daughter of his friend and first convert Abu Bakr, who became the first Caliph, fought Muhammad's cousin Ali, who claimed the Caliphate (656-61), in the Battle of the Camel (656).

No one can deny that within 25 years of the prophet's death Islam had been spread across North Africa westward and to the borders of China and the Indus Valley to the east. The Arab armies conquered by force, and the Islamic control of society was sustained by force. Many millions of people were slaughtered especially in a country like India where the Hindus worshiped hundreds of idols. Whole towns and villages were decimated including women and children, and thousands were impressed into slavery. Muhammad had taught that those who participated in Holy Jihad would be rewarded on earth with booty and in Paradise with all kinds of sensual delights including scores of glorified females called *houris*.

Muhammad commanded that all should submit to Islam and worship Allah. Jews and Christians or "people of the book" could submit to Islamic rule and pay tribute or a head tax called the *jizyha*. The only alternative for pagans who refused to become Muslims, however, was death. These are all intact Islamic rules, which are currently taught by orthodox mullahs, imams, and ayatollahs. The three choices were conversion, subjugation to Islamic law into a second-class citizenship called dhimmitude, or death.

This seems to contradict an earlier teaching in the Qur'an, *"There shall be no compulsion in matters of faith."* (Or "religion") (Sura 2:256) It is an example of the fact that portions of the Qur'an written while Muhammad was still in Mecca and portions written in Medina are sometimes very different. While still in Mecca Muhammad was favorable to Christians and Jews whom he sought to win to faith in Allah. He also was using persuasion in seeking to win his Quraysh brethren to Islam. When persuasion failed and Jews and Christians turned against him, Muhammad's message changed to a much harsher set of commands. The solution to these contradictions for orthodox Islamists is the simple principle that the later revelation always supersedes or abrogates the former teaching. It is a kind of progressive revelation.

(2) After six years of intermittent conflict, Muhammad signed a ten-year truce with the Meccans at Hudaybiyyah in 628. The agreement was unpopular with Muhammad's followers. So within two years Muhammad broke the truce. He accused the Meccans of unfaithfulness to their agreement because they had fought with a Bedouin tribe loyal to Islam.

Muhammad had had time to rebuild his army and was now strong enough to advance on Mecca with 10,000 followers. The Meccans were unprepared for this treachery. Apparently they believed that Muhammad would keep his word, and they were in no way prepared for this act of aggression. Muhammad promised that as long as the Meccans submitted to his and Allah's authority and did not resist, he would allow them to live and keep their goods and their lands. They had no recourse but to open the city gates and allow Muhammad and his followers to enter. He has been praised by his followers for this gracious act of generosity and compassion in forgiving the Quraysh. Muhammad's own treachery in not keeping the truce, however, is conveniently rationalized. In this deceit Muhammad set an example that is emulated by Muslims to this day.

Muhammad's deception has been used to this very day as an excuse by Muslims not to abide by treaties if it is not in their best interest.Truces are made to be broken. This explains why the Oslo Accords signed by Yasser Arafat were not worth the paper on which they were written. In fact, one of Arafat's own lieutenants let it be known that the Oslo Accords were really just a Trojan horse. Arafat himself speaking in Arabic to concerned Muslims cited the truce of Hudaybiyyah as a precedent for not taking the Oslo agreements seriously.

When it is to their advantage, Muslims will often propose a truce. Osama bin Laden, for example, recently offered the nations of Europe a respite from any terrorism if they would withdraw any and all support from the United States in the Iraqi conflict. This does not change the fact, however, that Muslims have always considered those outside the "House of Islam" as being a part of the "House of War." A profession of peace between orthodox Muslims and anyone outside the "ummah" or Islamic community is only a convenience. It is never a permanent viable option in the minds of the orthodox. Their ultimate ideal goal has always been the subjugation of the world.

(3) Muhammad administered very harsh justice. We noted above that when one of the Jewish clans of Medina, the

Qurayzah, sided with Mecca, Muhammad punished their treachery by cutting the throats or beheading all the men of the tribe, who numbered over 700. He distributed their wives among his followers, taking two for himself, and sold their children into slavery. All the property of these Jews was distributed among the Muslims. Muhammad took a 20% share for himself, which made him a very wealthy man.

Others who opposed or ridiculed him were also assassinated. Flogging, stoning and the cutting off of heads or body parts, such as hands or feet, was practiced in Arabia and is used as punishment in Arab nations to this day. (Sura 5:33) The Saudi ambassador to London Ghazi Al-Qusaibi in a recent interview in Arabic said that these practices, considered barbaric in the West, were the core of Islamic faith. (Internet site *memri.org*, Special Dispatch Series, #389, June 13, 2002) Over eighty criminals were executed by being beheaded in Saudi Arabia in 2001. The whole world has now been witness to the numerous beheadings of those captured by the terrorists in Iraq. This is not an aberration, but is "basic Islam."

(4) Muhammad was a polygamist, which practice was not uncommon in Arabia. As long as Khadijah was alive, however, she was his only wife, but after her death he took at least 12 different wives who were either closely related to his best friends and supporters, or even his enemies, or who were widows of his followers who had died or been killed in battle. One authority says that he had 16 wives, two slave wives, and 4 concubines. We cannot be certain. The Hadith says that numbers of women wanted to have a relationship with him. Two of his wives were Jewish and one was a professed Christian. It is certainly confirmed that at his death he was survived by at least nine wives.

It is true that in the Old Testament it was customary, as in many societies, for a man to have more than one wife. That this was not God's perfect plan for man is obvious from the fact that Adam and Eve were created as a couple. Abraham had one wife Sarah plus the concubine Hagar. Isaac had only one wife, Rebecca. Jacob, however, had two wives and two concubines—Leah and Rachel and their maid-servants Zilpah and Bilhah. On the basis of Jacob's example, the one from whom the nation Israel takes its name, rabbis permitted a Jewish man to have a maximum of four wives. David, however, had at least 26 wives and concubines and his son Solomon multiplied this by almost 40 times. However, God, in Deuteronomy 17:17 had specifically commanded that a king *"must not take many wives."*

Polygamy is always demeaning to the woman and a source of much conflict because the husband's heart and attentions are divided. The Biblical ideal is still a husband forming a family with only one wife, such as is commanded for leaders of the church in I Timothy 3:2,*"Now the bishop must be above reproach, the husband of but one wife."* Since the shepherd is to be the example for the flock, this command was extended to the whole Christian church.

According to Muhammad's teaching which followed the teaching of the Jewish rabbis, Muslim men are allowed four wives at a time, but they must treat them all equally. (Sura 4:3) They also could have as many slave girls as was practical in order to avoid fornication (Sura 4:3, 24).

Muhammad, however, did not follow this rule. He claimed that he was privileged by Allah to have many more wives as Sura 32:50 proclaims, *"This privilege is yours alone, being granted to no other believer."* It is an example of Muhammad's being above the normal law. In spite of this statement in the Qur'an, however, future caliphs followed Muhammad's example and had many more than four wives in their harems.

When Muhammad wanted Zeinab, the wife of his adopted son Zayd, Zayd at first refused. A convenient revelation from Allah, however, declared it legitimate to marry the divorced wife of an adopted son. Zayd divorced Zeinab so

Muhammad could marry her (Sura 33:37). Was this a genuine "revelation," or was it a manipulation by the prophet to
get his own way?

Muhammad also took into his household the six-year-
old daughter of his best friend and companion Abu Bakr
with his friend's blessing. Her name was Aisha, and by her
own testimony, the prophet consummated marriage with
her taking her to his bed when she was nine. Muhammad
was fifty-two years old. This is shocking by our standards,
and Muhammad would be punished as a pedophile in our
society today. She was not out of her teens before
Muhammad died. She became known as his favorite wife and
is prominent in Islamic history after his death. Because of
Muhammad's example, child brides are permitted in Islamic
countries to this day. Older wealthy Saudi sheikhs will go to
a Muslim center like Hyderabad in India and buy nine or ten
year old girls from poor parents for $200 and bring them
back to fill out their households. In the Sudan today wives
may be as young as seven years of age.

Finally, Muhammad permitted the soldiers in his army
to have a three-day temporary marriage called *muta*. This
practice avoided calling temporary cohabitation fornication.
It was practiced for a generation after Muhammad's death,
but is now a custom permitted only among the Shiite
Muslims. The Ayatollahs permit a man to have a temporary
contract of marriage for a specifically allotted amount of
time, e.g., one hour or one year, whatever is necessary. The
above rules covering multiple and temporary marriages
helped to control the male sexual drive by institutionalizing
the common sins of fornication and adultery within the
Islamic community.

Muhammad's Amazing Teachings About Women

Muhammad is said to have enjoyed the company of
women and often helped with his wives' tasks. He was not
averse to listening to their advice and even seemed to suffer

some occasional henpecking. It appears that at that time there was more equality practiced between the sexes than is true in most Islamic countries today. Women, however, used to play a subsidiary role in all Middle Eastern cultures including those of Jews and Christians. The first part of a Sura #4 in the Qur'an is devoted to the place of women in Islamic society, and one can evaluate for himself the justice of the teaching.

Perhaps the extreme submission of women in ultra conservative Islamic societies today is in part a reaction to the kind of equality and freedom women have achieved for themselves in other cultures in the world particularly in the West. The following passages from the Qur'an and the Hadith were the original teachings.

Sura 4:34—*"Men have authority over women because Allah has made the one superior to the other, and because they spend their wealth to maintain them. . . Those whom you fear will be rebellious, admonish; banish them to their beds and beat them."* Wife beating is permitted in Muslim societies today although it is to be humane. Sensitive parts of the body are never to be abused, usually only the buttocks and the legs are beaten.

Sura 2:228—*"Women also have recognized rights as men have, though men have an edge over them."* (Or "men have a status above women.")

Hadith 1:28—*"I was shown Hell-fire and the majority of its dwellers were women who were ungrateful."* 1:301*"O women, give alms, as I have seen that the majority of dwellers in Hell-fire were you women. . . I have not seen anyone more deficient in intelligence and religion than you."* 2:61 *"A horrible sight . . I saw that most of the inhabitants of Hell-fire were women."*

Hadith 3:826—The witness of a woman was equal to half that of a man. *"This is because of the deficiency of the woman's mind."*

Hadith 4:10—A woman received only one half of what a brother's inheritance would be. Wives received 1/4 of a man's estate if childless or 1/8 if there were children (Sura 4:12).

The above teachings are in contrast to the Apostle Paul's

Christian standard and admonition in Galatians 3:28: *"You are all sons of God through faith in Christ Jesus. . There is neither Jew nor Greek, neither slave nor free, neither male nor female, for you are all one in Christ Jesus."* Although there were some cultural rules common in the Roman Empire and in Judaism, which were supported in the New Testament, the overall teaching of the Scriptures is that men and women have equal value before God. This has been a positive influence enhancing the status of women in Christian oriented societies.

Women in orthodox Islam, however, are considered inferior to men although they are supposed to be treated justly and with kindness. Marriage has no particular spiritual significance and is only for this life. If a wife does not please a man, especially physically, he is allowed to divorce her simply with a word. He may have four wives at any one time, so presumably he could divorce them all and marry four different wives. In strict Muslim communities women are not educated. In Afghanistan under the Taliban, e.g., girls were forbidden to go to school. In Saudi Arabia they are not even allowed to drive a car. Women are baby producers and homemakers and are usually supposed to remain in seclusion. They are considered to be a man's property just like anything else he owns (Sura 3:14). For women to have recently attained the right to vote in Afghanistan, Iraq, and Kuwait is nothing less than revolutionary.

There is no command in the Qur'an that can be construed to teach that a woman's whole face should be covered such as with a burqa, which is the practice in some Muslim countries today. The Qur'an does teach that women should be reserved and modest. Sura 24:31—*"Tell the believing women to lower their eyes, guard their private parts, and not display their charms except what is apparent outwardly, and cover their bosoms with their veils and not to show their finery except to their husbands or their fathers* (and other male relatives). *. or male attendants who do not have any need for women* (eunuchs), *or boys not yet aware of sex."* This command suggests that women should cover their bodies in public as Sura 33:59 advises. *"O Prophet, tell your wives and daughters and the women of the faithful, to draw their wraps a little over them.* (Apparently this refers to when they go outside.) *They will thus be recognized and no harm will come to them."*

Muhammad certainly taught that women should be modestly dressed. Some kind of covering for the head was probably normative. Women in Mecca are said to have taken to wearing a veil in public in imitation of Muhammad's wives after his conquest of the city. The religious teachers in each individual Islamic community must decide the Islamic law commanding a specific dress for women today in Muslim countries.

In light of the teachings and example of Muhammad, their exalted leader, the current behavior of Islamic fundamentalists including the Palestinians can be more easily understood. One cannot deny that the radical and militant position of today's Islamists is a direct result of orthodox Islamic teaching and the historical example of practices of the 7th century Muslim world. The ultimate goal of militant Islam today is to force the entire world to submit to these teachings of the Qur'an and Muhammad—the will of Allah and the *shari'ah*—Allah's laws as applied to human society. An extreme example of Islamic law imposed on a society today was in Afghanistan under the Taliban. These literalists actually sought to recreate Muhammad's culture of 7th century Arabia.

Anecdotes from the Hadith and the Sunna

Besides the Qur'an, the basis for Islamic law includes the collection of sayings and actions of Muhammad called the *hadith*. Muhammad originally urged that none of his words be written down so that his teachings would not conflict with those of Allah in the Qur'an. His friends and family and Muslim leaders in the early years, however, gradually collected in many volumes stories and traditions concerning the daily events of his life including his words and instructions. Muhammad's wife Aisha herself kept a record of 2,000 of these teachings. These were eventually compiled in several collections. The two Hadith collections regarded as the most accurate are those by Al-Bukhari and Sayyid Muslim. Of the hundreds of thousands of recollections in existence Al-Bukhari, e.g., chose 7,725 Hadith published in 9 volumes. This is considered an authentic, authoritative edition of the prophet's life and sayings.

Drawing from these records we have a unique picture of the man who is regarded as the inspired founder of what has become the world's second largest religion. The reader can judge for himself from these published records as to Muhammad's personality and character. (I am indebted to Dr. Robert Morey for some of this material, which he has researched from the Hadith. Cf. *The Islamic Invasion*, pp. 177-208.)

(1) The Hadith clearly presents Muhammad as a "white man." This must be very disconcerting to many Black Muslims in America who have insisted that the prophet was black. Their leader Louis Farrakhan predicts that someday all white men will be eliminated. Black Muslims have insisted that Christianity is a white man's religion, but that Islam is a black man's religion, and that all white people are "devils." Muhammad, however, said that he had a dream about Jesus, and that he was white. This also contradicts the belief of many blacks that Jesus must have been black. Are Muhammad and Jesus therefore both "white devils?"

(2) Black people are disparagingly called "raisin heads" in the Hadith. (Vol. I. 662 and IX. 256) The only times that blacks are referred to at all, they are pictured as slaves. In fact, they are Muhammad's own slaves. Muhammad was a slaveholder, which explains why Saudi Arabia did not disallow slavery until 1962, and this was because of international pressures.

For all practical purposes slavery still is practiced in Islamic nations, especially in Mauritania and the Sudan. Christians in the southern Sudan have still been enslaved, women and children being sold on the slave blocks for $15 a head.

Islamic tribes and nations throughout history were the premier slaveholders and traders. At least 14 million slaves were taken from Africa and other nations to Muslim countries, most of them women and children. At least 25,000 slaves used to be sold in the markets of Mecca and Medina each year. The integration of children, who were half Arab and half black, has over the years resulted in the absorption of some Negroid genes into the Arab gene pool, which has modified their normal Mediterranean ancestry and appearance.

Incidentally the American colonies imported only about 500,000 slaves, whereas South America and the Caribbean imported up to 11 million. The emphasis here was on able-bodied male workers. The slave trade died out or was abolished in Christendom or the Western world in the 19th century, but it still thrives underground in the Islamic culture sphere.

(3) Muhammad is pictured in the Hadith as being easily angered, losing his temper with his face getting red. He was especially angered when he was questioned or contradicted. His words are in the record, *"Allah has hated you for asking too many questions."* (II. 555 and III. 591) He seemed to have had little sense of humor, and a man might fear for his life if he joked about the prophet or contradicted his teachings (II.173).

(4) Muhammad encouraged his followers to assassinate any who had greatly displeased him or who were his enemies. *"Who will kill Ka'b bin Al'Ashraf as he has harmed Allah and his Apostle?"* A volunteer promptly carried out the prophet's request. (III. 687) This kind of atrocity happened many times

especially to poets, both male and female, who satirized the prophet.

(5) Some in Islam claim that Muhammad was not a sinner. Since Jesus is portrayed even in the Qur'an as a sinless man, certainly Allah's final prophet must be just as good. The Hadith, however, is very clear in portraying Muhammad as a sinner in need of Allah's constant forgiveness. His followers and his family did not claim that he was sinless, but that Allah had simply forgiven all his past and future sins. (VI. 3) Muhammad admitted that only the prophet Jesus was not corrupted by Satan from birth. (IV. 506) All other men, including Muhammad, were admonished to seek forgiveness of sins in chanting the praises of Allah morning and evening (Sura 40:55).

The carnal side of Muhammad's nature was very evident. He was a barbarian in his treatment of others. He tortured people by cutting off their hands and feet, burning out their eyes, letting them bleed to death after cutting off their limbs or making them die of thirst. We have seen that he beheaded over 700 Jews in Medina distributing their wives to his followers and selling their children into slavery. To this day it is considered "basic Islam" to punish by cutting off fingers, hands and heads (I. 234; VIII. 794-96).

We have noted that Muhammad had anywhere from nine to twenty-two wives, concubines and slaves at one time. (The most accurate estimate is probably twelve to sixteen.) His child wife Aisha said that he could service all his women sexually in a single day before evening prayers. His superhuman side was supported by the belief that he had the sexual strength of thirty men. The sexual experience seems to have been regarded as the highest human delight and divine reward because Allah's Paradise consists of perpetual virgins called *houris* who will service men's physical needs in a never-ending orgy. A sensual society calls for a sensual Heaven. Muhammad had said that his three favorite things were "perfume, women, and the joy of prayers."

(6) Muhammad was superstitious. He believed in the evil eye, in good and bad omens, and was afraid of a strong wind as a sign of Allah's wrath. He feared that evil spirits might enter his body when he was urinating or defecating. He sincerely believed in the power of the black meteorite of the Ka'aba, which had been worshiped by Arabs for centuries. He made it the central object of the Hajj or pilgrimage to Mecca. The ritual of walking seven times around the black cubed building into which the black stone is set ends with everyone kissing the stone as a sign or devotion to Allah. (II. 667) Much of Muhammad's religion was geared to allaying Allah's anger to seek his mercy, his forgiveness, and rescue from hell fire. Islam is a religion based on fear not on love.

The prophet believed that people, especially Jews, could turn into pigs, rats and monkeys. (IV. 524, 569) He had a fear of magic and was superstitious about numbers. In particular he avoided even numbers. He believed that a mixture of camel urine and milk would heal diseases. He thought that placing a green leaf on a grave of a sufferer would cause the pain to ease as the leaf dried.

(7) He dyed his hair red to cover the gray. He had a large hairy mole or physical lump the size of a small egg below his left shoulder, which was regarded as the mark or sign of his prophetic office. Trying to find this in the Bible, Arab commentators have foolishly pointed to Isaiah 9 where it says, *"The government shall be upon his shoulder"* as a description of this identification. He was thought of as a *caching*, the Arab word for shaman, who could control the spirits called *jinn* that lived in rocks, trees, and bodies of water.

(8) Muhammad was a child of his age in that the hadith reveals that he had some truly crazy ideas and opinions. He taught that Allah created Adam 60 cubits or 90 feet tall (IV.

543). He hated dogs and said that they should all be killed (IV. 540). He said not to worry about a fly in your drinking water because Allah made one wing to cause disease and the other wing to cure it (IV. 537) Stars were created by Allah as missiles to throw at the devils. (IV. 282). If you have bad breath, God will not hear your prayers (I. 8,12-15). Yawning was from Satan. (IV. 509) Martyrs live in the bodies of green birds in Paradise and fly wherever they will (I. 28). The angel Gabriel has 600 wings (VI. 380). Satan stays in the upper part of your nose during the night and must be flushed out with water in the morning (IV. 516). Fever came from the heat of Hell and could be cooled with water (IV. 483-86). Satan urinates in the ears of those that fall asleep during their prayers (II. 245). Muhammad smeared dead bodies with his saliva and spit into the hands of his followers who smeared it on their faces (III. 891).

(9) Muhammad's revelations often came as a part of what some medical doctors have evaluated as an epileptic fit. This included a loud ringing in his ears, a rapid heartbeat, a very red face, and heavy breathing. After falling down half unconscious with both eyes open to the sky, he asked to be covered with a blanket. He would then receive a revelation. His lips trembled and he heard and saw things no one else experienced. He sweat profusely, would snore like a camel, and had vivid dreams.

He complained to his wives that he thought that he was sometimes possessed by demons, but his first wife Khadijah, and later Aisha, assured him that such a righteous and pious man could never be a host for demonic power. It had to be Allah. Muhammad's original insight, however, was without any doubt more accurate than he could have known.

(10) In light of militant Islam and the terrorist phenomenon today it is important to read in the Hadith what Muhammad had to say about physical violence in the name

of Allah. *"Allah's apostle was asked, 'What is the best deed?' He replied, 'To believe in Allah and his Apostle."* The next best deed was to *"participate in Jihad* (religious fighting) *in Allah's cause'"* (I. 25).

All infidels—pagans, Christians, and Jews—were to be fought against unless they embraced Islam. Pagans were to be killed and Christians and Jews could redeem themselves by submitting to Islamic law and paying a poll tax called the *jizya*. This tax was so burdensome that many decided that it was easier, and certainly cheaper, to change religions. In Saudi Arabia today some oil workers are forced to accept Islam or lose their jobs. Christians are not allowed churches or Bible studies or any kind of religious freedom of expression in the Saudi kingdom. Many have been executed in Saudi Arabia for practicing their faith. Eight of the ten nations that lead in persecuting Christians in the world today are Islamic.

Muhammad commanded that the violence of military force be used to convert non-Muslims. He said, *"I have been ordered (by Allah) to fight against the people until they testify that none has the right to be worshiped but Allah and that Muhammad is Allah's Prophet, and offer prayers and give obligatory charity, so if they perform all that, then they save their lives and property"* (I. 24). Only those who became Muslims would be safe.

He expressed this same warning to several leaders of other nations in letters where he stated that they would only be safe if they submitted themselves and their people to Allah. This had significant meaning for the future when these nations were attacked by Arab holy warriors almost immediately following Muhammad's death.

All who killed an enemy could keep the spoils or "the booty." We have seen that this is initially how Muhammad and his followers made their living. They raided scores of Meccan caravans and also confiscated the goods of all the people they killed.

No Muslim, furthermore, was to be punished for killing

an infidel. According to this doctrine, John William Muhammad and Lee Malvo, who killed 10 people as the Washington D.C. snipers, should be set free. The World Trade Center bombers also were innocent as are most suicide bombers and terrorists who target unbelievers.

Finally, any Muslim who renounces Islam and becomes an apostate or one who converts to Christianity or any other religion, must be killed. *"The Prophet said, 'If somebody discard his religion* (of Islam), *kill him"* (IV. 260). After Muhammad's death in 632, hundreds of the Quraysh tribe and other Arabs, who had accepted Islam under the military pressure of Muhammad's armies, apostatized from the faith. The new Caliph ("representative" of Muhammad) Abu Bakr pursued them and killed them all. These were the first of the Islamic wars, and they were fought against apostates in Arabia in obedience to the prophet's teaching.

About 20,000 Muslims in America become Christians each year. All of these converts stand in fear of retaliation some day in the future. It is taught that Allah hates them, and they will surely go to Hell. The Qur'an teaches that Jews or Christians, who have heard about Muhammad and do not believe in him, or in what was revealed to him, will also surely wind up in Hell.

Muhammad's Death and A Final Christian Evaluation

Muhammad died on his return from a pilgrimage to Mecca in 632. There is some suspicion that he was poisoned. He was in excruciating pain. It surprised his wives that a prophet would have to suffer so. He advised them that all prophets suffered. Then one of his last wishes uttered on his deathbed was, *"The Lord destroy the Jews and Christians. Let there not remain any faith but that of Islam throughout the whole of Arabia."*

We have noted that to this day there is no church in Saudi Arabia, and Bibles are forbidden. The presence of the infidel armies of the United States stationed in the land of

Muhammad during and after the Gulf War enraged Osama bin Laden and other fundamentalist Muslims. This was a primary cause for their declaration of war on America in 1996 and again in 1998. We had defiled the holy land of the prophet.

One reason for the invasion of Iraq ordered by President George W. Bush in 2002 with the goal of deposing Saddam was in order that our military presence in Arabia could be reduced. Because of Saddam's threat to the Saudis we were in Arabia primarily to protect the oil fields, which were coveted by Saddam. We have since been moving most of our forces to Qatar. We had hoped perhaps that this might lessen the radical Muslim attacks on America. For good or for ill our presence in Iraq has concentrated militant Islamic attacks on our forces there. This has preempted the radical Islamists' time and efforts to sabotage other American interests throughout the world.

In his final evaluation of Muhammad famed church historian Philip Schaff writes:

> To compare such a man with Jesus is preposterous and even blasphemous. Jesus was the sinless Savior of sinners; Muhammad was a sinner, and he knew and confessed it. He falls far below Moses, or Elijah, or any of the prophets and apostles in moral purity. However, outside of the sphere of revelation, he ranks with Confucius and Buddha among the greatest founders of religions and lawgivers of nations(*History of the Christian Church*, Volume IV, p. 171).

Don McCurry, a missionary to Muslims, in his recent, detailed examination of Muhammad and Islam writes:

> Muhammad stoutly maintained that he was neither of the Jews nor the Christians, but of the 'Religion of Abraham' (Sura 2:135). He borrowed from the

traditions of each, and separated himself from both, in order to supersede all his predecessors and become the Seal of the Prophets, that is, the end of the prophetic line, and therefore the final voice of God to the human race. What we have here is the effort on Muhammad's part to replace Jesus as the central focus of all Scripture, and take that place for himself. Muhammad reduced Jesus to being merely one of the prophets, and by making himself the last and the Seal of the Prophets, gave himself the place of preeminence. (*Healing the Broken Family of Abraham,* pp. 34, 55.)

Chapter 2

THE QUR'AN

Al-Qur'an (the recitation) is believed by Muslims to be the very words of Allah. Muhammad was simply the vehicle for Allah's message. Muhammad claimed that his revelations had been introduced to him by an angel whom he believed to be Gabriel.

The angel commanded him to recite. Originally, and at recurring times in his life, he wondered if evil spirits (jinn) or demons had inspired him. Sometimes Muhammad had what doctors today describe as possible epileptic seizures. In this state of semi-consciousness he uttered the words, which became the Qur'an. He was described by his followers as sweating profusely, shivering, foaming at the mouth and making loud noises. His wives Khadijah and later Aisha, however, assured him that a man so pious as he was surely being inspired by Allah. They convinced him that he was a prophet sent by Allah to his Arab brothers.

How Did the Qur'an Happen?

It is said that Muhammad was almost illiterate, so he had to memorize the earliest recitations. The utterances that came from his mouth were written down and memorized by his disciples. They were recorded on anything that was immediately available—for example, pieces of papyrus, pottery or leather, dried palm leaves, tree bark, the scapula or ribs of sheep, pieces of wood, and white stones. The recitations were then memorized as quickly as possible by his followers and were repeated orally and taught to others. These were regarded as revelations from Allah, and took place over a period of about 23 years. The first short recitation was

71

given to him by the angel in a cave on a mountain called Hira three miles north of Mecca. Muhammad had gone there to meditate and pray on a day during the sacred month of Ramadan in 610. The revelations began again in earnest in 613 and continued to the year of the prophet's death in 632.

It seems that Muhammad's wife Khadijah was literate and was very likely the first to record his recitations. After his wife's death in 619, Muhammad's disciples dutifully recorded everything they believed to be a revelation from Allah. Khadijah had a professing Ebionite Christian friend Waraqa, who was excited about Muhammad's revelations believing them to be from the true God. This has been mentioned often as an outside testimony confirming the truth of Muhammad's utterances. The Ebionites, however, held heretical beliefs, such as their teaching that Jesus did not die on the cross and that He was not the Son of God. Both of these heresies were adopted by Muhammad and are supported by the Qur'an. It is for reasons like this that Hillaire Belloc and others have called Islam one of the Christian heresies.

By the reign of the 3rd Islamic leader, Caliph Uthman, Muhammad's son-in-law, (644 to 656) there were several versions of the Qur'an in circulation in different parts of the Arab world. Disagreements arose as to which text was the true authority. Uthman settled the controversies by choosing the version kept by Muhammad's secretary Zaid ibn Thabit and commanded that all the variants, as many as 24, be destroyed. Four of these versions were by companions of Muhammad who had been called by him the "four greatest authorities on the Qur'an." One was Abdullah ibn Mas'ud who had compiled the official Qur'anic text used in Kufa in Mesopotamia. From the history of all of this recorded by Al-Bukhari, the compiler of the Sunna and the Hadith, we are impressed that the choice of Zaid's version seems to have been wholly arbitrary. It was simply the closest one at hand. Some Muslims, in fact, complained that the chosen text was inferior and less accurate than some of the others.

Islamic scholars acknowledge that many of the recitations did not get saved. Some who had memorized passages were killed in battle. Other sections were lost to decay or fire because of the fragile substances on which they were recorded. The Shiites claim that in his editing of the Qur'an Caliph Uthman failed to include about 25% of the available materials. Many variant readings were suppressed or lost. (For a detailed coverage of this history and a comparison of the Qur'an and the Bible see John Gilchrist, *Facing the Muslim Challenge*. Claremont/ Capetown, South Africa: Life Challenge Africa, pp. 17-61.)

A Recent Discovery of Ancient Fragments of the Qur'an

In 1972 a finding was made of tens of thousands of fragments from perhaps as many as one thousand old copies of the Qur'an in a grave in the famous Great Mosque of Sana'a in Yemen. The Qur'an was considered too sacred to burn, so just as the Jews buried old or imperfect copies of the Torah, Muslims apparently buried these worn and discarded copies of Qur'an. After being gathered into 20 potato sacks and put in a closet for seven years, the Yemeni Antiquities Authority enlisted the help of some German scholars to examine the find. Remarkably some of the fragments may date back to the 7th and 8th centuries or during the first two centuries of Islam.

There are some 15,000 sheets of material that have been flattened and restored and 35,000 microfilms have been made and taken for study to Saarland University in Saarbrucken, Germany. A specialist in Arabic writing and old texts of the Qur'an Professor Gerd-R. Puin is in charge of the project. Early conclusions from a cursory examination of the data indicate as mentioned above that there are many variant readings and materials not included in the Qur'an as it exists today. How a scholarly examination of this material will affect the Muslim world and the Islamic religion is yet to be determined. Some Muslims are enraged that the Qur'an—the very words of God—is being subjected to textual criticism. (Cf. "What is the Koran?" *The Atlantic Monthly*, January 1999) Any Muslim who would question the orthodox view of the Qur'an or the history of Islam is declared an apostate and in danger of death.

What are the Hadith and the Sunnah?

A distinction was made between the words of Allah, which became the Qur'an, and the teachings of Muhammad himself, which were also recorded, and became the tradition called the *Hadith*. These sayings attributed to Muhammad were accumulated and numbered in the hundreds of thousands. The Hadith, however, was subject over the years to apocryphal sayings so collections are of different lengths. There were eventual attempts to ensure accuracy, and six more or less authoritative collections emerged. These also recorded the traditions concerning the actions or behavior of Muhammad, which are called the *Sunnah*.

It is said that Muhammad did not want his teachings written down because he did not want them to be confused with the recitations or the words of Allah. So his disciples memorized them, and they were handed down from generation to generation. After 300 years Muslim scholars compiled them. Of the six major versions the two most widely accepted are the collections of Sayyid Al-Bukhari (7725 verses) and Sayyid Al-Muslim. It is said that the total collection gathered together and called *Sahih*, is the example of the fulfillment of the teachings of the Qur'an in the life of Muhammad. Together the *hadith* and the *sunnah* are very important in the formation of *shari'ah* or Islamic law, although they are not supposed to have the authority of the Qur'an. Islamic law is drawn from both the Qur'an and the Hadith as reasonably reconciled and interpreted by Muslim teachers and accepted by the community.

The Sanctity of the Qur'an

The language of the Qur'an is the Meccan version of 7th century Arabic. Muslims have always discouraged translations of the sacred book because they say it can only be fully appreciated in the Arabic language. They claim it is the only way its true beauty and majesty can be demonstrated, which is its primary claim to authenticity. The classical Arabic of the Qur'an is said to have a beautiful cadence or rhythm that has an almost mesmerizing affect on its hearers. Its potency is most easily experienced as an oral presentation. Muhammad always pointed to the Qur'an as the proof of his calling and his authority as a prophet of Allah. How could an illiterate person such as he have composed such a great collection of beautiful words was his argument. For Muslims it stands alone as the miracle upholding the truth of Islam.

The Qur'an is held in almost superstitious awe. It is believed to have been written in Heaven as God's final revelation and later dictated to his chosen prophet Muhammad. (Sura 85:22) Thus the Qur'an is considered the very words of Allah himself. We can say it is "super-sacred" to a devout Muslim. One must never approach it to read without a ritual washing called *wudu*. It must be held in a certain way with great reverence. It should always be on the highest shelf in the room and never put on the floor or left on a table where something might cover it. Muslims consider idolatry an abomination, and yet their treatment of the Qur'an, just like their extreme praise of Muhammad, seems to border on a kind of idolatry.

A Short Critical Analysis

The Qur'an is about four-fifths the length of the New Testament. It is divided into 114 chapters called *suras*. These are not organized in the order of the time when they were written down, but according to length. With the exception of Sura #1, the Prologue, which has only 7 verses, suras proceed from the longest to the shortest in automatic order. Sura #2

called "The Cow" has 286 verses and several suras are over
100 or 200 verses. The average, however, is much less than
100, and as the Qur'an proceeds the suras gradually become
shorter and shorter. The suras have been divided into verses,
called *ayats,* that literally means "signs." There are 6,116 ayats
or verses in the Qur'an.

The chapters are named according to the first line or
subject matter initially addressed in the text. After this
beginning there is no logical rhyme or reason to the Qur'an's
organization. Most chapters have many disparate or disconnected subjects. The Qur'an has no order, no beginning, and
no end. It appears as a hodgepodge of disconnected sections.
It can be very confusing. A Muslim scholar has said,
"Unfortunately the Qur'an was badly edited and its contents
are very obtusely arranged. All students of the Qur'an wonder why the editors did not use the natural and logical
method of ordering by date of revelation."

Muslim scholars have tried to chart the Qur'an chrono-
logically according to their understanding of the history and
traditions handed down about Muhammad. They believe
that the earliest is Sura #96 and the last to be recorded is
Sura #5. These studies are available to any Muslim who is
interested in knowing the approximate order of the revelations. At what period in Muhammad's life the *suras* were
recorded is very important, as we shall see. There is a considerable difference in the tone and teaching of the Qur'an, for
example, depending upon whether the revelations are from
Muhammad's time in Mecca (610-622) or in Medina (622-
632).

The Qur'an has been called "toilsome reading, a weari-
some confused jumble, crude, incoherent, desultory, inci-
dental." One problem, and perhaps a major reason for
Muslims resisting a translation of the Qur'an from the
Arabic, is the fact that, as Professor Puin points out, 20% of
the text is incomprehensible. Any translation of these sections therefore can only be tentative. Its actual meaning can

only be guessed at. This may be partly because the 7th century Arabic dialect of Mecca in which the Qur'an was written is no longer in use and is not fully understood. As Ahmed Ali, a Pakistani translator, says, "Some of its stylistic beauties are untranslatable and can only be suggested."

The Qur'an also assumes an historical background that most readers do not have. Also it was meant to be spoken and not just to be read. Perhaps it reads more easily in the original Arabic, but it is not always easy to decipher the exact meanings even in a good translation by a very knowledgeable Arabic/English scholar, such as Ahmed Ali, the Pakistani Urdu novelist, poet, and critic quoted above who taught in Indian, American, and Chinese universities. His work—*A Contemporary Translation*—was first published in Karachi, Pakistan in 1984 and later by the Princeton University Press in the United States in 1988. It is a translation frequently quoted in this book.

Muslims call the Qur'an "the greatest wonder of the wonders of the world." Claims that the Qur'an is perfect in every way, however, are just not true. It has many grammatical errors, incomplete sentences, foreign words, more than 100 aberrations from the normal rules and structure of the Arabic language, and is replete with scientific and historical mistakes. Its statements concerning the history and teachings contained in the Bible are filled with errors and misconceptions. It has little historical narrative, no chronological order, and mixes the time periods of what was revealed in Mecca and what was recited in Medina. This has allowed for many contradictions in teaching. There is endless repetition and a sense of disjointed incompleteness. It would be as if someone took the Bible and broke it up into more than 1000 parts, mixed them up, and indiscriminately put them together at random from the longest to the shortest sections. *McClintock and Strong's Encyclopedia* gives a blunt analysis, *"It is humiliating to the human intellect to think that this mediocre literature has been the subject of innumerable commentaries and that millions of men are still wasting time in absorbing it."*

There were major disputes within Islam in the early years concerning the nature of the Qur'an. Christians in the 8th century pointed out to Muslims the confusion in the text as proof that it had human origins. Muslim scholars studied the Qur'an and recorded the problems—strange vocabulary, grammatical irregularities, differing readings from other texts, apparent omissions in the text, and an over-all disorganization.

For a time in the 8th and 9th centuries a school in Islam called Mu'tazilism under the Caliph al-Ma'mun (813-833) treated the Qur'an as a human production rather than the "uncreated" Word of Allah. This resulted in a metaphorical rather than a literal understanding of the book. It was still regarded as a divine work issuing from Allah, but was considered imperfect like human beings are imperfect. It was denied that there was a literal copy in stone produced in Paradise by Allah and simply dictated to Muhammad. The teaching of the preexistence of the Qur'an in Heaven became orthodox Islamic dogma only by the end of the 10th century. From then on the sacred writings were considered to be the literal, uncreated Word of God, matchless, untranslatable from the Arabic, and incapable of being imitated.

Ten Examples of Contradictions and Strange Teachings

If the Qur'an was truly written by a god called Allah, he was lacking in the knowledge and understanding of many things. Here are a few examples:

1. Allah apparently did not understand the Christian meaning of the Gospel as defined in the Bible as the proclamation of the death, burial, and resurrection of Jesus Christ for the salvation of the world (I Corinthians 15). The Qur'an says that Jesus came to confirm the Torah (fulfill the law) and share the Gospel or good news (Sura 5:46). What constitutes

this Gospel the Qur'an neglects to say. It certainly is not the same as the Gospel proclaimed in the New Testament. The Apostle Paul said that any other "gospel" besides the one that he preached was an anathema (Galatians 1). Satan, of course, hates this Gospel of Christ and would seek to invent a substitute.

2. Allah did not even know who the Trinity is. The Qur'an proclaims that Christians teach that the true Godhead includes the Father, the Son Jesus, and his mother Mary, or God the Mother, rather than the Holy Spirit (Sura 5:116). It is on this basis that Christians are accused of worshiping three gods rather than one God in three persons (Sura 4:73 and 5:71).

3. Allah got the stories of Gideon against the Midianites and Saul against the Philistines mixed up. He has Saul's army being chosen by how the soldiers drank the water from the stream rather than Gideon's band of 300 fighting men (Sura 2:149).

4. Allah has the Sameri, or as the Muslims themselves identify the name, the Samaritans, making the golden calf idol for the Israelites when Moses is on the mountain (Sura 20:85). The Samaritans, however, did not exist until at least 700 years later.

5. Allah places the man called Haman by the side of the Egyptian Pharaoh who builds a tower to Heaven. In the Bible, however, Haman is the servant of the Persian King Ahasuerus who tries to kill the Jews. Also the building of the Tower of Babel in Sumer in Mesopotamia preceded the Pharaoh of Moses' time by many centuries (Sura 28:38).

6. Allah claims the death of Jesus by crucifixion was only the appearance of a death. Jesus was not crucified on the cross, so he was not resurrected from the grave (4:157). Satan, of course, hates the very idea of the crucifixion and resurrection because this is where he was unmasked and defeated by God (John 12:31 and I John 3:8). The historical facts of Jesus' crucifixion and resurrection are impossible to disprove. The very existence of Christianity, the witness of all Jesus' disciples, even the entire Bible, and the subsequent transformation of the Roman world are built on these historical truths.

7. Allah seems to contradict himself concerning the length of a day. In Sura 22:47 a day to Allah is 1000 years. In Sura 70:4 a day to Allah is 50,000 years. These are not just copyist errors in the omission of one letter as happens sometimes in the Old Testament record. The words for these numbers in the Qur'an are entirely different.

8. Allah cannot decide whether he created the worlds in six days or eight. (Compare Suras 10:3 and 25:59 with 41:9-12.) Also he can't seem to remember whether or not he created the earth first and then the heavens (Sura 2:39) or the heavens first and then the earth (Sura 79:27-33).

9. Allah doesn't remember whether or not he drowned Pharaoh with all of his followers (Sura 17:103) or whether Pharaoh repented and he saved him (Sura 10:88-92).

10. Allah created Adam from the dust in Sura 3:59, but elsewhere, in the Qur'an, Allah creates man from a drop of semen or a germ (Sura 16:3), from clots of

blood or an embryo (Sura 96:1), from "dry clay or black molded loam" (Sura 15:26), or all of the creation, including man, out of water (Sura 21:30).

Many other examples could be given of contradictions within the writings of the Qur'an or between the Qur'an and the Bible. It was inconsistencies like this, I am sure, which turned the Jews of Medina against Muhammad and caused them to declare him to be a false prophet.

Major Discrepancies Between the Qur'an and the Bible
The Story of Abraham

The story of Abraham and his family in the Qur'an shows one of the most dramatic differences and contradictions to the history of the patriarch in the Bible. Nowhere in the Qur'an does Abraham ever leave Ur of the Chaldees for Haran and then for the land of Canaan. When he sends Hagar and his oldest son Ishmael into the desert, it is to the area, which is now Mecca. Mecca is in the Arabian Desert and is hundreds of miles from Canaan, but it is almost 1000 miles from Ur of the Chaldees where we must assume from the Qur'an Abraham is living. The Bible says, on the other hand, that Hagar went into the Sinai desert, which is only a few days journey from southern Canaan. The account in the Qur'an is just not believable, not only because of the distance, but also because the desert, part of which is the formidable Empty Quarter, is virtually impassable.

In the Qur'an the baby Ishmael is still nursing when he is expelled with his mother, which means that he ordinarily would have been less than two years old. In the Bible Ishmael is 16 years of age when he and Hagar are finally sent away. The Qur'an mixes up two stories in the Biblical record about Hagar's exile. In the Bible Hagar is at first forced by Sarah to leave when she becomes pregnant, but an angel sends her back and Ishmael is born (Genesis 16:1-16). It is not until after Isaac is born at least 12 years later, and a conflict develops with

Ishmael, that God commands Abraham to send Hagar and Ishmael away for good.

In the Biblical narrative Hagar and Ishmael find a spring of water in the desert of Beersheba and later wander into the Desert of Paran in the Sinai (Genesis 21:1-21). In the Qur'an this spring of water is supposed to be hundreds of miles away near Mecca between the mountains. Visiting Hagar's spring today is a sacred duty for Muslim pilgrims as a part of the pilgrimage of the Hajj in commemoration of her discovery of the life giving water. There is, however, absolutely no historical basis for Hagar and Ishmael's presence at any time in the region of Mecca; in fact, the journey was virtually a physical impossibility either 1000 miles from Abraham's home in Ur or even the 600 miles from Canaan.

In the Bible Hagar finds a wife for Ishmael in Egypt probably from among her relatives. Egypt is near the Desert of Paran. In the Qur'an Ishmael finds a wife among the Bedouin tribes, which are drawn to the sacred cubicle of the Ka'aba. According to the Bible the descendants of Ishmael join with the descendants of Midian, a later son of Abraham by Keturah. It is only then that Ishmael's descendants along with those of Midian and even Esau (the Edomites) may have lived in or near Arabia.

According to the Qur'an and Muhammad, Abraham finally goes to live with Ishmael in Mecca, which is 1000 miles from Ur of the Chaldees across extensive, impassable deserts. They build the Ka'aba together, which is a sacred edifice to Allah. Here God commands Abraham to sacrifice his son. The son is not named in the Qur'an, but Muhammad tells us that it was Ishmael and not Isaac that was brought to the mountain to be sacrificed. The mountain, furthermore, is not Mt. Moriah, which is now part of the Temple Mount in Jerusalem, but one of the mountains surrounding the sacred city of Mecca. None of the history of Abraham in Canaan, which is extensively recorded in the Bible, is acknowledged in the Qur'an. There is, on the other hand, no

Biblical record or tradition of Abraham ever having been in Arabia.

The Biblical account of the Abraham story is consistent and believable. The account in the Qur'an is so obviously a fabrication, or a fable, that it is hardly worth refuting. The distances to Mecca from Chaldea or even from Canaan through interminable miles of desert are impossible to consider for Abraham's journey much less a trek by Hagar and a young son.

The entire Biblical narrative centers on Isaac who is the child of promise. It also tells of Rebecca, whom Abraham's servant Eleazar brings back from Haran in the north as a wife for Isaac. Then there is the story of Isaac's twin sons, Jacob and Esau. Finally the twelve sons of Jacob become the fathers of the twelve tribes of Israel. Meaning "prince with God," Israel is the new name given by God to Jacob, Abraham's grandson. The Bible calls God the "God of Abraham, Isaac, and Jacob" and the "God of Israel." He is never ever called the "God of Abraham, Ishmael, and Nebaioth" (Ishmael's eldest son).

The Bible is clear that Ishmael as a son of Abraham was to become a great nation (Genesis 21:13), but Ishmael was never to share in God's other promises to Isaac and Jacob that came to them through Abraham (Genesis 21:10-12; 25:5). The Qur'an, on the other hand, always insinuates Ishmael into the center of Abraham's family. Several times in the Qur'an Abraham, Ishmael, Isaac, and Jacob are linked together as being led and blessed by Allah (Sura 2:133, 136 and 3:84). They are also linked as prophets with many others, such as Jesus, Job, Jonah, Solomon and David (Sura 4:163).

We can only say that Muhammad either was completely deceived by his angelic teacher, or he made up the story to give an Arabian connection to Abraham whom God had called to leave his father's family and serve Him. We shall see that the Moon God, who was called Al-Ilah, or "the god," was worshiped in Ur of the Chaldees. In the Bible Abraham was

called away from that pagan worship by the true Creator
God, Jehovah or Yahweh. He was directed to the Promised
Land of Canaan where he lived all the rest of his life except
for a short sojourn in Egypt. There is no historical or written
record or archeological support whatsoever for Abraham's
ever having been in Arabia, much less in Mecca.

Muhammad says that Abraham was buried in Mecca. In
the Bible Abraham's burial site, and that of Sarah and his
descendants, was the cave of Machpelah near Mamre, later
Hebron, in southern Canaan, which Abraham purchased as
a burial ground for his family (Genesis 23). The Jews have
revered it to this day. It is called the Tomb of the Patriarchs
and is now in Hebron. One wonders why Muslims would
covet this site today when they are supposed to believe that
Abraham was buried in Mecca.

There is continuity in the historical records and traditions of Israel. This history goes back to nearly 2,000 B.C.,
which is 2500 years before Muhammad was born. There is
absolutely no proof of any contact of the Patriarchs with
either the area or the peoples of Arabia. The claims made by
Islam are incredible and cannot be taken seriously. They
seem to have been simply made up by Muhammad to give his
new religion authority and continuity with the past. It is very
easy to see why the Jews of Medina rejected him and even
mocked his strange teachings.

Comparisons and Contrasts with the Bible

The Qur'an was created from Muhammad's utterances
in many small parts and pieces within a very brief period of
23 years. The Bible, meaning "little books," was written over
a period of about 1500 years by many authors—prophets,
scribes, kings, and apostles. Its internal claim is not that God
dictated the exact words, but that it was inspired or "God
breathed" by the Holy Spirit. Muslims often say that the
Bible is written in the words of men, but the Qur'an is only
in the words of Allah recited by one man Muhammad, which

makes it obviously superior. Whereas hundreds of passages in the Bible, especially in the prophets are set forth as the very words of God, much is history and moral teaching, which God inspired men to write, keeping them free from error. The Bible is clear in its teaching. *"All Scripture is inspired by God* (God breathed),*"* (2 Timothy 3:16) and *"Holy men of God spoke as they were motivated by the Holy Spirit"* (2 Peter 1:21).

Although the Bible represents many different ages and nuances of culture, this Judeo-Christian revelation and authority exhibits a much greater unity than diversity. Purely from the naturalistic standpoint the Bible is more than just an amazing work. There is nothing comparable to it in history. It comprises the oldest living writings still in use. The 39 "little books" of the Old Testament are translated from the original Hebrew and a few chapters from the Aramaic, a similar Semitic language. The 27 "little books" and letters of the New Testament are translated from the Koine or conversational Greek of the first century. Together they comprise 1189 chapters.

Scholars are in almost universal agreement that because of meticulously careful copying through the ages, there is almost no corruption in the Biblical text. Any discrepancies are easily seen to be minor mistakes by copiers of the text. These, however, are very rare. For example, when the Dead Sea scrolls were discovered, the scroll of Isaiah was the oldest copy of this prophetic work in existence by over 1000 years. After all the centuries of copying by scribes there were virtually no significant differences. Only the ignorant or the severely prejudiced may claim the text of the Bible, as it exists today has been hopelessly corrupted. This is very important because there are many contradictions in historical facts and teachings between the Qur'an and the Bible. Simply to assert the claim that the Bible or earlier revelation of Allah was corrupted by Jews and Christians cannot explain these contradictions.

At the time the Qur'an was compiled, the Bible had

already existed for from over 500 to almost 2000 years. Muhammad himself recognized what is recorded in the Qur'an, that Jews and Christians had their own revelations from God, the Torah (Taurat) or Old Testament and the Gospel (Injil) or New Testament. Never is it stated by either the Qur'an or Muhammad that this earlier revelation had been corrupted. It is therefore impossible to suggest that the Bible was changed with Islam or the Qur'an in mind, and all the evidence points to the fact that the text of the Bible has remained the same as it has been for hundreds and hundreds of years.

For several hundred years, Muslim theologians in following Muhammad found no fault with the Bible. It was only when the Bible was found to contradict the Qur'an that Muslim teachers began to say that the Bible must have been corrupted because the Qur'an was Allah's final revelation to mankind. This belief is not based on any real evidence, but solely on the presupposition that, since the Qur'an is the final revelation, it must be superior. It is equally as logical to say, however, that the Qur'an was created later by a satanic power in order to usurp the authority of the Bible.

Muslims have always said that the Qur'an, written over 500 years after the Bible was completed, has precedence as the final revelation; and that if ever there is a contradiction between these two words of God, it is the Bible which has been corrupted. This is a completely untenable assertion based on no evidence of any kind at all. We are not arguing here of just doctrinal truth, but also of historical accuracy and consistency. How could two revelations that are so diametrically different and opposed to each other in detail have been produced by the same God?

In comparing the Bible, which is regarded by the Qur'an as an earlier revelation of Allah, with Muhammad's revelation, one will have to judge for himself as objectively as he can on the merits of the two sacred books. In the opinion of this author, who has read both, the Bible wins hands down for clarity, historical accuracy, moral superiority, and integrity. There really is no comparison at all.

The Qur'an, although warranted to be a masterpiece of Arabic poetry and literature, comes out much the poorer in every way. No matter how commendable are some of the teachings of Muhammad, they do not hold a candle to the teachings of Jesus or the apostles. It is *nolo contendere*—no contest at all. Just compare Jesus' teaching, *"You have heard that it was said, 'Love your neighbor, and hate your enemy.' But I tell you, Love your enemies, and pray for those who persecute you, that you may be sons of your Father in heaven."* (Matthew 5: 43-45) with Muhammad's saying, *"Whoever changes his Islamic religion, kill him"* (Hadith 9:57). Some Muslims are really afraid of the Bible. This is indicated by the fact that a nation like Saudi Arabia absolutely forbids any Bible being brought into the country. Disobedience to this law could result in a severe punishment such as a long-term imprisonment or even death by beheading.

The definition of "the Word of God" in Christianity is the communication of God, which comes in words that men can understand. Christians say that the Bible is the Word of God just as Muslims say that the Qur'an is the word of Allah. There is a dimension to the "Word" in Christianity, however, that is not found in Islam. The Apostle John wrote, *"In the beginning was the Word. . and the Word became flesh."* Jesus came as God's son incarnate and revealed God's words out of His own mouth to his disciples, and this Word has been passed on to us. He was the perfect communication of God. Muslims can only say, *"In the beginning was the word. . and the word became a book."* Thus the Qur'an is to the Muslim what the living Christ is to the Christian. We have the dynamic of a living Word versus a dead and powerless letter.

A Summary of Some Doctrinal Differences

The Qur'an teaches the laws that are to be observed by men in order to gain an uncertain future in Paradise. Jesus

Christ fulfilled the laws of God and becomes the righteousness of God, which is the provision of salvation and eternal life for us apart from keeping the law. The Qur'an shows men what Allah commands and what he wants men to do. Jesus Christ shows us who God is and what he wants us to become. The promise of God was that His law would be written in our hearts, and the keeping of His commands would be the testimony that we truly had been born again as the children of God. Our good works would not be the means by which we would achieve Heaven or eternal life, but would be evidence of our new life, express our new love for God, gaining for us rewards in the life to come (Ephesians 2:8-9 and Titus 3:4-8). The Qur'an only reveals Allah's law not Allah himself. This is a significant and riveting difference.

Christianity teaches that man, who is born in bondage to sin, is to be rescued from a life of sin and failure and given the grace, nature, and power to become like God, hence, godly. Islam teaches that man, who is not born a sinner, has the power to save himself just by adhering to the rules as revealed in the Qur'an. Muhammad's esteemed personal value is as an example, an embodiment of the Qur'an. He is called the *Perfect Model*, the example to all men in following Allah's rules for human behavior.

Jesus Christ is also an example for the believer, but God made the provision of salvation through Him because it was impossible for a natural, unredeemed man to follow His sinless example. We are given the life of Christ when we are born again by the Spirit of God so that we can learn to live as He did (2 Corinthians 5:17 and Colossians 1:27). Thus through Him and by His faith and power we are enabled also to "fulfill the law." This is the result not the cause of salvation. No man can imitate Jesus Christ without the power of the indwelling Spirit of God.

Muslims try to earn their way to Paradise. The Bible, however, teaches, *"But when the kindness and love of God our Savior appeared, He saved us not because of righteous things we had done but because of His mercy. He saved us through the washing of rebirth and renewal by the Holy Spirit, whom He poured out on us generously through Jesus Christ our Savior, so that having been justified by His grace, we might become heirs, having the hope of eternal life. This is a trustworthy saying, and I want you to stress these things, so that those who have trusted in God may be careful to devote themselves to doing what is good. These things are excellent and profitable for everyone"* (Titus 3:4-8). No man therefore can earn his salvation. *"For it is by grace you have been saved, through faith—and this not from yourselves, it is the gift of God—not by works, so that no one can boast. For we are God's workmanship, created in Christ Jesus to do good works, which God prepared in advance for us to do"* (Ephesians 2:8-10).

Historical Criticism

Perhaps the greatest difference between the New Testament and the Qur'an is that the Gospels are presented as current eyewitness accounts of the life and ministry of Jesus. The Book of Acts tells the contemporary history of the beginnings of the early church during the time that it was taking place. Finally the epistles are written to address current problems and situations in the various churches that existed within a generation of Jesus' death, burial, and resurrection.

The Qur'an, on the other hand, does not give any running narrative of the events of Muhammad's life and ministry. This biography and history was reconstructed two or three hundred years after his death by Muslim clerics and teachers from oral traditions handed down from past generations. We cannot be certain of the accuracy of their history because there are few, if any, eyewitness accounts of the day. Those that are appealed to are admittedly only a part of Islam's oral tradition. There are no contemporary documents.

We have already noted that many of the sayings and stories of Muhammad that were being circulated were considered apocryphal. Miracles were attributed to Muhammad, for example, to try to make him a more authentic prophet like Jesus. These are now denied, and those that gathered the Hadith and the Sunna genuinely tried to choose what they believed were true accounts. Even among all the compilers of Islamic history, we have seen that only two—Al Muslim and Al Bokhari—are regarded with the highest respect. There is no way, of course, to be sure. Also there is no document trail to show the accuracy or validity of the Qur'an itself that we have seen was originally in many different versions.

The Greek New Testament, however, has overwhelmingly the greatest mass of manuscript evidence of all of the writings from ancient times. Four whole New Testament manuscripts go back to from 325 to 450 A.D. all in existence before the time of Muhammad. Variant readings are few and unimportant. Many fragments date from the 2nd and 3rd century. There are in all over 5000 manuscripts extant from the 2nd through the 15th centuries. There are two fragments of Matthew's Gospel, the Magdalen Papyri, in fact, which have been identified by one papyri expert as dating from about 55 A.D. (See Carsten Thiede, *Eyewitness to Jesus*, New York: Doubleday, 1996) There is much more reason to have confidence in the sources of Christianity than in those of Islam. Just saying that the Qur'an takes precedence over the Bible doesn't make it so. These are only words with no proof or substantiating evidence. In fact, all the internal evidence points to the inferiority of the Qur'an.

Liberal historical critics of the Bible seek to deny that the New Testament record is contemporary or eyewitness testimony. This, however, is not based on any significant historical, archeological, or other external evidence. It is rooted solely on the presuppositions or unbelief of the critics in the supernatural as expressed in miracles, the presence of Satan and demons, the virgin birth, the resurrection, the ascension, and in general anything else that supports the deity of Christ as the incarnate Son of God and the Savior. These are all regarded simply as myths created to support the "faith" of the early church.

These skeptical critics teach that much that is in the Bible was made up, an invention of pious but deluded minds. In their criticism they believe that they are "demythologizing" the New Testament in order to make it palatable to the enlightened scientific mind. A recent example of this is a conclusion by members of the Jesus Seminar, a very small group of radical and vocal New Testament scholars, that only 18% of all of Jesus' words and teachings were authentic. They obviously are guilty of creating their own unsubstantiated myths, which are rooted in their own presuppositions concerning reality. It is a highly suspect, subjective exercise with no credible basis in fact. Thousands of more traditional New Testament scholars heartily disagree with them.

Muslims often argue against the validity of the New Testament testimony to Jesus from the writings of these liberal critics. They cannot reasonably base their claims on the arguments of infidels, however, because Muslims would have to accept the infidel's rejection of the supernatural to validate their own objections. They would have to reject many of the Biblical records of the Old Testament, such as Noah and the flood, and a New Testament event like the virgin birth, which are mentioned in the Qur'an. Muslims, however, do not share the anti-supernatural presuppositions of these whom they must consider infidels, but this is the only real basis for the liberals' late dating of the New Testament documents, and their rejecting them as eyewitness accounts. Thus, Muslims cannot use these criticisms at all as grounds for their arguments against the historicity and accuracy of the New Testament record, because when applied by these same liberal scholars to the origins of Islam, conclusions would be similar or even more devastating to Islam's authenticity.

Finally, there is no evidence of any major corruption of

the New Testament Greek text. Even liberal Greek scholars like Dr. Edgar J. Goodspeed of the University of Chicago have admitted that 99.9% of the text is the same as it was originally written. The records of the origins of Islam, on the other hand, are on very shaky ground in comparison to the record of the origin of Christ and Christianity.

"Two Islams" in the Qur'an—The Doctrine of Progressive Revelation—Militants vs. Moderates

There are two major periods during which the revelation of the Qur'an came to Muhammad. The very different emphases in these two periods account for most of the apparent contradictions in teachings and spirit portrayed in the book. This also accounts for the two different characters or perspectives of Islam: (1) what can be called moderate or "soft" Islam and (2) the expression of radical or militant Islam. The Qur'an seems to teach both. The first period encompasses the twelve years when Muhammad lived in Mecca (610-622) and also his first year in Medina (623). The second period comprises the remainder of his time in Medina. (624-632).

During the first thirteen years in Islam's development Muhammad was on the defensive and suffered much opposition and even persecution in Mecca. It is obvious that the prophet sought to make his religion attractive to Christians and Jews, calling them the "people of the earlier revelation" who had been blessed by Allah. He at first claimed that the God of the Christians and Jews was the same as Allah whom He was proclaiming (Sura 29:46). He even portrayed the Jews as those having Allah's special favor through whom He had sent prophets into the world (Sura 2:47 and 5:20).

Muhammad believed that especially the Jews would support him in what he thought was his resurrection of the ancient monotheism. This certainly was his reason for choosing Yathrib, later Medina, as his new home where there were three prosperous Jewish clans. He immediately sought the friendship and support of the Jews. It is during this period that the Qur'an teaches that there should be "*no compulsion in religious faith*" (Sura 2:256). Another example of Muhammad's initial tolerance was that originally during prayer times Muslims were supposed to face toward Jerusalem.

The Jews, however, reacted with scorn to Muhammad's account of the Old Testament history and teachings of the Torah. They did not recognize Allah as the God of Israel. They taunted and ridiculed him and supported those who stood against him. One Jewish woman even tried to poison him.

Serious Christians also could not have been happy with Muhammad's description of Jesus as only a prophet and not God's Son or the Second Person of the Triune Deity. These rejections and humiliations made Muhammad very angry, and he retaliated with fierce actions and militant teachings.

In the second period of the revelation of the Qur'an, therefore, the "softness" and conciliatory tone of the first period was officially abrogated by Allah in the Qur'an. Allah's revelation was taught to be a progressive revelation or what is called in Arabic the doctrine of *nasikh*. Note Sura 2:106, "*When we cancel a message or cause it to be forgotten, we replace it with one better or one similar. Do you not know that Allah can do (has power over) all things?*" Muhammad himself admitted to changing his teaching because Allah had revealed to him a different message (Sura 16:101).

All Islamic sects teach the doctrine of *nasikh* or progressive revelation. It is convenient, to be sure, to have both conciliatory and militant teachings in the same book. When in the minority and when seeking to curry favor especially in America and in the West, Muslims emphasize the "tolerant" teachings toward non-Muslims in the Qur'an. When in the majority or when seeking to extend Islam's power and influence, Muslims can appeal to Holy Jihad against non-Muslims, citing the example as well as the teachings of Muhammad.

The basic principle of *nasikh*, furthermore, is that the later teaching cancels out the former teaching, and newer revelation abrogates all previous revelations. The declarations of war against unbelievers in the text of the Qur'an come largely from the second period of Muhammad's revelation. These are the teachings, which today motivate the militants, the extremists, the radicals, the fundamentalists, the jihadists, and the terrorists in their eternal fight against all the infidels in the world as well as against those who espouse a secular, a moderate, or a "soft" Islam. (See the chapter on Holy Jihad.)

Moderate Muslims, however, cling to those verses in the Qur'an, which seem to teach the more tolerant approach. The majority of Muslims in the world today are still considered to be moderate, but militants are daily gaining ground through their teachings in Islamic schools and preaching in the mosques. These have been supported all around the world primarily by the Wahhabi sect of Saudi Arabia with oil money from some members of the royal family in that nation. As we shall see, these militants do have support for their ideas and beliefs from the literal words in portions of the Qur'an and from Muhammad's own teachings in the Hadith.

Many have hoped that a reform movement might sweep the Islamic world comparable to the Reformation of the Christian church in Europe or reforms in other movements, which brought more moderation and rationality to their systems. From the standpoint of orthodox Islam and the teachings of the Qur'an and Muhammad, however, such reform would have to bring about a change in what is called "basic Islam." According to a Canadian Muslim journalist Irshad Manji, most Muslims have no idea how to "debate, dissent, revise or reform" where the Qur'an and Islamic law is concerned. They simply have never been encouraged to ask questions or interpret the Qur'an freely, and they fear to do so.

(Quoted in Blankley, *The West's Last Chance*, pp. 45-46) Both Judaism and Christianity have been much more free and open in their discussions and understanding of their religious faiths. Islam is an extremely closed system in comparison.

This kind of change would have to be more similar to the old modernist or liberal movement within the Protestant denominations, which actually began with denying the basic doctrines of Christian faith and the authority of the Bible. It does not seem likely that such a movement, which would include a denial of the unquestioned authority of the Qur'an, would gain a very wide acceptance in the Islamic world. Most would be afraid to voice their doubts. Any who promoted this kind of "unbelief," furthermore, would certainly be in danger of being killed.

The only hope for the peace of the world is that Muslims will not actually put into practice the logical consequence of their basic teachings, which is to bring every people and nation by force as well as persuasion in subjection to Allah and Islamic law. Since as many as one tenth of over one billion Muslims in the world have been infected with these radical teachings, however, it is likely that militant Islam will be with us for many, many years to come.

The irony of the matter is that although most Muslims will not participate in terrorist acts, neither will the majority of them speak up against the extremists. Many believe that the Qur'an really supports the vision and actions of the jihadists and give their silent support.

Others who disagree do not speak up because they fear for their own safety and the security of their families. King Abdullah of Jordan's recent bold condemnation of Muslim terrorists who sacrifice the lives of innocent people was a breath of fresh air and a singularly courageous act by a moderate Islamic ruler who sincerely wants peace and to be a friend to the West. May more Muslim leaders dare to follow his example.

We might want to encourage moderation, but it seems to

me to be an insoluble problem. Many Muslims believe that
we are living in the last days, as do evangelical Christians.
This means that as the Day of Judgment nears Muslims
believe that it is their holy responsibility to conquer and
obliterate the Jews and finally to impose the law of Allah on
all infidels in the entire world.

Chapter 3

ALLAH—THE GOD OF ISLAM

In the Introduction to this book we cited a PBS-TV's *Frontline* documentary on Islam in America. The community of Palos Heights, Illinois was featured where Muslims have sought to buy a church building and turn it into a mosque. This was opposed by the citizens of the area, and we witnessed a discussion between Christians and informed Muslim leaders concerning the issue. The most important claim made by the Muslims was, "After all, we worship the same god." Although this claim is also made in an early revelation in the Qur'an, it is not true. The god depicted in the Qur'an just is not the same as the God of the Bible. The God of Abraham, Isaac, and Jacob and Moses and the Father of our Lord Jesus Christ is not the same being as the Islamic god. There are certainly some similarities, but they differ in character, in purpose, and in their relationship with man.

Al-Ilah means "the chief deity" or "the god" in Arabic. The specific word for god in Arabic is *Ilah* and is related to the Hebrew *Elah* the singular of *Elohim*. The article "al" is simply the article "the." Al-Ilah contracts to Allah. The belief in this chief of deities predates Muhammad's revelation. His own father was called a "servant of Allah" or Abdallah. The most important god of the western Semitic tribes, who was the head of their pantheon of many gods, was usually not identified by his name, but was simply called "the god." There were many Arabs influenced by Jews and Christians in Muhammad's time who were already thinking that perhaps the one they called "Allah" was the only real deity.

Muhammad's teaching simply confirmed that conviction that there was only one Al-Ilah.

Allah as the Moon God

For hundreds of years before Muhammad the designation "Al-Ilah" was applied to the Moon god of the western Semitic peoples from the Euphrates to the Nile. Archeological evidence from Arabia of amulets and idols representing the Moon god indicated its primary place in pre-Islamic religion.

The Arabs worshiped this Moon god as the most important of all the hundreds of idols at the Ka'aba, the sacred cubed building in Mecca. He was not identified by his name, but simply by the generic term "Allah." Allah was the designation for this highest deity in their pantheon of gods. There were idols on display for worship at the Ka'aba representing the 360 gods of the Arab pantheon, one for each of the days of the lunar year. The Moon god was "the chief deity" of them all or Al-Ilah, "the god."

The Moon god's name was *Nanna-sin* or simply *Sin*, and he was worshiped for centuries before the advent of Islam. Originally therefore Allah was the designation for *Nanna-sin*, who was worshiped as the head of a pantheon of lesser gods.

The Romans were also polytheists and had a pantheon of gods led by their chief god named Jupiter. He was therefore the "Allah" of the Roman pantheon. The Greek god Zeus was comparable to both Jupiter of the Romans and to the Moon god Nanna-sin of the Arabs. Zeus could therefore also be characterized as Allah, or the chief god of the Greek pantheon of gods.

There is some confusion, however, where Islam is concerned because the designation god or Allah has been used since the time of Muhammad as if it were a name like Jupiter or Zeus. The Arabic words "the god" or "allah" therefore usurp all names used to identify the highest deity including the revelation of "the Most High God" in the Bible.

The Ka'aba was dedicated to Allah long before Muhammad's time and was a center of Arab pilgrimage and worship. Mecca had therefore become the most important town in Arabia. The Quraysh, the principal tribe in Mecca, became the wealthiest and most prominent people in all of Arabia because of the wealth and trade derived from the thousands of Arab pilgrims from other areas who came to pay homage to their gods.

The Moon god was considered by the Arabs to be a male god whose female consort was the Sun. Together they had three daughters—Al-Lat, Al-'Uzza, and Manat—who are mentioned in the Qur'an (Sura 53:19-20). These were representations of planets including Venus, and were the next most important deities in the pantheon. In the 5th century B.C. the Greek historian Herodotus makes mention of an important god of the Arabs called Al-il-Lat or Al Lat.

The worship of these gods therefore predated Muhammad by more than 1000 years. Muhammad, at first, in deference to the merchants of Mecca, his Quraysh brethren, allowed the three daughters of Allah to be included in his religion as offspring gods. This was later said to have been a temptation of Satan, and the teaching was revoked.

Salmon Rushdie, the British novelist wrote about this lapse of Muhammad in his novel *The Satanic Verses*. For his irreverent impertinence in defaming Muhammad, Rushdie was placed in mortal danger by a condemnatory *fatwah* issued by the Ayatollah Khomeini of Iran authorizing any Muslim to kill him. After several years it was revoked, and Rushdie was able to surface from his hide-a-ways.

The Qur'an, referring to the three daughters of the Moon god in Sura 53:23, says, *"These are but names which you and your fathers have invented. Allah has vested no authority in them."* One might ask that if the ancestors of the Semitic peoples had invented the names of the daughters of Allah as the Qur'an asserts, why could it not be concluded that they had also invented the name and person of Allah as well? The fact that the three names remain in the Qur'an, furthermore, provides certain indication that the Allah of Islam was originally the old Moon god of the western Semitic tribes.

The archeologist Sir Leonard Wooley discovered a temple to the Moon god Nanna-sin in the Sumerian city of Ur dating back at least to 2800 B.C. There was a trench around the monument, which displayed drawings and cuneiform inscriptions showing that it had been filled with snakes, maybe pythons. Markings of the cobra were also prominent. The snake or serpent in the Bible is a symbol for Satan.

This was the city out of which Abram was called by his own personal God. The worship of Nanna-sin the Moon god is condemned in the Bible as just another idolatrous pagan practice. It is obvious that the god of Abraham was neither Nanna-sin, the Moon god of the ancient Semites nor the Allah of Islam. The God of Abraham became the "God of Israel" revealed also to Moses, and we shall see that He has His own name, and it is not Nanna-sin.

There are hundreds of archeological finds in Arabia— idols, amulets and inscriptions. Some show the crescent moon with three stars, which symbolize Allah and his three daughters. The crescent moon, which was a symbol of the Moon god going back to the times of the Sumerians and the Babylonians, is still a symbol of Islam today. It is also significant that the month of Ramadan, which is sacred to Muslims, begins and ends at the time of the crescent moon.

Arabs used Allah in naming their children like Abdallah, the name of Muhammad's father. The word for god in Arabic has therefore taken on an identity as a name. This was similar to the Jewish practice of naming their children with the suffix referring to Yahweh, the actual name of "the Most High" or "the God" in the Old Testament; for example, Jeremiah or Nehemiah, or Zechariah. The modern spelling for the suffix -iah is -yahu as in Netanyahu.

No Muslim scholar can deny that the Allah that

Muhammad claimed was the Creator god originated in the chief god of the Arab pantheon of gods. Muhammad believed that the lesser gods represented by the idols of the Ka'aba were false gods and that only Allah was the true god. He claimed thereby to be resurrecting the original monotheism—the ancient worship of the one true god. Islam is a religion sprung out of an ancient idolatry, which was cleansed of its pluralism by Muhammad.

The Old Testament prophets spoke out against the worship of the heavenly bodies, which was the practice of the neighboring Semitic tribes. Moses gave the first warning in Deuteronomy 4:19: *"And when you look up to the sky and see the sun, the moon, and the stars—all the heavenly array—do not be enticed into bowing down to them and worshiping."* (See also Deuteronomy 17:3.) Job said that if he gave the kiss of homage to the sun or the moon, *"I would have been unfaithful to God on high"* (Job 31:26-28). In his cleansing of the Temple, King Josiah removed the priests who burned incense to the moon (2 Kings 23:5-6). The prophet Jeremiah severely criticized the kings, officials, priests, prophets and people of Jerusalem who served, followed, consulted with, and worshiped the sun, moon, and the planets of the heavens. God said that He would judge them and expose their bones (Jeremiah 8:2).

We can surmise from this evidence that the prophet Muhammad was deceived in his choice of Allah, who was originally the ancient chief pagan deity, the Moon god Nanna-sin. The Bible expressly forbids this worship. Satan, depicted in the Bible as an *Angel of light*, is also the *Great Deceiver* and seems, without doubt, to have been the author of this deception.

Allah and the God of the Bible

Muhammad concluded that his god Allah was the only true *Ilah* or god. He identified Allah with the God of the Bible or the one God of the Jews and Christians. He claimed that Abraham worshiped Allah as did all the prophets including

Jesus and His disciples. In the Biblical story, however, Abraham was called away from the worship of the Moon god in Ur of the Chaldees by a different God who revealed Himself to him as the true Creator God. God (*Allah* in Arabic) later identified Himself to Moses as the "*I am who I am*" (Jehovah is the common translation, but *Yahweh* may be the closest transliteration.) or "the God of Abraham, Isaac, and Jacob." (See Exodus 3.) This name identified Him as the preexisting, existing, and eternal God. This means that He was not the same as the god of Muhammad who was the chief god of the Ka'aba.

Muslim teachers or mullahs struggle to find Allah in the Bible because it is claimed that he was the author of this earlier revelation. There is, however, absolutely no reference to a god like the Allah of the Qur'an in the Bible although, as we have seen, there are many negative references to the Moon god. Muhammad had originally tried to tie his religion into the traditions of the Jews and Christians, but was rejected. In anger before he died, he demanded that all Jews and Christians be expelled from Arabia. The orthodox directive was eventually given to kill even the "people of the book" or "the people of the earlier revelation" if they would not submit to the laws of Allah.

Referring to "the people of the book," an early statement in the Qur'an says, *"Our God and your God is one, and to Him we submit"* (Sura 29:46). On further detailed examination, however, many Islamic teachers today do not believe that Allah is the same as the God of Abraham, Isaac, and Jacob depicted in the Bible. They think that the Bible has a corrupted view of the true God. They believe that the only accurate and true picture of God is to be found in the person of Allah described in the Qur'an. Some Muslim teachers even suggest that the Yahweh of the Old Testament was a demonic manifestation.

Jews and Christians, of course, hold exactly the opposite view. To them Allah is a caricature of the true Creator God. Allah is believed to be a false god, a usurper without a name.

His anonymous character arose out of pagan beliefs and has been given a new description in keeping with a new claim that he alone is the true God. Some Orthodox Christians in the most oppressive Muslim nations, who have lived as second-class citizens under the threat of a Muslim majority, have come to regard Allah as a personification of Satan.

Where Muslims live as a minority in a nation with Christian origins, it is often that they will say, maybe with tongue in cheek, "After all, we worship the same god," but this is not orthodox Islamic doctrine today. This deceitful approach simply avoids conflict and provides grounds for acceptance of Muslims in the community. It also provides a convenient, common ground on which to begin to try to win new converts to Islam.

Some may argue that no matter what the origins of the concept of Allah, today both Muslims and Arab Christians regard him as the Supreme Being or Creator of the universe, earth, and man. The word simply means "the god" in Arabic. Allah therefore should be respected as such. This does not answer, however, the many troubling and even devastating differences between Allah of Islam and the Judeo-Christian God as He is revealed in the Bible.

It is unfortunate and confusing that the Arabic translations of the Bible, and Bible translations in other Muslim countries, use the name Allah for God. The proper translation would be to use the word Ilah as it is also used in the Qur'an to refer to God in the generic sense. Sura 2:255 says, *"Allah, there is no god* (Ilah) *but him, the living the eternal one."* Also the *shawadah* or declaration of Islamic faith says, *"There is no god* (Ilah) *but Allah, and Muhammad is his prophet."* Although Allah means "the god" in Arabic, it has for all practical purposes become the name of the god of Muhammad and Islam—separate and distinct from the God of Abraham, Isaac, and Jacob, the God of Israel, of the prophets, of Jesus and his disciples, and of all orthodox Jews and confessing Christians today.

Although Allah is used as the word for God in the Arabic Bible, many who are converted to Christianity from Islam feel very uncomfortable in identifying the God of the Bible with the name Allah. An Egyptian university professor, for example, who was converted to Christianity after being disillusioned by Islam, explained the awful conflict in using "Allah" for "God" in the Arabic translation of his Bible. Dr. Mark Gabriel (his western name) was a former professor at Al Azhar University in Cairo, which is Islam's premier educational and theological institution. His knowledge of his old faith is profound. He had memorized the entire Qur'an by the time he was twelve years old. He expressed deep concern in the use of the name "Allah" to translate Jesus as *"Allah the Son"* or in passages like John 3:16, *"For Allah so loved the world. . ."* He wrote, *"For myself, I hate this feature of the Arabic Bible. I was delivered from Islam and have no desire to read the name of Allah in my Bible. Hatred, destruction, killing, anger, deceit, racism, and hopelessness—this is the name Allah to me."* In its origins in the Middle East before Islam, *"the name Allah has never referred to the one true God of heaven"* (*Islam and the Jews*, p. 179).

This is a genuine problem for Christians in Arab countries; namely, how to differentiate the "Allah" in the Bible from Allah in the Qur'an. As we shall see they are certainly two different beings with many conflicting characteristics. Although in some ways similar, the differences are greater than the similarities.

The best way to differentiate the God of the Bible from the Allah of Islam would be simply to call Him by His name Yahweh or Jehovah meaning, "I am who I am," or "the God of Abraham, Isaac, and Jacob," which God Himself said would be His name. Note Exodus 3:15—*"God also said to Moses, 'Say to the Israelites—The Lord, the God of your fathers—the God of Abraham, the God of Isaac and the God of Jacob—has sent me to you.* ***This is my name forever, the name by which I am to be remembered from generation to generation.'"*** In light of this statement, why is this name never used for God in the Qur'an if the Qur'an was inspired by the true God?

This name in the Hebrew is comprised of four consonants YHWH and is known as a tetragrammaton. Vowels are not included in the original Hebrew texts so the exact rendering and pronunciation of this name is unknown. The Hebrew people considered it too sacred a name to use, so whenever it appeared in the text of the Old Testament, it was pronounced *Adonai* meaning Lord. This name is shown in the English Bible as LORD in capital letters translating the Hebrew tetragrammaton YHWH, *"I am who I am."* It is the name appearing most frequently in the Old Testament to designate the God of Israel, where it is used over 7,000 times.

Allah of the Qur'an and the God of the Bible are two different beings. They are portrayed as having very different characteristics. Allah is utterly transcendent. He is not a personal God and cannot be known by his followers. The God of the Bible can be known as a Person. Allah is a monolithic being, whereas the God of the Bible is described as a composite Being in both the Old and New Testaments. This unique plurality is revealed in the New Testament as God having three persons, which Christians call the Triune God or the Trinity. To Muslims, and even to traditional Jews who do not understand the teaching of the composite unity of God in the Old Testament, the Triune God is an idolatrous teaching.

Because Allah and the God of Jews and Christians are so different, well-taught Muslims believe that the latter worship a false god. Also in objecting to the Trinity taught in the New Testament, Muslims claim that Christians worship three gods. To a Muslim this means that Christians are infidels because they are committing the most serious sin of *shirk*, which is the idolatrous offering of competition to Allah. They will therefore be punished by fires in Hell unless they repent, bow the knee to the one god Allah, and become Muslims.

Well-informed Christians, on the other hand, would

consider the worship of Allah to be an abomination—the worship of a creation of Satan and therefore tantamount to a worship of Satan himself. There is no possibility of any kind of common ground here. The differences between Allah of Islam and the God of Christians and Jews cannot be reconciled.

What are the Differences Between Allah and Jehovah?

Of the 99 names, which describe Allah's attributes, only one says he is loving. Also none of them identify Allah as Father, which shows God's love to us in the Bible. Allah is never characterized as a god of unconditional love. He does not love those who are corrupt (Sura 5:64). He does not love unbelievers (Sura 3:32). He does not love the unjust or evildoers (Sura 3:57). In other words, Allah only loves those who submit to him, obey him, and do good works. He does not love the sinner.

The Bible, however, teaches that as a part of the general revelation of His character, the true God distributes his blessings to the righteous and sinner alike. Specifically Romans 5:8 teaches, *"But God showed His love for us, in that when we were still sinners, Christ died for us."* Both Old and New Testaments depict God as a God of love and the Apostle John predicates God's very character as *love* when he writes, *"God is love"* and *"This is love, not that we loved God but that He loved us and sent his son as an atoning sacrifice for our sins"* (1 John 4:6, 10).

The Apostle Paul teaches us that when we were God's enemies, *"we were reconciled to Him by the death of His Son,"* and that *"Christ died for the ungodly."* The Bible, of course, also depicts God as a God of justice who doles out punishments as well as blessings. It emphasizes, however, that *"God is not willing that any should perish but that all should come to repentance"* (2 Peter 3:9b).

The names of Allah primarily describe his exalted majesty and his overwhelming power, which is expressed in his will. He can be merciful and forgiving to those that repent, and he is pictured as loving only those who submit completely to him. As the creator of all things, however, he can do anything he pleases. He is the direct creator of both good and evil. He can even cause men to sin and then punish them. From the human point of view, however, his decisions and actions can be arbitrary. Allah can break his word and not keep his promises because he is absolutely sovereign, which has great implications for dealing with some Muslims in the world of business, diplomacy, and even social contact. His most important characteristic is his will, and no one has the right to question him. This precludes the concept of freedom from being a major value in Islam.

Allah predetermines everything. True freedom of the human will is discarded since everything is predestined to be as it is by Allah, the almighty. Allah's will has no limitations. It is Allah alone who determines who goes to heaven or hell. Man can do all kinds of good works, but ultimately he can do nothing short of martyrdom to influence Allah's sending him to heaven. Human freedom or liberty is not highly valued in Muslim societies, whereas it is a major component in the teachings of Judeo-Christianity. It finds its most emphatic expression in the teachings of Jesus and the Apostle Paul. *"If the Son shall set you free, you shall truly be free."* (John 8:26), and *"Where the Spirit of the Lord is there is liberty"* (2 Corinthians 10:29).

The God of the Bible is limited by His character, which is absolute purity, righteousness, honesty, longsuffering, patience, goodness, kindness, faithfulness, and unconditional love. He has permitted evil to come into the world, but He is not its direct Creator. In fact, He seeks to turn evil to good purposes (Romans 8:28). He manipulated the evil works against Joseph in Egypt and Jesus in order to ultimately bring salvation for His people and the world. In fact, God's eyes are even too pure to look upon evil (Habakkuk 1:3). His mercies are pictured as eternal. Even His judgments are combined with blessings. In His mercy he postpones the times of judgment. He has made covenants with men, promises that He cannot break. He therefore limits Himself, but in so doing demonstrates His wisdom, His fairness, His longsuffering, and His love. Allah is depicted in the Qur'an as being merciful, but even in this role he is a poor caricature of the God of the Bible.

Allah is completely transcendent. He is utterly unknowable and can never be comprehended. He is a "remote, vast, and unknown god." No human being can ever know Allah because he is so different from us and so far away from us. One can know that he exists and can know some of his rules for human behavior. We can describe some of his attributes, but we can never know him in a personal sense. He is totally beyond our comprehension, and we can have no personal relationship with him. It would be like an ant trying to have fellowship with a human being. There is an element of the ludicrous about the very thought.

To have an intimate relationship with Allah is an absolute impossibility and actually is an insult to Allah because it sullies his greatness and demeans his transcendence and his majesty. The Sufi Muslim sect has tried to overcome this obstacle by seeking a relationship or union with Allah. Sufis are regarded as the mystical branch of Islam and remain only a very small percentage of Muslims worldwide. They demonstrate, however, man's hunger for a more intimate connection to his Creator.

Allah has not revealed himself as a person, but reveals only his will, which must be obeyed. In no way is Allah to be identified with or in any intimate way to be dependent on his creation. The concept of God being a personal loving father to his children is incomprehensible to a Muslim.

The God of the Bible, however, can be known intimately by His children. He claims to be their Father in both Old and New Testaments. Quoting the Old Testament promises, Paul writes *"Come out from among them and be separate says the Lord, and touch not anything unclean; and I will receive you and will be a*

Father to you and you shall be my sons and daughters, says the Lord Almighty" (2 Corinthians 6:16-18).

Getting to know God is one of the greatest privileges possessed by a child of God. The Scriptures are full of the idea, the teaching, and the desirability of seeking to know God. There are too many passages throughout the Word to even begin to list them. Paul prayed that the Ephesian Christians would learn to know God better (Ephesians 1:17). Jesus, whom Muslims say is a prophet of God, said in his prayer of intercession for His disciples, *"This is eternal life, that they may know Thee, the only true God, and Jesus the Messiah whom thou hast sent"* (John 17:3). The Apostle John taught that we can know that we know God if we obey His commandments and are filled with His love. *"Everyone who loves has been born of God and knows God"* (I John 2:3 and 4:8). Paul testified, *"I know whom I have believed"* (2 Timothy 1:12).

The Triune God of the Bible

In contrast to the monolithic, indivisible nature of Allah, the God of the Bible in both the Old and New Testaments is a composite unity. In the famous *Shema Israel* ('Hear, O Israel') quoted in every synagogue from Deuteronomy 6:4, God is declared to be "one Lord." *"Hear O Israel: The Lord our God, the Lord is one."*

The Hebrew word for "one" in this passage is **'echad**, which refers to a composite or combined unity. It comes from a root word meaning to unify or collect together. It is used in other passages in the Torah, and it often refers to a combining of two or more elements. *"The two shall be one flesh"* (Genesis 2:24). The two dreams that Joseph interpreted for Pharaoh (Genesis 41:25-26) were described as being *one*. In both instances **'echad** is the Hebrew word for *one* used to describe this combined unity. It is often translated in the Old Testament in the sense of being together, such as the whole congregation in Ezra 2:64 or those Israelites who worked on the house of God *together* (Ezra 3:9). *Together* they were *one* or *'echad*. This Hebrew word is used to describe many kinds of collections of human beings in groups, societies, or a nation. God in the Old Testament is never pictured as a monolithic, indivisible Being as is claimed for Allah by Islam's teachers, or even in the official doctrines of Judaism.

Also the Hebrew word for God, *elohim*, found throughout the Torah is the plural form of *Elah* or God, which is comparable to the word *Ilah* in Arabic. Genesis 1:1 reads, *"In the beginning God (Elohim) created the heavens and the earth."* On the sixth day God created man, and Genesis 1:26 describes the deliberation within the godhead. *"Let **us** make man in our own image, in our likeness."* There are many passages like this in the Old Testament, which indicate some kind of plurality within the unity of God. Although it was the meaning of their Hebrew language, most Jews have not understood this underlying truth or have even tried to explain it away.

It is not until the New Testament, however, that we fully understand this revelation. Beginning in the four Gospels we find the teaching of the Triune deity—one God in three persons—Father, Son, and Holy Spirit. At least this is how God revealed Himself through Jesus, who was declared to be God's Son, who taught us about His Father God and said that He and the Father were One. He finally taught us about the Holy Spirit through Whom God would manifest Himself and continue His work in the world after Jesus ascended to His Father.

Those who received this teaching of Jesus were all Jews, and no objection to this teaching is ever expressed in the New Testament or by the early church, which was primarily Jewish. This is probably because some of the ancient rabbis did understand that there was a composite unity in God's nature taught in the Torah, and the idea was not unknown to devout Jews.

The teaching concerning the Triune God—God the Father, God the Son, and God the Holy Spirit—is not something that Christians invented. God is described in this fashion throughout the entire New Testament. This teaching is present, for example, from the very beginning at the annunciation of the angel to Mary. Luke writes, *"The angel answered, 'The Holy Spirit will come upon you, and the power of the Most High will overshadow you. So the holy one to be born will be called the Son of God'"* (Luke 1:35). Here we have the Holy Spirit, the Most High (the Father), and the Son.

This trinity of persons in the Godhead is present at Jesus' baptism, the Transfiguration, the Crucifixion, and the Resurrection. Jesus Himself attests to it in the Great Commission where the disciples are commanded to baptize *"in the name of the Father and the Son and the Holy Spirit."* (Matthew 28:19). Jesus also made reference all the time to His Father, referring to the God of the Jews, and identifying Himself as His Son (Matthew 16 and John 10). At both His baptism and on the Mount of Transfiguration, God the Father's voice is heard coming from above saying, *"This is my beloved Son in whom I am well pleased."*

In the classic passage in John 14, the disciple Philip asks Jesus to show them the Father. Jesus answered, *"Don't you know me, Philip, even after I have been among you such a long time? Anyone who has seen me has seen the Father. . Don't you believe that I am in the Father, and that the Father is in me?"* Earlier Jesus had also told the Jews who wanted to stone Him, *"I and My Father are One"* (John 10:30).

He then predicted the coming of the "Comforter," the Holy Spirit, who would "come upon" His disciples and empower them to do His work. The Greek word translated "Comforter" is *parakletos* and, as we have seen, means "one called alongside to help." The work of the Holy Spirit is ever-present in the ministry of the Apostles and the life of the church depicted in the New Testament. He is presented, not just as an influence, but also as a Person sent from the Father to help his children and glorify the Son.

All three Persons of the deity are mentioned throughout the New Testament, each of them having a special work, position and responsibility and yet being one God. The Apostle Paul concludes his second letter to the Corinthian church with the benediction, *"May the grace of the Lord Jesus Christ, and the love of God, and the fellowship of the Holy Spirit be with you all"* (2 Corinthians 13:14). He taught the Ephesian church, *"For through Him* (the Son) *we both have access to the Father by one Spirit"* (Ephesians 2:18). Paul then refers to the new "household of God" which is built on the foundation of the prophets and apostles. Jesus Christ is called the chief cornerstone or capstone of this new creation. Paul concludes that we are joined with Christ in a new holy temple to God *"built together to become a dwelling in which God lives by his Spirit"* (Ephesians 2:19-22).

Often the phrase "Spirit of God" is used in the Old Testament (e.g., Psalm 51:11 and Genesis 2:1), but most Jews did not understand this as an expression of God in His capacity as a separate person. God in his capacity as Father is also mentioned many times in the Old Testament (Psalm 103:13). *Yahweh* or Jehovah is the name most widely used for the deity, which is the name Jesus identified with Himself. One can therefore find indications of the Triune God throughout the entire Old Testament.

Most Christians do not try to explain the Triune God, but simply accept the revelation by faith. There is, however, a significant illustration from the entire creation, which is exemplified best by the three atoms of the water molecule (H2O) in its three states as solid, liquid and gas. These can be present all at the same time. This characteristic, furthermore, is true of every element in the universe. Each substance can be either found or made into these three states at varying temperatures. In this sense all matter can be described as three-in-one and reflects the nature of its Creator.

Also we live in a universe having characteristics of time and space. Time has three parts—past, present, and future; and space has three dimensions—length, depth, and height. Light is composed of three primary colors—red, blue and yellow.

Einstein also determined that energy, matter and time could not be separated, but were all interrelated. To natural man the new theories of matter and the universe are incomprehensible. So is the Triune God. There are other examples of this revelation concerning God's nature in the creation. It seems as though the composite nature of God is built into and illustrated by everything He created.

The prophet Isaiah had a vision of God seated on His throne *"high and lifted up."* He saw six winged seraphs or angels who were calling to each other, *"Holy, holy, holy is the Lord Almighty. The whole earth is full of His glory."* We can interpret this as saying that each person of the Triune God is declared to be Holy and the whole earth manifests His glory by mirroring His very triune nature (Isaiah 6:1-3).

Allah, on the other hand, is regarded as having an absolutely indivisible unity. The concept of the Trinity, therefore, is considered an idolatrous anathema. It is asserted that Christians teach idolatry. Therefore Muslims claim that the Bible is a corrupt book. Anyone bringing a Bible into Saudi Arabia or studying or teaching the Bible within the borders of the kingdom is in danger of severe punishment, even execution by beheading.

This division of the unity of God is regarded in the Qur'an as a very grave sin, which will certainly send the infidel to hell. He who says, *"'God is the Christ, son of Mary'. . his abode shall be Hell. Unbelievers say, 'God is the third of the trinity;' but there is no other god other than God the one, and if they do not desist from saying what they say, then indeed those among them who persist in disbelief will suffer painful punishment"* (Sura 5:72-73). And *"They speak blasphemy who say that Allah is the third of three. There is indeed no god except the one God"* (Sura 5:73).

This ascribing of partners to Allah was committing the sin of *shirk* or *association*, which was the only sin mentioned in the Qur'an, which cannot be forgiven. *"Truly Allah will not forgive any associating with him but will forgive anything else. . For whoever associates with Allah verily commits a grave sin"* (Sura 4:48).

The Dome of the Rock, which was constructed on the Temple Mount in A.D 691., is covered with quotations from the Qur'an in the Arabic script. Right over the area of the door as one enters is the statement, *"Allah has no son."* Sura 9:30 says, *"Christians say, 'Christ is the son of Allah' May they be damned by Allah. How perverse are they!"* We have seen that the Qur'an, because of Muhammad's limited knowledge of Christianity, describes the Trinity as God the Father, the Mother Mary, and the Son Jesus. This is one example of one of over 100 blatant historical inaccuracies, which make the Qur'an much less than a revelation from an all-knowing Creator god.

"Only a lord" versus "A Lord and Father"

Allah is often referred to as *rabb*, meaning lord. He is never ever referred to as *abb* or father. Allah has no partners and no family. To call him "father" would reduce him to the level of the human, and this is unthinkable. In rejecting this picture of God, Islam has missed one of the most beautiful and comforting pictures which the Bible in both the Old and New Testaments gives of the true God. Psalm 103:13 pictures Him as a Father who has compassion on his children. Psalm 68:5 says that He is the Father of the fatherless. The prophet Isaiah writes, *"You, O Lord, are our Father, our Redeemer from of old is your name"* (Isaiah 63:16). And again, *"Yet, O Lord, you are our Father. We are the clay, you are the potter; we are all the work of your hand"* (Isaiah 65:8).

More than in any other role, God is pictured as our Father in the New Testament. Jesus Himself said, *"I and my Father are One"* (John 10:30). He is called *"the Everlasting Father"* in the prophetic words of Isaiah. (9:6) Jesus called Him my Father and your Father (Luke 12:32) which means that we can have a personal relationship with Him. We are taught by Jesus to address him as *"Our Father in Heaven"* (Matthew 6:9 and Luke 11:2).

The Apostle Paul says that all fathers on earth are named

after the Father in heaven (Ephesians 3:15). He calls God the *"Father of our Lord Jesus Christ, the Father of compassion and the God of all comfort, who comforts us in all our troubles"* (2 Corinthians 1:3-4).

One of the most beautiful statements in the writings of the beloved Apostle John is found in his first letter (1 John 3:1). *"How great is the love the Father has lavished on us, that we should be called children of God! And that is what we are!"*

In contrast the relationship of Muslims to Allah is only as servants or slaves to a master. The Qur'an asserts, *"There is no one in the heavens or the earth who can come to the Compassionate except as a servant"* (Sura 19:93). This is the highest position that a man can have in the presence of Allah. The relationship of true Christians to the true God, on the other hand, is always pictured as children to a loving Father to whom we have access in prayer for love and fellowship through our Lord Jesus who broke down the barrier that existed between man and god. For Muslims that barrier is still there.

Next to the God of the Bible, Allah seems a very rigid, cold, and distant being.

Chapter 4

MUHAMMAD'S RELIGION

Islam means submission. The Qur'an says, *"The only true faith in Allah's eyes is Islam"* (Sura 3:19). A Muslim is one who submits to the will of Allah. Belief in this one transcendent deity, who is the creator, and then seeking to do his will is the fundamental tenet of Muhammad's faith. Everything in Islam grows from the belief that man is to be a servant or slave (*abad*) of Allah. Worship is called *ibadah*—service or slavery. A continuing daily awareness of Allah and a conscientious desire to do his will is the ideal. Every part of one's life is to be religious. There is no separation of the state and religion or society and religion in Islam. All are cut out of one cloth from top to bottom. Islam therefore is a sociopolitical religious system. Question: Should Islam then merit an equal recognition as a religion in America under our freedom of religion doctrine? Fundamentalist Islam's goal is to overthrow all secular governments including America. It bears repeating that Orthodox Islam will always be a potential "5th column" in any non-Muslim society where it resides.

Muhammad claimed that Islam was the ancient and original monotheism. He taught that Islam was not a new religion, but the restoration of what had been the religion of Adam, Noah, and Abraham, and that the ancient monotheism had deteriorated into paganism and false religion. Allah was the true Creator god whom Muhammad sought to restore as the one and only god to his rightful place.

He taught that Judaism and Christianity had grown out of the ancient monotheism and had departed from the whole truth. Jews and Christians therefore held to perverted and corrupt teachings and needed reconversion to Islam. If

117

they would not convert they should either be destroyed with the pagans or be in submission to the law and governance of the Islamic community and pay the special head tax or *jizya*.

Islam's Requirements of Practice and Belief

In order to become a Muslim one has only to repeat the statement of belief before witnesses. *"I declare that there is only one God, Allah, and Muhammad is his prophet."* From then on a Muslim has four more main responsibilities. Together with the above testimony they comprise what are called the five pillars of Islam.

1. A Muslim must make the statement of faith (*shahadah*) mentioned above.

2. A Muslim must pray five times a day (*salat*) kneeling on his face toward the sacred city of Mecca. One who does not believe he has to do this is no longer a Muslim. The muezzin who calls the people to prayer reminds the faithful five times a day of their commitment to the one god Allah whose prophet is Muhammad.

3. A Muslim must give alms (*zakat*) amounting to about 2 1/2% of his income. This money can go to a local mosque or to a charity of one's choice. It has even become the basis for millions of dollars from all over the world being funneled to terrorist organizations.

4. A Muslim must fast during the month of Ramadan (*sawm*) to commemorate the revelations to Muhammad which began in that month in A.D. 610. This is a daytime fast with accompanying prayers as a sign of devotion to Allah ending at sunset. Eating in moderation is allowed after sundown.

5. If financially able a Muslim must make at least one pilgrimage (*hajj*) in his lifetime to Mecca to participate in communal worship around the sacred Ka'aba. More than three million Muslims make this journey each year usually early in the spring.

A Muslim's life is also to be dedicated to a struggle (*jihad*) for Allah and Islam. This requirement is sometimes considered like a "sixth pillar" or requirement. It calls for resistance against everything that is evil including (1) one's own selfishness and compromises with the world system; (2) the secular lust for things, pride, evil desires; and (3) the enemies of Allah in the world. It can therefore take the form of a holy war in the forcible spread of submission to Allah. That this idea was considered by Muhammad his most important teaching is what motivates the revival of Holy Jihad in Islam today.

The Muslim is to submit himself to the law of Allah and Islam as practiced in the *ummah* or Islamic community. The *shari'ah*, or Islamic law, is a combination of the teachings of the Qur'an and the example of Muhammad (the sunnah) and his sayings (hadith). These are interpreted by the mullahs or imams (religious teachers and leaders) to be applied in any specific period in history in order to sustain a well-ordered, moral, and prosperous society.

Some have called the religion of Islam an "orthopraxy," which is a religion, based primarily on actions or works rather than an "orthodoxy" which is a religion based upon teachings or doctrines. Muhammad did not permit theological controversies. There is only a short and simple list of beliefs to which Muslims must subscribe.

1. The existence of only one god Allah whose will is supreme.

2. The existence of angels, jinn (good and evil spirits) and Satan.

3. The revelation of Allah in holy books. (Muslims
    believe that the Bible was given by Allah, but was cor-
    rupted and supplanted by the Qur'an, which is writ-
    ten in the very words of Allah himself.)

4. The existence of prophets sent by Allah to proclaim
    his will. (The most important prophets are seven in
    number—Adam, Noah, Abraham, Moses, Jesus,
    Muhammad, and the future al-Mahdi who comes at
    the end of the age. Tradition teaches that there have
    been 124,000 prophets of which 26 are mentioned in
    the Qur'an.)

5. Predestination: Everything in the universe is deter-
    mined by the will of Allah, predestined by him, and
    man can do nothing about it. "Whatever Allah wills,"
    is a common phrase.

6. The certainty of final judgment when everyman's
    works will be judged by weighing them in Allah's
    scales.

Allah will provide scales at the Judgment where he will
weigh each man's works, whether good or evil, and assign
him his place in eternity in either heaven or hell. No Muslim
can possibly have assurance or be certain of how Allah will
judge him or what his eternal destiny will be. Only if he sac-
rifices his life for the cause of Islam as a martyr can he be
assured of heaven with all its promised pleasures. This
explains the willingness of radical Muslims to become suicide bombers in their Holy Jihad against Israel, America,
other infidels and unfaithful Muslims.

Specific Teachings About Life After Death

Allah rewards good and punishes evil deeds. He is merciful and is easily propitiated by repentance. The punishment

of the impenitent wicked will be fearful, and the reward of the faithful great. All men will have to rise from the dead and submit to the universal judgment. The Day of Resurrection and of Judgment will be preceded and accompanied by seventeen fearful signs in heaven and on earth, and eight lesser ones, some of which are identical with those mentioned in the New Testament. The Resurrection will be general and will extend to all creatures—angels, jinn, men, and animals. The torments of hell and the pleasures of Paradise, especially the latter, are proverbially crass and sensual.

Hell

Hell is divided into seven regions: Jahannam, reserved for faithless Muslims; Laza, for the Jews, Al Hutama for the Christians, Al-Sair for the Sabians, Al-Saqar, for the Magians; Al-Jahim, for idolators, Al-Hawiyat, for hypocrites. As to the torments of hell, it is believed that the damned will dwell amid pestilential winds and in scalding water, and in the shadow of a black smoke. Boiling water will be forced down their throats and will "tear at their bowels." They will be dragged by the scalp, flung into the fire, wrapped in garments of flame, and beaten with iron maces. When their skins are well burned, other skins will be given them for their greater torture. While the damnation of all infidels will be hopeless and eternal, the Muslims, who, though holding the true religion, have been guilty of heinous sins, will eventually be delivered from hell after expiating their crimes.

Paradise

The joys and glories of Paradise are as fantastic and sensual as the lascivious Arabian mind could possibly imagine. As plenty of water is one of the greatest additions to the delights of the Bedouin Arab, the Qur'an often speaks of the rivers of Paradise as a principal feature. Some of these streams flow with water, some with wine and others with honey. Besides there are many other lesser springs and fountains, whose pebbles are rubies and emeralds, while their earth consists of camphor, their beds of musk, and their banks of saffron.

All these glories, however, will be eclipsed by the resplendent and ravishing girls, the *houris* of Paradise, the enjoyment of whose company will crown the happiness of the faithful. These maidens are created not of clay, as in the case of mortal women, but of pure musk and free from all natural impurities, defects, and inconveniences. They will be beautiful and modest and secluded from public view in pavilions of hollow pearls.

The pleasures of Paradise will be so overwhelming that Allah will give to everyone the potentialities of a hundred individuals. To each individual a large mansion will be assigned, and the very meanest will have at his disposal at least 80,000 servants (slaves) and the 72 bashful dark eyed virgins called houris as his wives and loving companions. While eating, he will be waited on by 300 attendants, the food being served in dishes of gold, whereof 300 shall be set before him at once, containing each a different kind of food, and an inexhaustible supply of wine and liquors. There will be an eternal abundance of fruit and eternal shade (Sura 3:15 and 13:35). The magnificence of the garments and gems will conform to the delicacy of their diet. They will be clothed in the richest silks and brocades, and adorned with bracelets of gold and silver, and crowns set with pearls. They will make use of silken carpets, couches, pillows, and other comforts. In order that they may enjoy all these pleasures, Allah will grant them perpetual youth, beauty, and vigor. Music and singing will also be ravishing and everlasting.

In other words, in Islam's Paradise, one may indulge in every sensual pleasure, which on earth might be considered sinful. It sounds more like an idealized replica of Hugh Hefner's mansion. The longest, most involved passage in the Qur'an describing these delights of Paradise is in Sura 76:10-21.

Rules, Ethics and Values

The number 1 rule in Islam is one's absolute and unequivocal submission to Allah. This includes obedience to Allah's commands, which means observing the Five Pillars and Holy Jihad. Neglecting to observe any of the Five Pillars is a sin, but rejection or disbelief in any of them is apostasy. To run away from fighting the infidel or unbelievers is a sin worthy of death and hell, (Sura 8:15-16) because Allah has commanded Muslims to fight on his behalf. It is not just an option or a choice. (See chapter on Holy Jihad.) There are to be no other gods but Allah. Islam absolutely will not tolerate the addition of any other idols or deities within their belief system. The worship of Jesus or a Triune god, for example, is an anathema and is considered the sin of *shirk*, the gravest of iniquities.

2. The second most important rule is to respect, honor, and obey the prophet Muhammad. Criticism of the prophet is dangerous because it is believed that the prophet's life was a perfect example of the fulfillment of all the requirements and recommendations of the Qur'an. To deny the prophet therefore is to deny Islam itself. Muslims were commanded by Allah to obey Muhammad completely (Sura 4:65). The Qur'an also taught that opposition to the prophet meant that one's final destination would be hellfire. During his own lifetime Muhammad ordered that many of those who scorned, insulted, and opposed him be assassinated.

3. There are other specific rules or disciplines, which make up *shari'ah* or Islamic law. Most important of these include abstaining from drinking alcohol, eating pork, and avoiding fornication. Also a Muslim is not allowed to charge interest on a loan, which inhibits capitalistic enterprise. He is to reject

licentious behavior, which includes carousing and gambling. Women are to be modest to the point of covering most of their body, usually including their heads and faces, in public. They may not leave home unless accompanied by a male relative. In Saudi Arabia they are not allowed to drive a vehicle. The details of these rules may differ from nation to nation or among the sects of Islam as they are laid down by the religious teachers (mullahs, imams, ayatollahs) in each community.

The ethics of Islam as expressed in moral values or principles is very close to Judaism, Christianity, and numerous other religions. This is because there is a way of life, which is necessary for human survival, and the prosperity of human societies. Even the Apostle Paul recognized pagans who "do by nature the things required by the law" because the requirements of the law are *"written on their hearts, their consciences also bearing witness and their thoughts now accusing, and now even defending them"* (Romans 2:14-15).

The ethics of Islam therefore will approximate in many ways the moral values and principles of other religions.

One list of Islamic ideal values sounds like virtues listed in the Bible: faith, justice, forgiveness, compassion, mercy, sincerity, truth, generosity, humility, tolerance, modesty, chastity, patience, responsibility and courage. One can have no argument with these professed virtues. Things to be avoided include hypocrisy, cheating, backbiting, lying, pride, envy, anger, divisiveness, excess and extremism. It is interesting that the Qur'an commands men not to go beyond the truth (Sura 5:77) and says, *" Commit no excess. God loves not those given to excess."* These words are intriguing considering what has been perpetrated by Muslim militants in recent days.

Islam teaches no need of redemption, just discipline. There is no doctrine of the fall, which says that all men are *"by nature children of wrath"* (Ephesians 2:3). The story of Adam and Eve and their disobedience in the Garden of Eden is never mentioned in the Qur'an. It is both a story of Satan's duplicity and man's fall into a life of sin and consequent death. The author of the Qur'an certainly did not want to reveal himself in this kind of light nor is the consequence of man's inherent sinfulness and mortality, which showed Satan to be a liar, something he wanted to publicize. It is fascinating that several Muslims in reading the Bible have been startled by the story of the fall of man into a state of sinfulness. They had never heard the story before, and it helped to lay the groundwork for their understanding the origin of their own sinful nature and their need of a Savior. Muhammad taught no means of salvation or man's need for a Savior.

Paradise is achievable by human agency. Man is expected to save himself. The faith of Muhammad was that man was adequate. Man could earn his own salvation. He was responsible to exercise his own discipline. "Allah is great," but Islam has always been a man-centered faith. Muslim chaplains in American prisons have capitalized on the concept that a man should be strong in himself. Christians are said to be weaklings dependent on Jesus for salvation, whereas in Islam a man can save himself by good behavior and a disciplined keeping of Allah's rules. The Bible teaches that good works are a product of a life transformed by being born again and receiving a new nature. They are never God's provision to earn God's forgiveness or receive eternal life. Good works are a fruit of the Holy Spirit's influence in our lives to make us more like Jesus.

The most important members of the government of a truly Islamic state are the judges. The executive and legislative functions are not nearly as important—hence there is no democracy, no liberty, and no due process, only submission to law. There is no such thing as the separation of church and state. The church is the state. Muhammad was prophet, priest and king.

There are no true democracies among Islamic nations to this day except maybe Turkey, which is secularized. Representative government was forced on Turkey by the strong man Kemal Ataturk in 1924. He suppressed the power of the clerics and abolished the allegiance to shari'ah law. This shocked the Muslim world. Ataturk's "heresy" was the principle catalyst, which brought about the founding of the Muslim Brotherhood in Egypt. This was the first of the Islamic fundamentalist terrorist organizations and was a major influence in the founding or promotion of all modern Islamist groups including Hamas, Islamic Jihad, and al-Qaeda.

Are we being overly optimistic if we think that we can very easily erect democracies in Afghanistan and Iraq? The jury is still out on whether or not democracy can find permanent root in these nations in spite of the fact that they have had their first elections. This will probably prove to be only window dressing. Islamic nations have no tradition of representative government; in fact, it is really against the whole spirit of their religion since only Allah is sovereign and man can have no place in creating laws. The law should always be the law of the Qur'an, which is Allah's word. There is also the 1,370-year-old tradition of the Caliph and the Sultan which is why all Islamic nations tend to dictatorships.

Muslim governments are supposed to reflect the teachings of the Qur'an and the prophet. When they do not measure up to this standard, which is true of most of them that have been influenced by western culture, they are the targets for Islamic fundamentalist terrorists as much as Israel or America. This is certainly true, for example, of the Saud family rulers in Saudi Arabia. The 6,000 princes are walking a tightrope between trying to stay friends with the West and placate the militant Islamists. The Egyptian president Anwar Sadat was assassinated in 1979 because he made peace with Menachem Begin and Israel, which was regarded as a betrayal of Islam's destiny. Other Muslim leaders like Presidents Mubarak of Egypt and Musharraf of Pakistan must constantly guard against threats of assassination. At least nine attempts have been made on the life of Musharraf alone.

Ethical conduct is enjoined, and good Muslims, by worldly standards, are good people—hospitable, honest, dependable, friendly, and loyal. Those elements of human conduct, which are necessary for human society to exist, are found among Muslims as they are found among people generally around the world. Peace, justice, and tolerance in Islam, however, are only really found within the *ummah*. The logical consequence of Muhammad's teaching does not allow the condition of peace to be extended to the world as a whole. Every nation outside Islam is a part of the "House of War."

A state of truce often has existed, but there has always been a potential state of warfare between Islam and the rest of the world from the beginning. Following Muhammad's example in the Truce of Hudabiyyah, Islamists will declare what they consider simply a temporary peace or truce in order to regroup or avoid fighting everyone at once. Osama bin Laden offered a truce to European nations if they would stay out of the war in Iraq. Otherwise they would be objects of Allah's wrath in attacks by Muslim terror groups. France and Germany have been left alone. Nations like Spain and Britain, who sent troops to Iraq, suffered bombings. Ultimately, however, Islamists want to take over all of Europe. This has been a Muslim goal since the 8th century when they invaded Spain and France and since the 16th century when, after they had conquered the Balkans, they fought European armies all the way to the gates of Vienna.

We are simply experiencing in Islamic terrorism today what has been normative for Islam in the past. Islam was quiescent for years being handicapped in not having the wealth or military capacity to continue their original goal of world conquest. Things are much more volatile today because of the great wealth produced by the oil fields in the Muslim nations of the Middle East. This was pointed out by the Ayatollah Khomeini of Iran, who in 1979 proclaimed that the oil was Allah's treasure and called for a resurrection of Islamic militancy and the goal of world conquest.

The radical Pakistani Muslim teacher Syed Abul Ala Maududi gave the Islamic philosophy behind Khomeini's call for Holy Jihad. He said, *"Islam requires the earth—not just a portion, but the whole planet—not because the sovereignty over the earth should be wrested from one nation or several nations and vested in one particular nation, but because all of mankind should benefit from Islam which is the program of well-being for all humanity."*

Maududi said that non-Muslims have *"absolutely no right to seize the reins of power in any part of God's earth nor to direct the collective affairs of human beings according to their own misconceived doctrines."* In other words non-Islamic nations have no right to exist. Believers in Allah are *"under an obligation to do their utmost to dislodge them from political power and to make them live in subservience to the Islamic way of life."* This way of life means subjection to shari'ah law. No non-shari'ah nation should be allowed to exist and must be fought.

There are only two conclusions possible from this philosophy—death or victory for the Muslim believers. No negotiations, compromise, or peaceful coexistence can even be considered. This strict Muslim belief helps us understand what went on in Afghanistan and also the basis for the never-ending conflict in Palestine today. It is also the basis for the all-consuming hatred and declaration of war against the United States. It seems that the West as a whole does not take words like these very seriously. It could be our undoing.

Divisions in the Muslim World Community

The Muslim community or *ummah* includes all Muslim societies as a whole throughout the world. This is to be a community of peace. Warfare among Muslim states is absolutely forbidden. This is why more than 80% of American Muslims when polled concerning the Gulf War in

1990 said that they were against America's attacking Iraq, and that they would never send their sons to fight in such a war. Saddam Hussein, however, was guilty of declaring war on the Shiite nation of Iran. This incurred little objection in the Muslim world because of the division in Islam between the Sunnites and the Shiites, the latter numbering only about 10% of all Muslims. Even Saudi Arabia has persecuted Shiites as heretics more than they have persecuted Jews or Christians. Just recently the second most sacred mosque to the Shiites was car bombed in Najaf, Iraq and their leading ayatollah Muhammad Al Bakir Al Hakim was blown to pieces. Mostly likely the perpetrators will be found to be Sunnite, even Saudi, radicals like al-Qaeda who hate the Shiite separatists.

Shiites believe that the first four caliphates in the history of Islam were not legitimate, but that the rightful heir to Muhammad as his representative was his son-in-law Ali. Therefore the entire Sunnite tradition, or 90% of Islam, has a false foundation. The Iranian Shiites tend to be more radical than Sunnites in militantly advancing the cause of Islam. They do not accept the consensus of the community, but rather the spiritual leadership of holy imams or teachers whom they believe speak with the voice of God. *Ayatollah*, a title given to Iranian imams, means "sign" or "shadow of God." The Iranians have been regarded as fanatics, extremists, and even terrorists by the majority of Muslims, although since the pronouncements of the Ayatollah Khomeini this militant philosophy has come to be shared also by Sunni Muslims.

Iran may be the most dangerous Islamic foe the West faces. A nation of 70 million people, almost three times the size of Iraq, she may soon be a nuclear power. Former Israeli Prime Minister Benjamin Netanyahu shared with friends recently that he had information to the effect that Iran has employed Russian scientists to help with the design and eventual manufacture of missiles, which will be able to reach Jerusalem, London, and New York.

Because of the influence of the Shah and his introduction of western customs to Iran before the revolution, however, there is a great division among the Iranian people. Because of this westernization and the education of thousands of Iranians in the United States, many Iranians, in contrast to most Arab peoples, expressed genuine sympathy for the tragedy of 9/11. In fact, all 19 terrorist bombers were Sunnites, 15 of them Saudis.

A very large number of people in Iraq, as many as 60%, are also Shiites, which explains why Saudi Arabia was against deposing the Sunnite leader Saddam Hussein during the Gulf War. Our military action was curtailed after Kuwait had been liberated, and America called on rebels within Iraq to unseat Saddam. Then we withdrew our military and refused to participate in the liberation of Iraq; so Saddam ruthlessly put down the Kurdish and Shiite rebels, killing as many as a million Iraqis, burying them in mass graves. Considering we had already abandoned Afghanistan in 1989 following her liberation from the Soviet Union, it etched another black mark on the reputation of America among the Islamic peoples.

Our recent conquest of Iraq and removal of Saddam Hussein has created a potential impasse. Many Iraqis say that they want a democracy. The Shiites wanted an immediate vote because they are in the majority. Shiites finally did receive 48% of the vote, and arrangements have been made for the sharing of power in Iraq. How long this truce will continue cannot be known, but there is a danger of a government eventually dominated by Shiites in league with Shiite Iran. At first only Shiites and Kurds okayed the constitution, but the Sunnis forced a concession that the constitution could be amended soon, if unsatisfactory, so some supported it. The constitution was accepted by the voters with this qualification for amendment.

It appears that instead of a true democracy, Iraq will create an Islamic state of some kind. Saddam, who was a

Sunnite, although a ruthless dictator, had established a secular state. Our intervention may have resulted in a jumping out of the frying pan into the fire. A future civil war still remains a possibility.

Echoes From the Ancient World:
Celebrating the Past in Iraq, Syria, and Iran

Islam was created simply by cleansing or rechristening the pagan polytheism of Arabia by giving it a new monotheistic focus. Muhammad kept the sacred Ka'aba, the sacred meteorite, and the ancient rituals of the pilgrimage. All pagan rituals and practices did not disappear. In light of this fact, it is significant that the three major ancient empires of Babylon, Assyria, and Persia have been resurrected in spirit today by Muslim leaders, demonstrating their roots in paganism, which is significant for prophecy.

Saddam and Babylon

Iraq under Saddam Hussein al Tikriti (i.e., from the town of Tikrit) resurrected Babylon. In 1989 he held a great celebration at which Muslims of every description gathered at a lavish pagan festival of the ancient Mesopotamian goddess of fertility Ishtar, who has been identified as one of the daughters of the moon god, probably Manat. A bronze talisman of the goddess was unveiled—incense, music, lights— Saddam stepped onto a strobe lit platform and announced the beginning of a new world order. "I will wash my hands and my feet in the blood of the infidels for the glory of Mesopotamia forever." Nebuchadnezzar, who conquered Judah and Jerusalem in 606, 597 and 586 B. C., was reincarnated in Saddam's mind. He said that the modern jihad had begun. The world would once again feel the scourge of the Dar al Harb—the "House of War." Babylon was reborn.

Iraq was one of the original five nations to attack Israel in the 1948 war. The army was disorganized and poorly directed and was no match for angry farmers of the Jewish kibbutzim who fought with their backs against the wall. The Iraqis staggered home in defeat. With the help of the Soviet Union, however, Iraq rearmed under Saddam and reorganized what seemed to be a formidable fighting force. He fought a fruitless war with Iran from 1979 to 1989 and then decided to attack Kuwait, which he considered an old Iraqi province. He wished to claim the Kuwaiti oil fields for Iraq.

To counter this highhanded territorial grab by Saddam, President George H.W. Bush and America led a coalition of nations against Iraq in 1991. During this Gulf War called Desert Storm they quickly and easily turned back Saddam's vaunted forces and liberated Kuwait. This physical insertion of the American military into the Middle East, however, immediately triggered active terrorist attacks against our nation in many parts of the world.

Saddam regrouped and called his armed forces "The Jerusalem Army." He was the unspoken leader of the three nations—Iraq, Iran, and Syria—in their future war plans to invade Israel and recapture Jerusalem. The British Intelligence Digest said in 1998 that Saddam had made peace with Iran and Syria, his former enemies, in an alliance, which would allow Iran to cross Iraq with her armies. This has all been foiled, or at least postponed, by the most recent American victory in the war on Iraq and the deposing of Saddam and the Baathist Party in that country.

American actions, however, further provoked the Islamic radicals, and it appears that *mujaheddin*, the "holy warriors" of Islam who began to be trained in the Soviet/Afghan conflict, are crossing the borders into Iraq by the thousands to avenge Saddam and engage the 150,000 troops of the United States in a costly guerrilla type war. Iraq will continue to be a disordered and dangerous place for many months, and even years, to come. America may have bit off more than we bargained for; on the other hand, our presence in Iraq will tend to concentrate the terrorists where they may be more easily controlled. As President George W. Bush has reiterated, "It is better to fight the terrorists over in Iraq than here in America."

Hafez al Assad and Assyria

Syria under Hafez al Assad celebrated at a week-long festival in 1978 the 2750th anniversary of the conquest of Israel by Sennacherib in 722 B.C. There was lavish activity and earthly pleasures. A gold statue of Ashur, the Assyrian deity, was unveiled as a symbol of Syrian nationalism and dedication to the destruction of the Jews. Assad said, *"We are the heirs of Shalmaneser and Sennacherib—the greatest heroes of our nation. . We have inherited their glory, wisdom and valor . . . and most of all their cause. Assyria must once again unite the Arab world against the imperialism of the Infidel, the interloping of the West, and the encroachment of the Jew."* It all seems somewhat incongruous, however, because Assyria and Nineveh whom they were celebrating were really in northern Iraq and never headquartered in what is modern Syria.

Syria has been an antagonist of Israel in every war since 1948. She lost the Golan Heights to Israeli armies in the 1967 war. This high ground overlooks Galilee and was a strategic spot from which Syria could shoot down on Israeli settlements. It is one of the points of conflict in any talks between the two countries to normalize relations. A main problem is that Syria like every other Muslim nation adamantly refuses to recognize that Israel is even a legitimate State.

Syria has made the return of the Golan Heights a condition for making peace with Israel. It would be unwise for Israel to give up this high ground, however, and put their faith in the word of Arabs who are eternally pledged to her eventual destruction.

Syria also is the headquarters for Hezbollah and Islamic Jihad—two of the five major terrorist organizations attacking Israel. Hezbollah has its origins in Iran, but now has rooted itself in Lebanon with armed forces poised just across the northern border of Israel. Recent reports have placed Saddam's weapons of mass destruction possibly in the Bekaa Valley of Lebanon, which has been under the control of Syria and the Hezbollah. There is evidence that they may have been spirited out of Iraq in trucks and ambulances while the world was waiting for a resolution by the United Nations, which delayed America's preemptive military intervention.

Will the recent withdrawal of 14,000 Syrian troops from Lebanon open the Bekaa Valley to inspection in the search for weapons of mass destruction? If they were ever there, did the Syrian army take these buried WMD's with them when they returned to Syria? Even though Syria has withdrawn troops and there have been Lebanese elections, Syria still has much influence in Lebanon, and Hezbollah, the Iranian terrorist group, has much power.

The Shah of Iran and Persepolis

Iran, under the Shah, celebrated over a five-year period—1967-71—the 2500th anniversary of the reign of Cyrus from Persepolis. Many acres of the city were restored and an imperial coronation was conducted for the Shah with unheard of wealth in clothing and jewelry. Gathered for this was the greatest assemblage of the heads of royalty and world leaders that the world had ever seen in one place at the same time together. This was designed by the Shah to set the course for the nation. He proclaimed, *"The glory of Persia is merely represented in the embellishments you see about you. In fact, the essence of that glory is yet to be fully realized as our nation only now begins to assume its proper place among the great nations of the earth. Persia shall arise."*

The Shah was deposed in 1979 because he wanted to westernize Iran. The Ayatollah Khomeini, however, who became Iran's new clerical and political leader, continued the charade. He declared, *"These symbols shall give new impetus to the export of our revolution. Soon the spirit of Allah will sweep the faithful Umma of the Persian hoards across the earth—first Jerusalem, then the Great Satan, and finally, our Ji'had will free the oppressed masses on every continent."*

Iran or the ancient nation of Persia is not an Arab country. The Persians came originally from India and most speak Farsi, which is an Indo-European and not a Semitic language. In 1979 the revolution against the western ways of the Shah put the religious leaders—the ayatollahs—in power with the Ayatollah Khomeini taking the lead. It was the time of the storming of the American embassy in Tehran and the taking of over 50 embassy personnel as hostages. Under President Jimmy Carter's ineffective leadership nothing was accomplished except a futile attempt at rescue that wound up crashing in the desert. The hostages were returned after Reagan became President, but liberals accused him of having bribed the Iranians with the promise of arms. It was a time of internal conflict as America tried to assess its own purposes, function, and influence as a superpower in the Middle East.

Iran has never yet been a part of a war against Israel, but her current number one foreign policy goal, according to some observers, is to reconquer Jerusalem for Islam. Persia is the first nation mentioned in Ezekiel's prophecy (chapters 38-39), which is a prediction of the confederacy of nations that we now recognize as Islamic' that will make a final attack on Israel in order to recapture Jerusalem and obliterate the Jewish nation.

Iran seems to be the closest of any Islamic nation in the Middle East to possessing nuclear arms. In this quest she has had the cooperation of Russia in building nuclear reactors, which can supply the raw materials for weapons. More recent intelligence has uncovered the fact that Iran was also helped by the leading Pakistani scientist who developed Pakistan's atomic arsenal. North Korea and Russian scientists have also aided Iran in the production of missiles. This has all been of great concern to the United States. President George W. Bush labeled Iran along with Iraq and North Korea an evil triumvirate of nations.

The ultimate goal of these Muslim states has been the resurrection of a new caliphate combining all the principal Islamic nations under one banner into one community or *ummah*. However, first the United States and Israel—the Great Satan and the Little Satan—must be dealt with. Islamic militants from various Muslim states declared war on America in both 1996 and in 1998. President Bush's declaration of War on Terror in 2001 was simply a belated response to this aggression.

The recent invasion of Iraq, the subjection of Saddam Hussein and the Baathist party and the attempt to establish some form of democracy in that nation has inhibited the efforts of Islamic militants to achieve their goals. People being allowed to vote in Afghanistan, Iraq, Palestine, and now in Lebanon has given some hope for change in the Middle East. We should not expect, however, any dramatic or permanent innovations. As we have seen, Islamic teaching does not harmonize well with western notions of freedom and democracy. The recapture of Jerusalem and the destruction of Israel is still the ultimate goal of Muhammad's religion.

The relentless antagonism of Islamic militants will continue, and Biblical prophecies concerning the final major conflict of the Islamic nations joining together to try to destroy the new nation of Israel will be fulfilled, but the timetable for the end has been slowed down. This fulfills a prediction and principle of the Scripture highlighting the patience and longsuffering of the true Creator God, who, in contrast to Allah, loves sinners and *"is not willing that any should perish but that all should come to repentance"* (2 Peter 3:9).

Chapter 5

HOLY JIHAD

The term *jihad* means "struggle" in Arabic. "Jihadists" can be translated "strugglers." Holy Jihad is the "holy struggle" conducted by "holy strugglers." Most Muslims in the West will claim in the defense of *jihad* that its primary meaning is a moral struggle against sin or against the weakness of the flesh. This is the Sufi interpretation, but it is condemned by the Islamists who are predominantly Sunnite and Shiite.

For Muhammad its more important implication was struggle in the cause of Allah against the world. In the Hadith it says, *"Allah's apostle was asked, 'what is the best deed?"* He replied, *'To believe in Allah and his Apostle'"* Then he added that the next best was to *'participate in Jihad (religious fighting) in Allah's cause'"* (Hadith, 1.25). He said, *"Paradise is under the shades of swords."* And the scimitar or curved sword is still one of the symbols of Islam.

Muhammad taught that 24 hours of fighting for Allah was better than one month of fasting and prayer. If a man did not participate in some military campaign during his lifetime for Allah and Islam, he would die as a kind of infidel. He said, *"I have been ordered to fight against the people until they testify that none has the right to be worshiped but Allah and that Muhammad is Allah's Prophet, and offer prayers and give obligatory charity, so if they perform all that, then they save their lives and property"* (Hadith, 1.24). He went so far as to warn the leaders of the nations whom he contacted that, if they would embrace Islam, they would save themselves. He meant save themselves from a Holy Jihad mounted against them.

Muslim apologists in the United States will not acknowledge this teaching today. Muslim organizations, such as The Council on American Islamic Relations (CAIR) have sent out speakers like Hussam Ayloush to our universities to claim that jihad means only the exertion of effort for the sake of Allah and has no implications of war or violence. This is a complete misrepresentation of the truth for obvious reasons. (CAIR is notorious for its secret connection to Muslim terrorist organizations. It is wedded to the technique of the big lie which was employed by both Hitler and Stalin.)

From the time of Muhammad most Muslim writers have exalted holy warfare to be the most important exercise of jihad. Ibn Khaldun, the famous Muslim thinker of the 14th century (1332-1406) wrote, *"In the Muslim community, the holy war is a religious duty."* The obvious proof of this definition is in the history of Islam's expansion during the first 100 years of the religion's existence. There were no soldiers in history that demonstrated greater bravery or abandonment to possible death in battle than the Muslim armies who conquered an area larger than the Roman Empire within 100 years. What made them almost invincible was their emphatic belief that to die in battle was the door to all the pleasures of Paradise.

If they lived through the battles, their reward would be all the loot or booty that they could appropriate for themselves from those they had killed or enslaved.

Driven by dreams of a victorious Islam in ages past, orthodox Muslims are being very frank today about their own goals of world conquest in the name of Allah. Their ultimate purpose is to impose *shari'ah* law, or the commands of Allah, upon all nations as Muhammad instructed.

The Sunni Jordanian-Palestinian Abdullah Azzam, beginning about 1979, preached Holy Jihad in many Muslim nations. He also spoke to rallies of Muslims in the United States urging them to support Islam's conquest of the world. When he was killed in Pakistan in 1989, his disciple Osama bin Laden expressed the same zeal and goal and organized the thousands of *mujaheddin* who had fought in the Afghan war against the Soviets. He created a data base in his computer with the names of all these holy warriors. It became known as simply "the base," which in Arabic is al-Qaeda.

At the same time in 1979 the Ayatollah Ruhollah Khomeini, the Iranian Shiite mullah, fomented the Iranian revolution against the Shah and helped engineer the takeover of the American embassy in Teheran with over 50 American hostages. His words present a classic example of the aims of orthodox Islam today. He wrote, *"Islam makes it incumbent on all adult males to prepare themselves for the conquest of countries so that the writ of Islam is obeyed in every country in the world."* The Islamic Council in Chechnya said that the purpose of jihad was so that *"the religion of Islam could be above all, so that all areas of life could be guided by Islam, and so that the earth could be cleansed from unbelief."*

Islam's Authority for Holy Jihad

The following is a selected list of quotations from the Qur'an and the Hadith, which are the authoritative support for militant Islam today. They come largely from the parts of the Qur'an that were written in the Medina period from 623 to 632. There are over 120 verses in the Qur'an that use the Islamic law's meaning of Jihad; namely, fighting and killing in the name of Allah. They are being taught in mosques and schools all over the world. Here are a few of these.

Words Attributed to Allah Himself

Sura 2:193— *"Fight them on, until there is no more tumult, seduction, or oppression, and there prevail justice, faith in Allah, and the religion becomes Islam."*

Sura 4:74— *"Let those who would exchange the life of this world for the hereafter, fight for the cause of Allah; whether they die or conquer. We shall richly reward them."*

Sura 4:95-96— *"The believers who stay at home—apart from*

those that suffer from a grave disability—are not the equals of those who fight for the cause of Allah with their goods and their persons. Allah has exalted the men who fight with their goods and their persons above those who stay at home. Allah has promised all a good reward; but far richer is the recompense of those who fight for Him. . ."

Sura 8:13, 17— *"I will instill terror into the infidels, smite them above their necks; smite all their fingertips off them. It is not you who slay them but Allah."*

Sura 9:5— *'When Ramadan is over, slay the idolaters wherever you find them. Arrest them, besiege them, and lie in ambush everywhere for them."*

Sura 9:14— *"Kill the infidels, God will torment and cover them with shame."*

Sura 9:41— *"Whether unarmed or well-equipped, march on and fight for the cause of God, with your wealth and with your persons. This will be best for you if you but knew it."*

Sura 9:73— *"Prophet, make war on the infidels and the hypocrites and deal rigorously with them. Hell shall be their home: an evil fate."*

Sura 9:26— *"Fight against those to whom the Scriptures were given as believe neither in Allah nor the Last day who do not forbid what Allah and his prophet have forbidden and do not embrace the true faith until they pay tribute and are utterly subdued."*

Sura 48:29— *"Muhammad is Allah's prophet. Those who follow him are ruthless to the infidels but merciful to one another."*

Sura 66:9— *"Prophet, make war on the unbelievers and the hypocrites, and deal sternly with them. Hell shall be their home, evil their fate."*

Quotations from Muhammad's Teachings

Habit 1:13— *"I have been ordered by Allah to fight with people till they bear testimony to the fact that there is no God but Allah."*

Hadith of Sahih Muslim 19:4294— *"Fight against those who disbelieve in Allah. Make a holy war."*

Hadith 1:35— *"The person who participates in Allah's cause (namely, in battle). . will be recompensed by Allah either with reward or booty or will be admitted to Paradise."*

Hadith 9:4— *"Wherever you find infidels kill them; for whoever kills them shall have reward on the Day of Resurrection."*

Hadith 9:50, 57— *"No Umma (a member of Muslim community) should be killed for killing a Kafir (an infidel). . Whoever changes his Islamic religion, kill him."*

Holy Jihad is to continue until the entire world is in submission to Allah. His law, the *shari'ah*, must be imposed on the whole world under Muslim dominion. All those outside of the House of Submission (*Dar al Islam*) are part of the House of War (*Dar al Harb*). Islam is in potential conflict with all who are not Muslims. Times of truce, even if they last for decades, are regarded as temporary. Since it is believed by Islamists that these are the last days, it is the duty of <u>all</u> Muslims to participate in Holy Jihad. It is the final effort and the last chance to conquer the whole world for Islam.

Hatred is required of those who would defend Allah's cause. One may not embrace, support or love what stands in the way of Allah imposing his law throughout the world. One should not love what Allah hates. Those who apostatize from Islam are especially hated. No Muslim has the right to forgive an apostate. This is why, if their children leave the faith, devout Muslim parents will disown them completely or even attempt to kill them. Because Allah hates all apostates, they must hate them too. Death is the only prescribed penalty for one who rejects the Islamic faith.

Just exactly as Lenin commanded his followers to hate the bourgeoisie and any group that stood in the way of the communizing of the world, orthodox Islam teaches a hatred of its enemies or any who would stand in the way of Islam's conquest of the world. This is why America is hated. This is why Israel is hated. Fortunately, only a minority of Muslims embraces this teaching to this extreme, although it explains the growing strength of the terrorist movement and the thousands of Islamists who are rallying to the support of Holy Jihad resurrected by the militants today.

No matter how much moderate Muslims may regret it, inveigh against it and not wish to participate in it, Holy Jihad as warfare and conquest is basic Islam. The head of the war department in Egypt is, in fact, called "Chief of Jihad." *Jihad* as fighting in the cause of Allah has been an integral part of Qur'anic teaching and the actions of the prophet and his followers from the beginning. Moderate Muslims, who are today friends of the West or the infidels, are considered by the militants as if they were apostates and enemies of Islam. Holy Jihad will also be directed against them.

Death while participating in Holy Jihad is rewarded by Allah with forgiveness of all sins and immediate admittance to Paradise with all its promises of sensual delights. No other activity of a Muslim, not even the most generous almsgiving or charity, gives this assurance of Paradise. This indicates the high priority of Holy Jihad in Muhammad's teachings. It helps us understand the many who are willing to become suicide bombers to defend or advance Islam. It explains the abandon with which Muslim armies fought their battles, not caring if they died, because of the promise of Paradise. This carefree devotion virtually assured their long string of victories in their early conquests of the Middle East, North Africa, and Spain. Islamists believe that because of their revived dedication similar victories can continue to be reaped today. The Holy Warriors were encouraged in this conviction by what seemed a miraculous victory over the Soviet Union in Afghanistan in 1989.

Islamists anticipate that Allah will give them a victory over the United States of America as he did over the Soviet Union. This is why thousands of holy warriors have been trying to sneak into Iraq. Osama bin Laden has urged the Holy Warriors to engage the United States in Iraq and defeat the coalition armies like the Soviets were defeated in Afghanistan. They are pledged to fight to the death. In a recent ambush attack on an American army convoy in Samara, Iraq, for example, it was observed that Saddam's old

Fedayeen warriors did not care if they lived or died. They were wearing their unique white and black uniforms underneath their outer garments. As many as 50 of them were killed while wounding only 5 American soldiers (12/1/03).

The Saga of the Christian Crusades—A Comparison with Islamic Jihad

The Crusades of the 10th to the 13th centuries in the West were very much a copy of the Islamic Holy Jihad. They both had religious motivations. They both aimed at military conquest in the cause of God. And they both granted participants some kind of special forgiveness of sins.

The Crusades were initiated by Pope Urban II in 1095 by a call for Christians to liberate Jerusalem and the Holy Places from the Islamic infidels. Popes as early as the ninth century had offered forgiveness for the temporal punishment of sins, called indulgences, for war against the Muslims. It was not until over 200 years later, however, that the idea caught fire and became a popular movement. Its immediate provocation was both the terrible persecution of Christians by Al-Hakim, Fatimid caliph in Egypt, and then the massacre by Muslims of 7,000 Christian pilgrims on their way to Jerusalem in 1064-1065. The Crusades might be viewed therefore as armed pilgrimages. They were certainly considered a just retaliation for Islam's attacks on Christian lands.

The Crusades were a belated reaction of European Christians against 450 years of Islamic imperialism. Specifically the Roman Catholic leaders of Christian Europe felt they could no longer stand by and let Muslims retain control of Christ's birthplace and the site of his ministry, death, and resurrection. Again a plenary or complete indulgence was offered to those who would join the fight. This meant that the temporal punishment for sin, which included suffering in Purgatory before entering the bliss of Heaven, would be forgiven. Any warrior killed in battle therefore would go straight to Heaven. This wasn't much different from what Muhammad had taught his Muslim warriors 500 years earlier.

Also the slogan of the Crusades *Deus vult*, "God wills it," is reminiscent of the Muslim "As Allah wills." Christians developed a new idea of religious orders, which were military in their organization and purpose. These included, for example, the Knights Templar and the Hospitallers also called the Knights of St. John. The former were to protect pilgrims, Jerusalem, and the Holy Land. The latter supported a hospital in Jerusalem and cared for the sick.

Jerusalem was conquered during the First Crusade in 1099. Most of the inhabitants were massacred by the Crusaders even the Jews whose synagogues were burned. This is one of the many blots on the history of the church in the Middle Ages. Even though it was in retaliation for centuries of Muslim attacks and massacres of Christians, there is no justification for this kind of behavior in the teachings of Christ and His apostles.

If they had been able to read Arabic, the Crusaders might have destroyed the Dome of the Rock, which stands on the Temple Mount as a testimony against the main doctrine of Christianity; namely, the deity of Jesus Christ. Over the door in Arabic were written the words from the Qur'an, "God has no son." Instead they used it as a church.

Jerusalem was reconquered by the Kurdish leader Saladin and the Muslims 85 years later in 1184, but the Crusaders held on to the famed fortress at Acre until 1291. The Crusades therefore lasted less than 200 years. Militant Muslims, however, are still fighting the Crusades in their imaginations. Saddam Hussein pictured himself as a modern Saladin, and the terrorists have labeled the American armies with the name *Crusaders*.

Historians have joined Islamists in condemning Christianity for the Crusades. Pagan European historians have judged the Muslims to be tolerant while picturing the Christians as brutal, violent and absolutely intolerant. They seldom make the distinction, however, that whereas

Muhammad and the Qur'an commanded Holy Jihad, the Crusades were an aberration for the Christian church. The Crusades as a holy jihad of Christians against Muslims was a far cry from the teachings of Jesus and were in direct contradiction to Christian teaching in the New Testament. Holy Jihad is basic Islam, but the Crusades were not basic Christianity. (Note Daniel Johnson, "How to Think About the Crusades," *Commentary Magazine,* July-August 2005, pp. 46-51.)

Islam's Early History
Bloody Conquests in the name of Jihad

With the exception of the Crusades and the most recent war against Iraq, which was a preemptive strike by the United States against the threat of Saddam Hussein's dangerous regime, Muslims have initiated all wars with the West. Western culture and Christianity are an anathema to traditional Muslims. There is no middle or common ground. This most recent call for Holy Jihad against Islam's enemies is going to be a threat for many, many years. As the Apostle Paul warned his disciple Timothy, *"In the last days, dangerous* (or terrible) *times will come"* (2 Timothy 3:1). Holy Jihad is here in the world to stay. Islamists want to finish the job that was begun in the first three hundred years of the expansion of their faith.

Within ten years of the Prophet Muhammad's death in 632, aggressive Islamic armies had conquered most of the Middle Eastern nations. None of these wars were defensive. Muslims plundered foreign peoples for economic gain and forced conversions all in the name of Holy Jihad.

The earliest major city captured was Damascus in 635. Then Iraq fell in 636, Jerusalem in 638, Caesarea in 641, and Armenia in 643. By 709 the Muslim armies had conquered all of Christian North Africa as far as modern Morocco. In Egypt alone eventually over four million people were slaughtered, many of them Coptic Christians. By 711 Muslims had overrun Spain and crossed the Pyrenees Mountains into what is now southern France. They were finally turned back in defeat by Charles Martel (the Hammer), the grandfather of Charlemagne, in 732 in the battle of Poitiers near Tours, exactly 100 years after the death of Muhammad.

Muslims first besieged the Byzantine or Eastern Roman Empire capital of Constantinople in 716, but this city did not succumb for over 700 years until in 1453, when it was conquered by the Ottoman Turks who had converted to Islam. By 827 Muslims had invaded Sicily and by 846 they threatened to take the much beleaguered city of Rome itself. They were turned back, but the Mediterranean Sea was to become a Muslim lake. Finally, the conquest of parts of India by the Muslims is considered one of the most bloody military campaigns in history. The Hindus and Buddhists were pagan idolaters and had to be killed if they would not immediately convert to Islam.

From the very beginning it had been an Islamic goal to conquer Europe. Europe and Africa were considered the two barbarian frontiers, infidel backwaters that were destined someday to become Muslim. Ottoman Turks tried twice more in the 16th and 17th centuries to conquer Europe advancing both times to the gates of Vienna where they were turned back. From this time on the rapid economic, technological and military advance of the West made its conquest by the more stagnant Islamic nations impossible.

The Islamist Call to the Renewal of Holy Jihad Today

Today, Muslims boast that they will conquer Europe from the inside by immigration and reproduction. They say, "Thanks to your democratic laws we will invade you. Thanks to our religious laws we will dominate you." Muslims number more than 7% in France, over 4% in Germany and Britain, and 5% in Holland. They are concentrated in the cities. Brussels, the capital of the European Union, is 15% Muslim. In Paris 20% of the young people are Muslim. Muslims are actively campaigning to gradually take over England, but believe that they have the best chance to eventually win a majority in Holland. The libertarian Dutch pride themselves on their tolerance for everything and everybody, but it has recently been sorely tested by Muslim terrorist acts, which has promoted a call for restricted immigration and new laws.

A Muslim understanding and modification of Western democracy stated in the words of one militant is "one man, one vote, one time." This idealized internal "5th column-like" takeover is as much Holy Jihad as a hot war. It is part of the struggle by militants to impose Allah's law on all of the free world. It is even the long-range goal of dedicated Muslims in the United States of America.

The Islamic nations that are the most religious are the most militant and the least peace promoting. Islam claims to be a "peaceful religion," a phrase that we have even heard leaders like President George W. Bush echo, but it is a charade. The true teaching is that peace can only really exist within the Muslim community or *ummah*. Outside of the *ummah* there must be either a continuing, potential struggle—a kind of cold war or truce—or there will be a state of hot war or jihad. Which one of these alternatives is chosen will be determined by how numerous and strong Islamists consider themselves to be.

The most secular Islamic nations are those that are the most peaceful and want to cooperate with the West; namely, Turkey, Malaysia, and Qatar. Saudi Arabia, as the home of the Wahhabi sect of Islamic philosophy, is the most religiously orthodox and the most active in quietly supporting the advance of Islam with missionary zealots and billions of dollars in oil money. The latter sustains radical mosques, schools, and even activities of terrorists throughout the world. Most of the 9/11 terrorists were Saudis.

Iran led by Muslim clerics called *ayatollahs* is also a very active supporter of terrorism. It harbors al-Qaeda cells and is permitting jihadists to cross into Iraq over its border to fight the American infidel "enemy." It is supporting the insurgents in Iraq with funds. Most are agreed that it is also trying to develop a nuclear capability to enhance its chances in a war against Israel or even Europe.

Islam teaches that Holy Jihad must always be declared in defense of an Islamic territory and people. It is Islamic law that Muslims must come to the aid of a brother community, which is under attack by infidels. We are therefore observing jihadists from all over the Muslim world coming to the aid of the Iraqis. They are sneaking into Iraq, coming from nations throughout the entire Muslim world and even from Muslim enclaves in Europe. As much as possible they are crossing into Iraq over the borders of Syria, Iran, and Saudi Arabia. They join with Iraqi insurgents and will continue to foment fear, disorder, and violence with hundreds of terrorist attacks throughout this nation. Many will never stop unless they are killed.

This militancy will escalate as long as an American military presence exists in that country. President Bush speaks with sincere personal determination when he says that America will never give up in the fight against terrorism including counteracting the many assaults in Iraq. No matter how seriously resolute we are, however, we must face the possibility that we are in effect confronting the possibility of hundreds of thousands of fanatical enemies. Although President Bush asserts dogmatically that we are not at war with the religion of Islam, for orthodox Muslims this is a religious war—a Crusade or Holy Jihad. Many Islamists doubt that America has the moral commitment or fortitude to persevere indefinitely.

Democratic elections on January 30, 2005 in Iraq were largely successful in spite of militant opposition. As many as 60% of the population made it to the polls in spite of terrorist threats. It seems that most Iraqi's do not share the Islamists' commitment to Holy Jihad. One reason is that Saddam's regime was a secular one, and religious fanaticism was discouraged. Whereas Islamist militants who have invaded Iraq as holy warriors from other nations have a religious motive, the Baathist Party insurgents are fighting a political not an ideological battle. The Iraqi people also had a level of education that was greater than most other Islamic nations including the education of women.

We must come to realize that all the horrendous recurring aggression that has gone on in Iraq, Israel, Bali, Somalia, Algeria, the Sudan, Kenya, Pakistan, Yemen, and Afghanistan and even in Saudi Arabia is the fruit of orthodox Islamic teaching and must be considered basic Islam. *"Soon we will cast terror into the hearts of the unbelievers. . their abode will be the fire,"* is a promise from the prophet Muhammad. Most Muslims in the world have not yet acted on these teachings, but the influence of the Fundamentalists is growing every day.

Although the majority of Muslims may still be benign in their outlook, the ranks of the militants are growing as these radical beliefs motivating terrorists are being taught at mainstream mosques and Islamic schools called *madrassas* all over the world. There are many of these schools even in America and Europe financed with Saudi oil money. They saturate the preaching and teaching of Muslim clerics and educators. The Muslim American serviceman Sergeant Hasan Akbar, e.g., who killed soldiers of his own company in Iraq, had apparently been indoctrinated at a Wahhabi mosque in Los Angeles.

Few so-called moderate Muslims are willing to take a stand against Islamic terrorists. In fact, American Muslims claim that they are being made the scapegoats for a few radicals. They object vigorously to the Patriot Act, which permits law enforcement to conduct internal surveillance of suspects in America or racial profiling of Middle Eastern types.

Organizations, which have been labeled terrorist support organizations by the investigative reporter Steve Emerson (Cf. *American Jihad*), are especially vocal against these protective measures. They include Muslim groups, such as the Council of American Islamic Relations (CAIR), the American Muslim Council (AMC), and the Islamic Society of North America (ISNA).

Most of these apologists try to claim that Holy Jihad refers to an internal moral struggle and not to violent attacks on infidels. None of these groups, however, are teaching that acts of political violence are antithetical to Islam. Neither are they publicly objecting to the radical anti-Israel and anti-American teachings in mosques and schools. Nor are they attempting aggressively to teach American Muslims that all this terrorist behavior is evil. They are primarily crying out against the violation of Muslim civil rights in the United States. Even if they do begin to teach against violence, we would do well not to take their words at their face value.

All of these organizations, furthermore, have been discovered to have either supported terrorist groups by raising funds or in turn been supported by movements such as Hamas or Islamic Jihad. Their pious declarations are rank hypocrisy. None of them would really pledge that they would not like to see the United States Constitution replaced with the *shari'ah* or Islamic law. It has been demonstrated over and over that most are involved in their hearts in a silent holy jihad against all that is American or western, especially evangelical Christianity and Judaism. There is a strong ambivalence that exists in many quarters of the Islamic community in this country.

Islam claims 150,000 converts a year in America. On this very day Muslim chaplains in our prisons are teaching mostly black prisoners how to become Muslims, to applaud the 9/11 attackers, to hate America, and are even recruiting for al-Qaeda. A military chaplain and Arabic translators at Guantanamo have recently been detained on either suspicion or charges of treasonous behavior. This is their contribution to Holy Jihad—the House of Submission versus the House of War.

In the aftermath of 9/11, President Bush attributed this act of Holy Jihad to radical extremist Muslims. He said to the American people and the world, *"Islam, as practiced by the vast majority of people, is a peaceful religion, a religion that respects others."*

Even if we grant, however, that a majority of Muslims may not want to get involved in Holy Jihad, can we truthfully call

Islam a peaceful, tolerant religion? It holds a worldview, which says that all humanity **must** obey Islamic law as taught in the Qur'an and Hadith, and that all other religions are infidel. Also the history of Islam shows that the practice of Islam is not to convert simply by persuasion, but also by force.

In the final analysis, furthermore, strict Muslims show little deference or respect for the religions of others, all of whom are considered infidels. Peace and tolerance as taught in orthodox Islam exist only within the *ummah* or the Islamic community. The goal of Islamists is to impose this community and its beliefs on the whole world. This is certainly not tolerant. This is not peaceful. All the world outside of Islam is called "The House of War."

Those Muslims, furthermore, who would show openness to Christianity or Judaism are themselves considered apostates and worthy of execution by the fundamentalist radicals. No church or synagogue can be built in Saudi Arabia, and especially never in the sacred city of Mecca, because that would defile the land of Muhammad. Bringing a Bible into the Kingdom is absolutely forbidden, and conducting Bible studies or sharing the Christian faith is punishable by imprisonment or execution by beheading.

Pope John Paul II, on the other hand, encouraged the building of a prominent mosque in Rome and tried to show his tolerance by publicly kissing the Qur'an. Muslims take great advantage of their opportunities in free societies, but do not reciprocate. They offer little or no religious freedom to others in their own communities. The law of Allah must prevail and be supreme. Nothing else will be tolerated.

The response to 9/11 by Muslims in Europe, except in Kosovo where America is respected for our defense of their nation against the Serbs, was silent at best and jubilant at the worst. Just note one example of Muslim demonstrators north of London in October 2001. A banner carried by a marching crowd read "Islam will Dominate the World." Most Muslims thought the act of the terrorists legitimate and that the perpetrators were heroes. The so-called moderate Muslims in France and Britain, supposedly opposed to extremism, uttered not a whispered word of dissent.

One Muslim reaction to our recent invasion of Iraq has been the uniting in heart and spirit of all the *mujaheddin* from all the terrorist groups in Holy Jihad against the United States. For them this is a religious war. We need to take them at their word. This is not a war because of poverty, or benign neglect, or specific wrongs committed by the United States, or for any other reason other than the Qur'an and Muhammad have commanded such actions. It is a revival and continuation of the aggressions of Islam, which began during the life of Muhammad and continued for 100 years until the Muslim caliphate controlled much of the civilized world outside of Europe.

Muslims believe with orthodox Jews and Christians that these are the end times, and therefore Muslims worldwide are being called by militant Islamists to unite and conquer the world for Allah. The authoritative Egyptian writer and teacher Sayyid Qutb echoed the ideal of every orthodox Muslim fundamentalist when he wrote, *"The foremost duty of Islam is to depose the government and society of unbelievers (Jahiliyyah) from the leadership of man."*

It is against the law of Allah for any nation to be governed by infidels, the unclean, or the secular. Neither do orthodox Islamists believe that any nation should be governed by and for the people as a republic. This has from the beginning been the teaching and the dream of Islam embedded in the *ummah* (the greater Muslim community) more or less in every place and in every age. This struggle will now be with us for many, many years. This is an enemy that is not going to go away.

For those who want to know what Muslims are saying in Arabic among themselves need to consult *www.memri.org* This stands for the Middle East Media Research Institute which has its headquarters in Washington D.C. They cover TV, radio, newspapers, and periodicals throughout the Arabic world and publish significant pertinent materials translated into English on the Internet. One will find major contradictions between what the Arab world is saying among themselves and what they say to the outside world. It demonstrates a kind of wolf in sheep's clothing phenomenon.

Although it has been politically incorrect to call attention to these differences, to neglect to do so is not only foolish but also perilous. A good example of this is Egypt that the United States has favored with 50 billion dollars in aid over the past 25 years. Fully 96% of the Egyptian people today regard America unfavorably, or even as the enemy, because of propaganda in the Egyptian press. Diatribes against the United States are not really discouraged by the present Egyptian government, which professes to be our ally. The Muslim press in most of the Arab nations is notoriously anti-American. Their words have been conditioning the minds and attitudes of the Islamic masses to regard America as their archenemy. This supports the Ayatollah Ruhollah Khomeini's declaration in 1979 that the United States is the Great Satan and must be neutralized or destroyed.

Finally, Khomeini gave the lie to the notion that Islam is primarily a religion of peace. He made the following bold and unmistakable declaration of war against the world:

Those who know nothing about Islam pretend that Islam counsels against war. Those people are witless. Islam says: 'Kill all the unbelievers just as they would kill you all!' Does this mean that Muslims should sit back until they are devoured by the infidel? Islam says: 'Kill them, put them to the sword and scatter them.' Islam says: 'Whatever good there is exists thanks to the sword.' The sword is the key to Paradise, which can be opened only for the Holy Warriors! Does all this mean that Islam is a religion that prevents men from waging war? I spit upon those foolish souls who make such a claim.

This is in distinct contrast to Christ's statement that they who live by the sword shall perish by the sword. Christianity has believed that there are just wars, but force is not the means by which the kingdom of God will be established or the church extended. Jesus said, *"My kingdom is not of this world,"* and *"The kingdom of God is within you."* In other words, God rules in the universe but He rules specifically on Earth where He rules as King of the individual human heart.

The most famous of all Islamic historians Ibn Khaldun in the 13th century recognized this difference and also Holy Jihad as an Islamic institution. He wrote in *The Muqadimmah: An Introduction to History:*

> In the Muslim community, the holy war is a religious duty, because of the universalism of the Muslim mission and the obligation to convert everybody to Islam either by persuasion or force. . The other religious groups (Christianity and Judaism) did not have a universal mission, and the holy war was not a religious duty to them, save only for purposes of defense.

Ibn Khaldun was writing just at the end of the time of the Crusades. Apparently he did not interpret them as Christian holy wars, but just what they were, an effort to recover the holy places in Jerusalem. He was also doubtless aware of their defensive nature, because Islam had made incursions into Christian lands for centuries and had annexed the Greco-Roman Christian provinces of North Africa and the Middle East which eventually remained their permanent possession. Muslims also ruled in the Mediterranean having conquered Cyprus, Malta, Sicily, southern Italy and France and most of Spain. The Crusades, as we have seen, must be viewed in the context of Muslim conquest of Christian territory from 632 to the time of the First Crusade in 1095. During this period of over 400 years there had been no retaliation by any Christian armies.

Probing the Motivations for Holy Jihad: The Testimony of a Jihadist Suicide Bomber

I think we can understand the idea of Holy Jihad most accurately if we listen to the words of a Muslim jihadist committed to suicide for the glory of Allah. A *Time Magazine* reporter had just such an opportunity in Iraq. His interview with a masked young man calling himself Marwan Abu Ubeid was published in *Time*, July 4, 2005, pp. 22-29.

A 20 year old Iraqi Sunni from Fallujah and a member of Al Zarqawi's al-Qaeda, Marwan expressed great eagerness and joy in the anticipation of killing as many infidel Americans as possible with the help of Allah. His motivation is his unquestioning belief in his religion, in the teachings of the Qur'an, much of which he has memorized, and in Allah who has commanded the mujaheddin (holy warriors) to kill all infidels. He looks forward to martyrdom and the certain promise of Paradise. He says, "The only person who matters is Allah, and the only question he will ask me is 'How many infidels did you kill?'"

Marwan not only expects to wake up in Paradise after his suicide, but also expects to find all his holy warrior friends there. Also as a martyr Allah gives him the privilege to name 70 family and friends who will be guaranteed Paradise through his sacrifice.

He is not ashamed to be called a terrorist because the Qur'an says, "*Against them* (the infidels) *make ready your strength to the utmost of your power. . to strike terror into the enemy of Allah and your enemy*" ("The Spoils of War," Sura 8:12). He regrets the killing of any innocent victims of his mission, but knows he will be forgiven for these unintended consequences, because all victims like this are also assured Paradise. The killing of Iraqis who have cooperated or compromised with the infidel, however, is justified. These disloyal Muslims are to be considered as infidels.

We learn that suicide bombers go through a long period of preparation including purification of soul and body. They testify to a glorious euphoria in anticipating the sacrifice of their lives. They believe with all their hearts that they are obeying the Qur'an and Allah. So giving your life to kill infidels and traitors is a religious experience, a good work, and a noble act. Sacrificial death in killing for Allah is the highest possible achievement that one can attain in this life. It is known as "the pure path." Muhammad taught that Holy Jihad was more important even than prayer.

Marwan claimed that the jihadists are the most religious people among the Muslims. They can quote relevant sections of the Qur'an to apply to any subject. Islamic schools or madrassas including those in the United States emphasize the memorization of the entire Qur'an. Often this is the only subject. An important goal of this kind of education is to prepare thousands of young men to give their lives as Holy Warriors for Allah. This is being encouraged today all over the world wherever Muslim schools are found.

Holy Jihad is not a fringe Muslim teaching. We must realize that it is basic Islam for all who can be persuaded or are willing to pay the price. When it is exalted as the most important good work of all, it becomes the supreme goal of thousands of young Muslim idealists. This is what we are facing in the world today, and it reminds us again of the prophecy of the Apostle Paul given to his disciple Timothy, "*In the last days dangerous times will come*" (2 Timothy 3:1).

Chapter 6

ISLAM AND CHRISTIANITY

Truly Allah and the God of the Bible are not the same being. Also there is really only a superficial common doctrinal ground between Islam and the teachings of the Bible. There are major disagreements. The Qur'an, however, teaches that the earlier revelation of the Bible was given by Allah and is to be received with reverence. How can this be? Primarily these contradictions between the Qur'an and the Bible can be attributed to the illiteracy of Muhammad, who was badly misinformed and had an impaired understanding of the writings of the Old and New Testaments. He especially had a warped knowledge of the history and teachings of Christianity due to his acquaintance with the Ebionite heresy which taught that Jesus although sent by God was only a great teacher and prophet.

Muslim teachers try to explain the differences by boldly teaching that the Bible as we have it today has been hopelessly corrupted. Even the most agnostic and liberal of Biblical scholars, however, cannot point out any significant changes in the text of the Bible in the 700 years between the time of Muhammad and the Old Testament evidence in the Dead Sea scrolls and the earliest New Testament manuscripts. The text of the Bible that Muhammad claimed Allah inspired is the same text that we have today.

A Major Discrepancy—Works vs. Grace

Islam originated in Arabia and for years was primarily an Arab faith. Arabs consider themselves and the Arabic language the heart of Islam. They claim a history going back to

Ishmael, the son of Abraham by Sarah's maidservant or slave woman Hagar who was from Egypt. They probably also include in their ancestry other offspring of Abraham that became Semitic desert tribes, such as the Midianites and the Edomites

Coming from a setting that goes far back into Old Testament history, Islam's teachings are a warped reflection of the Old Testament dispensation of law. Islam teaches a pure religion of works with no concept of grace. Amazingly, over 500 years before the advent of Muhammad, the Apostle Paul had some very significant teaching, which can be directly applied to Islam. Although in his letter to the Galatians Paul was writing about the legalistic Judaizers who were insisting that Christians be made to keep the Law of Moses for their salvation, his illustrations and admonitions can be directly applied to the teachings of Muhammad and the Qur'an.

Galatians is believed to be about the earliest of the New Testament writings. It was probably written from Ephesus and addressed to the Christians in the churches of Galatia in Asia Minor as early as A.D. 51, which was only 20 years after the time of Jesus. The Apostle had heard that the Galatians were perverting the Gospel by reverting to a doctrine of works from the teaching of grace. His explanation and admonitions are stunning in their application to the religion of Muhammad. This letter to the Galatians reads as though it were written to Muslims. It seems almost to be prophetic of this religion, which began 560 years later.

"Tell me you who want to be under the law, are you not aware of what the law says? For it is written that Abraham had two sons, one by the slave woman (Hagar) *and the other by the free woman.* (Sarah) *His son by the slave woman was born in the ordinary way* (Ishmael)*; but his son by the free woman was born as the result of a promise* (Isaac).

"These things may be taken figuratively, for the women represent two covenants. One covenant is from Mount Sinai (the law) *and*

*bears children who are to be slaves. This is Hagar. Now Hagar stands for Mount Sinai **in Arabia** and corresponds to the present city of Jerusalem because she is in slavery with her children. But the Jerusalem that is above is free, and she is our mother.* (Paul is saying here that the Jews of his day had reverted to a works salvation and therefore were in bondage just like the slave Hagar and her son Ishmael.)

"Now you brothers (referring to the Galatian Christians) *like Isaac are children of promise. At that time the son born in the ordinary way* (Ishmael) *persecuted the son born by the power of the Spirit.* (Isaac) *It is the same now. But what does the Scripture say? 'Get rid of the slave woman and her son, for the slave woman's son will never share in the inheritance with the free woman's son.' Therefore brothers we are not children of the slave woman, but of the free woman."*

Here is a very distinct contrast between both the Judaizers and Islam with Christianity. It is a difference between bondage and freedom. This passage also has prophetic implications for the disposition of the land of Palestine. Ishmael always wanted to usurp Isaac's inheritance because he was the firstborn. The sons of Ishmael today are determined to possess the Promised Land, or Isaac's inheritance, which God gave to Israel.

The teaching of the Gospel is that God wants to set men free, which is in stark contrast to Islam's teaching and practice. *"It is for freedom that Christ has set us free. Stand firm, then and do not let yourselves be burdened again by a yoke of slavery"* (Galatians 4:21-5:1).

Ishmael is pictured here as the son of bondage illustrating the doctrine of works for salvation. The Arab descendants of Ishmael who are Muslims subscribe to this exact teaching, which the Apostle Paul condemns. The emphasis for the Jew and the Christian is that God has set us free by His grace and wants us to live as free men.

The Word of God teaches, *"Where the Spirit of the Lord is, there is liberty"* (2 Corinthians 10:29). *"It is for freedom that*

Christ has set us free. Stand firm, then, and do not let yourselves be burdened again by a yoke of slavery. . You, my brothers, were called to be free. But do not use your freedom to indulge the sinful nature; rather, serve one another in love. The entire law is summed up in a single command: Love your neighbor as yourself" (Galatians 5:1, 13-14). *"So if the Son sets you free, you will be free indeed."* (Jesus words in John 8:36.)

These teachings in the Bible are completely alien, even heresy, to fundamentalist Islam. Human freedom would violate Allah's sovereignty. The really major difference here, however, is the concept of grace. Because Allah does not have unconditional love and does not love the sinner, grace is an alien idea to the Muslim. The teaching of God's grace therefore may be the primary teaching of Christian faith, which can touch the heart of a seeking Muslim who has no sacrifice for sin and no assurance of salvation apart from martyrdom.

The idea of a "grace greater than all our sin" is a beautiful revelation of our Father who loves us with an unconditional love and seeks to reach us through the work of His Son in order to set us free. Grace means that we have God's favor even though we didn't deserve it or earn it. It is a free gift of God, which we receive by faith after repentance. This is called our redemption. To be redeemed means, in the Greek language of the New Testament, to be purchased out of the market place where slaves were chained to stakes in bondage.

As a part of this redemption a man is born again by the Spirit of God. He receives a new life, a new heart, and a new mind in Christ by grace through faith (Ephesians 2:8-9). The good news is that man can be released from bondage and set free by the Holy Spirit. He discovers true freedom and peace when his inner being and desires are changed and in harmony with God's will and the reason for which God created him. He is enabled now to choose what is right and more easily avoid what is wrong, but as the Apostle Peter warned the church, *"Live as free men, but do not use your freedom as a cover-up for evil"* (I Peter 2:16).

Our Founders were well aware of the bondage and disorder that an unchecked freedom resulting in gross sin can produce. Benjamin Franklin said, "Only a virtuous people are capable of freedom. As nations become corrupt and vicious, they have more need of masters." John Adams added, "Our constitution was made only for a moral and religious people. It is wholly inadequate to the government of any other."

Freedom to do as you please was never the kind of freedom, which our Founding Fathers fought for in the Revolutionary War. Their idea of freedom had come right out of the New Testament, which taught a responsibility to God the Creator. It was defined as "freedom to do as you ought" under the authority of the Creator who had authored the Ten Commandments and the commands given by Jesus Christ. Jesus said, *"My yoke is easy and my burden is light"* (Matthew 11:29, 30). It was still a yoke of obedience, but all of God's commandments were given in order that man might find success, prosperity, and the purpose for his life. (Deuteronomy 4:40; 6:2-3,24; 7:12-15; 28:1-14, et.al.) When a man is born again into the family of God, these commands are simply the way he learns to live his new life. As he grows in grace and knowledge of Christ, they become, as it were, part of his very nature blending with his character as he becomes a new man.

Islamic clerics like the Ayatollah Khomeini, however, are correct to point out that in America many have turned our doctrine of freedom into license or licentiousness. This is one reason that he called America "The Great Satan." The prevalence of sexual immorality, pornography, broken families, greed for money, drugs and crime are evidence that something is not working. Freedom is defined by pagan liberals in America today as a freedom to do as you please. This kind of freedom eventually results in social disorder and bondage.

This freedom to do as you please is neither the kind of freedom taught in the Scriptures nor that understood by the

Founders of our nation who laid our foundations on the principles of the Bible. John Quincy Adams, our 6th President, who growing up knew all of the Founding Fathers, reminisced at a 4th of July celebration in 1821. He said, *"The highest glory of the American Revolution was this: It connected in one indissoluble bond the principles of civil government with the principles of Christianity."*

Islam's Suspect Origin

From the standpoint of the Bible, the religion of Islam has a very curious origin. By his own testimony, Muhammad said that he was taught by an angel, although at times he wondered if he were possessed by demons. When he had doubts, he was reassured by his first wife Khadijah and later by another wife Aisha and his followers that his revelations must be from the Creator god, because he was, after all, a pious and good man. It is true that the ethical teaching he received is similar in part to the teachings of the Torah and the prophets, but it is far from the heart of the Gospel of Christ. Yet, Muhammad claimed that it was the final truth, which superseded anything else that had ever been revealed.

The Apostle Paul taught something that applies very specifically to the origin of Islam. To these same Galatians who were practicing a "works salvation" very similar to the teaching of the Qur'an, he wrote,

> *"I am astonished that you are so quickly deserting the one who called you by the grace of Christ and are turning to a different gospel* (good news), *which is really no gospel at all. Evidently some people are throwing you into confusion and are trying to pervert the gospel of Christ. But even if we **or an angel from heaven** should preach a gospel other than the one we preached to you, let him be eternally condemned. As we have already said, so now I say again: If anybody is preaching to you a gospel other than what you accepted, let him be eternally condemned"* (Galatians 1:6-9).

The logical conclusion from the Apostle Paul's teaching is that Muhammad and all of his followers are adhering to a false revelation and are eternally condemned by the true God of Abraham, Isaac, and Jacob. Islam has perverted the Gospel or the "good news." Who then was this "angel" who taught Muhammad? To anyone familiar with the Bible, the answer is devastatingly obvious. *"Satan himself masquerades as an angel of light"* (2 Corinthians 11:14).

Satan's Religion

There can be no doubt that Islam is a satanic creed. It was Satan's effort to mimic as closely as possible Judeo-Christianity and create a substitute religion, which would be his vehicle in the world. If Satan were to create a religion, what would it be like?

It would have to be moral in order to sustain a viable society. After all, Satan had lived in the presence of God and knows right from wrong and the moral from the immoral. At the same time his system would appeal to man's sensual nature similar to Satan's temptation of Eve in the Garden of Eden where he appealed to her desires—a tasty fruit and the opportunity to be like God.

So the Islamic Paradise is a place of sensual, physical delights. Muslim men can have as many as four wives in this life if they treat them equally, but they are promised scores of beautiful virgins called *houris* in Paradise plus unending physical delights.

1. Satan's religion would have to recognize a Creator, but make him unknowable. Satan does not want to be "known."

2. There would have to be the closure of a final judgment, an evaluation of this life.

3. Satan is an angel, so he would emphasize that there are angels.

4. He would build his religion on a foundation of pagan beliefs, which he had authored for millennia, which explains the Moon god and the Ka'aba, an original center of pagan Arab idolatry. He would draw out from this background a doctrine of monotheism to compete with Judeo-Christianity. He would also create a new god made in his image, a caricature of the Creator, because Satan himself wants to be worshiped.

5. He would make it a religion of works, because he knows nothing about grace; but he would keep it simple and practical.

6. He would emphasize power and will tempered by a conditional love and forgiveness. There could, however, be no teaching of unconditional love because this is not part of Satan's nature.

7. He would spread his religion by both stealth and force. Deceit, hatred, lying and destruction would be his tools, but the victors would be commanded to live in peace and follow a system of rules in the new religion.

8. He would be ruthless in dealing with his enemies.

9. Finally he would emphasize much prayer because he knows better than most Christians and Jews the intrinsic power there is in the combined prayers of thousands of people. Muslims pray together all over the world five times a day.

Satan would also demonstrate an implacable hatred of God's people, both Jews and Christians. A principal desire and goal of most Muslims in the world today is the total annihilation of Israel. Arabs sided with Hitler in his perverted vision of a "final solution" for the elimination of the Jews. Hitler's blue print for the world *Mein Kampf* has been a best seller in the Middle East. During the Second World War the Baath political parties of Syria and Iraq were modeled after the Nazi party in Germany, and Saddam Hussein patterned himself after Hitler's example. When he was imprisoned as a young militant, Saddam studied the techniques of both Hitler and Stalin in how to sustain a totalitarian regime.

Saddam claimed that Allah revealed to him in a dream or vision that he was a reincarnation of Nebuchadnezzar who conquered Jerusalem and Israel in 606-586 B.C. This was Saddam's primary foreign policy goal in which he was joined in heart by the 250 million Arab Muslims who surround the 4 to 6 million Jews in Israel. According to the *British Intelligence Digest*, Saddam had given permission to his old enemies the Iranians to cross Iraq when they would join together to obliterate Israel and reconquer Jerusalem. He had also made peace with Syria since they would have to cooperate together in obliterating the Jews. Recent information suggests that Saddam may have sent some WMD's to Syria before the United States army invaded Iraq.

Satan's hatred of Jews and Christians, who are called God's children on Earth, has never been more apparent than in these Last Days. One of Jesus' signs to his disciples that the end was near was that all his people would be hated and persecuted by all the nations (Matthew 24:9). There has been more persecution and martyrdom of Christians and killing of Jews in the world during this past century than in the entire previous 1900 years.

Out of the ten leading persecuting nations today eight are Islamic. Recently the most nefarious has been the Sudan where as many as two million professing Christians have been killed or enslaved. In many of the Islamic nations, if a Muslim becomes a Christian or changes his allegiance to any other faith he will more than likely be murdered according to the command handed down by Muhammad. Christian evangelism is absolutely prohibited, the Bible banned, and more and more Christian teachers and preachers are being punished in many Muslim nations.

Saudi Arabia is the strictest. A Filipino Christian was caught having a Bible study in his own home. He was arrested and eventually beheaded. Recently in Pakistan a Christian church was invaded, and its parishioners including women and children were gunned down. Similar atrocities have been committed in Indonesia and in Nigeria. There is no freedom of religion where Muslims are in control. Muslims can be more ruthless than Communists who are followers of another satanic creed.

Islamic fundamentalists today hate Christians perhaps more than Jews. Although the Qur'an commands Muslims to respect the upright who recite the Bible (Sura 3:113), Christians who believe Jesus is God are considered idolaters, and Muslims are to *"fight the idolaters to the end as they fight you in like manner."* This war of Islamic militants against America, which to them represents Christianity as well as secular humanism and Judaism, is a war to the death.

Even though the Qur'an says in Sura 5:82 that the people who say, *"We are the followers of Christ"* are closest to Muslims in belief in that *"they are not arrogant,"* Sura 5:51 commands, *"O believers, do not hold Jews and Christians as your allies. They are allies of one another; and anyone who makes them his friends is surely one of them; and God does not guide the unjust."*

And again the Qur'an in Sura 9:29 says, *"Fight those people of the book* (the Bible) *who do not believe in Allah and the last day, who do not forbid what Allah and His apostles have forbidden, nor accept shari'ah."* (Allah's law as interpreted by Islam's teachers) Whoever does not believe Muhammad's revelations and denies that they are true will become a resident of hell. (Sura

5:86) If the infidels resist, *"So fight them till all opposition ends and obedience is wholly Allah's"* (Sura 8:39).

Islamic militants understand the Qur'an and Muhammad to teach that ultimately Jews and Christians, who do not submit to Islamic law, must be eliminated. This demonstrates Satan's hatred of all of God's people. He knows that they will eventually replace him and all the spiritual beings—principalities, powers, thrones and dominions—who have rebelled against God (Ephesians 3:10 and 6:12) as God's representatives on the Earth.

Satan motivates this Islamic movement, which seeks to destroy Israel and America. Fundamentalist Islam hates democracy, hates freedom, hates the West, hates the secular society, and hates everything about the civilization called Christendom. Take a good look at the Taliban society of Afghanistan and you will see their ideal "ummah" or community. Their vision or ultimate goal is to return all the world to a retrograde society like 7th century Arabia when it was dominated by the prophet Muhammad and the religion of Islam in the year 630.

Who is Jesus in the Qur'an?

The Bible teaches that Jesus is the final revelation of God to mankind. He is the fulfillment of His covenants with Abraham, Isaac, Jacob and David, and of all His promises given to Israel through the prophets. He is called the Alpha and the Omega, the beginning and the end. He is the wisdom and righteousness of God incarnate in human form, and is in the express image of the Father. He is the Savior and Redeemer of the world and the beginning of the new creation of God, which is His family who are those called out of the world system to live forever with God. *"God was in Christ reconciling the world to Himself"* (2 Corinthians 5:19). He was declared to be the Savior and the Son of God through His sacrifice of Himself on the cross, where He became a curse for us and took our sins *"in his own body on the tree,"* and through His resurrection from the dead. This was to prove His identity and His authority assuring us that our sins can be forgiven and washed away and that we can have a new life in Him.

All of the above was prophesied over and over again in the Old Testament and is the heart of every one of the books of the New Testament. It was the core teaching of the disciples of Jesus, who testified not only to His words and His miracles, but also to His crucifixion, His resurrection, His ascension and the testimony of God Himself to His Sonship— *"This is my beloved Son in whom I am well-pleased."* Several times the disciples heard this audible testimony of the Father (Matthew 3:17 and 17:5).

When Jesus asked Peter about His identity, his disciple answered, *"You are the Messiah, the Son of the Living God"* (Matthew 16:16). Later on immediately following his personal encounter with the risen Jesus on the road to Damascus, Saul (later called Paul, the Apostle), who had persecuted the Christians as heretics, was found testifying in the Jewish synagogue of the city that *"Jesus is the Son of God"* (Acts 9:10).

In the wilderness that was the Hijaz in western Arabia where Muhammad grew up, the Bible was virtually unavailable and this message had not been heard very clearly. So now, in spite of all the testimony of the disciples of Jesus and the clear message of the Gospel, according to Islam and Muhammad, if you believe that Jesus is the Son of God you will be punished in Hell. To Muslims His name is "Isa," and He is only a great prophet.

Islam's Misunderstanding of the Meaning of *Gospel*

What does Islam teach about Jesus? There is nothing in the Qur'an about Jesus being sent by God to be a Savior or Redeemer. There is nothing about His providing salvation or a way to God. The Qur'an says he was sent by God simply as an "anointed one" (the meaning of *Messiah*) to be a sign to mankind (Sura 23:50), to fulfill the Torah and to bring the Gospel. There is, however, no definition of the Gospel or recognition of what is meant by the Gospel except to say that it is *"guidance and light, corroborating what was revealed before it in the Torah: a guide and an admonition to the righteous"* (Sura 5:46). This is very strange and speaks volumes about Muhammad's own illiteracy and lack of knowledge of exactly what Christianity was all about.

If the Qur'an is the word of the Creator God, it is very awkward that Muhammad or Allah seem to understand so little about the meaning of the Gospel. The Apostle Paul is very clear that the Gospel or good news is not just an explanation of the Torah, but is specifically the message of the death, burial and resurrection of Jesus the Messiah so that we can have forgiveness of our sins and be saved from eternal death (I Corinthians 15:1-8). This is the good news of God to the world, which is exactly the meaning of the word Gospel. This is the heart of the teaching of the New Testament. It is proclaimed over and over again that now men may be reconciled to the Creator God and have salvation through Jesus Christ by His sacrifice on the cross and His resurrection. This is never mentioned in the Qur'an except to deny that Jesus was crucified.

Who is responsible for this travesty, this lack of knowledge and understanding of the truth? The Scriptures speak clearly, *"The god of this age has blinded the minds of unbelievers, so they cannot see the light of the gospel of the glory of Christ, who is the image of God"* (2 Corinthians 4:4). This is exactly the way it is. Satan himself has afflicted Islam and its followers with spiritual blindness.

Islam's Denial of the Crucifixion and the Resurrection

Muhammad hated the symbol of the cross. This seems to have been a peculiar obsession, which separates Muhammad from all Christians—his rejection or fear of the cross. According to a friend Al Waqidi, who witnessed these things in Mecca, Muhammad broke everything that came into his house that had the form of the cross. It was this same man who testified to Muhammad's fear that he was possessed of a demon, but was dissuaded of this thinking by his wife Khadijah.

The Qur'an teaches the Jews are supposed to have uttered a monstrous falsehood when they said to Mary, *"We have put to death the Messiah, Jesus son of Mary, the apostle of God."* The Qur'an continues, *"They did not kill him, nor did they crucify him, but they thought they did. . they knew nothing about him that was not pure conjecture; they did not slay him for certain. God lifted him up to Him . . On the Day of Resurrection* (referring to the time of the final judgment) *he* (Jesus) *will bear witness against them"* (Sura 4:157-158). Are we expected to accept this brief statement denying all the historical evidence for the crucifixion of Christ, just because Muhammad said it or because a questionable deity called Allah revealed it? This is enough evidence right here for a Christian to immediately recognize that Islam was not revealed by the God of Abraham, Isaac and Jacob, but by Satan himself.

This denial of the crucifixion of Jesus by the Qur'an almost 600 years following the life and death of Jesus is absurd. Every witness to Jesus life over and over again testifies to the historical fact that he was executed by the Romans on the cross at the insistence of the Jewish leaders. The details of his apprehension in the Garden of Gethsemane, his trial before the Sanhedrin, his trial before Pilate and Pilate's misgivings, the cries of crucify him and the release of Barabbas, his cruel beatings and crown of thorns administered by the Roman soldiers, the Via Dolorosa where Jesus fell under the weight of the cross probably because of loss of blood, all the many details surrounding the crucifixion itself including the seven words or Jesus utterances, and the details of his being taken from the cross to the tomb would have been impossible to simply make up as a piece of fiction. There would have been hundreds of objections by eyewitnesses to such false representations.

To deny the crucifixion is more outrageous than to deny

the facts of the prophet Muhammad's life and death. The entire New Testament is a testimony to the death of Jesus on the cross. The Apostle Paul wrote, *"I am determined not to know anything among you but Jesus Christ and Him crucified"* (I Corinthians 2:2). Every one of Paul's epistles to the churches testifies to the crucifixion. To the Galatians he wrote, *"You foolish Galatians who has bewitched you? Before your very eyes Jesus Christ was clearly portrayed as crucified"* (3:1). This statement was made no more than 20 years following the crucifixion.

Paul had persecuted the church before his Damascus road conversion. He knew the original disciples of Jesus. He was an educated man. He certainly would never have accepted anything but the testimonies of eyewitnesses. It is too monstrous a lie and too ridiculous and insane to fathom a claim made 600 years after the fact in a remote desert of Arabia that what happened in Jerusalem all those years before was just a myth, but Muhammad lived in a desert backwater and was no student of history. He did not realize that it was this testimony and belief in the crucifixion and resurrection of Jesus Christ, which had birthed the religion that broke the back of the pagan Roman Empire.

Jesus not only told His disciples that He was going to die (John 12:7, 20-33), but He indicated at least twice that His death would involve being lifted off the ground. He said, *"'But I, when I am lifted up from the earth, will draw all men to myself.' He said this to show the kind of death he was going to die"* (John 12:32-33). To a ruler of the Jews and member of the Jewish governing body Nicodemus Jesus said, *"Just as Moses lifted up the serpent in the wilderness, so the Son of Man must be lifted up so that everyone that believes in Him might have eternal life"* (John 3:14-15). In the midst of a terrible plague, Moses had erected a pole on which he placed a serpent fabricated from bronze, and all the Israelites who had been bitten by a poisonous snake and were dying only had to turn and look at the snake on the pole, and they would be healed. (Numbers 21:8-9) This event prefigured Jesus' crucifixion and also the salvation, which would be granted to those who believed in his sacrifice on the cross for their sins.

No event is more emphasized in the New Testament besides Christ's resurrection than the death of Jesus on the cross. It is through the cross that Jesus unites both Jew and Gentile into one body erasing their hostility (Ephesians 2:14-16). One of the earliest creeds dating back to the earliest days of the church is quoted by the Apostle Paul in his letter to the Philippians which teaches that Jesus' going to the cross was an act of obedience to the Father for which he receives *"a name that is above every name"* and the worship and obeisance of all the created universe (Philippians 2:8-10).

Paul prophesies that the "enemies of the cross of Christ" will reap destruction (Philippians 3:18). He certainly could be speaking here of the followers of the false god Allah when he warned, *"Their destiny is destruction. . and their glory is in their shame."*

If there had been no crucifixion, certainly all that was written and preached about this fact could have been denied by the hearers of the day. Paul's letters were recorded within 20 to 30 years from the time of Jesus' death on the cross, or within the lifetime of many of the witnesses. His accounts and those of the Gospels would have been challenged vigorously if this history had been fabricated. Nothing speaks louder to the falseness of the Qur'an and the religion of Islam than this foolish denial of Jesus' crucifixion. It makes sense, however, if we realize it is Satan's effort to deny this very event, which God used to *"destroy him who has the power of death"* and *"destroy the works of the Devil"* (Hebrews 2:14 and I John 3:8).

The Witness to Jesus' Resurrection

An even more important testimony of Jesus' disciples, and central to their faith and teaching, was their witness to His resurrection. They knew that He was a living Lord. Paul says that the risen Christ was seen of more than 500 brethren all at one time and by many, many others (I Corinthians 15). This first letter of Paul to the church in the city of Corinth was written about 55 A.D. perhaps before any of the Gospels were widely distributed and within 25 years of Jesus' death and resurrection. There were many eyewitnesses to these events who were still alive who could have contested his claims. Paul rests the entire truth of Christian faith on the fact of the resurrection. It is the event upon which all our faith, our forgiveness and our new life in Christ hangs. He says frankly, *"And if Christ has not been raised, our preaching is useless and so is your faith. More than that, we are then found to be false witnesses about God, for we have testified about God that he raised Christ from the dead. . And if Christ has not been raised, your faith is futile; you are still in your sins"* (I Corinthians 15:14-17).

John testified, *"our hands handled him"* or *"we touched him"* (I John 1:1). Every recorded sermon of the apostles after the ascension of Jesus to the Father testified to the fact that He had been raised from the dead to prove that He was the Son of God and to declare the certainty of believers being justified by God. For their belief in this truth—that Jesus was alive—all the disciples gave their lives in martyrdom. Would they have died for a fraud? The Apostle Paul wrote, *"That if you confess with your mouth 'Jesus is Lord' and believe in your heart that God raised him from the dead, you will be saved"* (Romans 10:9). Belief that Jesus is alive and that He was raised from the dead is necessary to receive God's gift of forgiveness and salvation.

Islam's Denial of the Deity of Christ

The Qur'an constantly refers to Jesus as the "son of Mary." The central teaching here concerning Jesus is a negative one; namely, that He definitely, dogmatically was not the Son of God. Mary was not God's consort but was an unmarried virgin when Jesus was born (Sura 6:101). How could the Creator have a consort? The Bible never implies, however, that this Greek idea of a sexual relationship between a God and a human being was possible, and it certainly is not implied concerning Mary.

The Qur'an repeats its denial that Jesus is the Son of God over and over again. *"Those who say: 'The Lord of Mercy has begotten a son,' preach a monstrous falsehood, at which the very heavens might crack, the earth split asunder, and the mountains crumble to dust"* (Sura 19:88). *"Jesus, son of Mary, was no more than God's apostle and his word which He cast to Mary: a spirit from him. So believe in God and his apostles and do not say 'Three.' God is but one God. God forbid that he should have a son"* (Sura 4:171-72).

"They say, 'God has begotten a son.' God forbid! Self-sufficient is he" (Sura 10:68). *"Infidels* (unbelievers) *are those that say: 'God is the Messiah, the son of Mary.' For the Messiah himself said: 'Children of Israel, serve God, my Lord and your Lord.' He that worships other deities besides God, God will deny him Paradise, and the Fire shall be his home. None shall help the evildoers."* (Sura 5:71-72; see also 5:16.)

"Admonish those who say that God has begotten a son. Surely of this they could have no knowledge, neither they nor their fathers: a monstrous blasphemy is that which they utter. They preach nothing but falsehood" (Sura 18:4-5). *"God forbid that he himself should beget a son! When he decrees a thing, he need only say 'Be,' and it is. Truly the wrongdoers are today in evident error"* (Sura 19:35, 38). These utterances of Muhammad are supposed to be the very words of Allah. In truth, they are the words of a defeated and disillusioned Satan himself.

Islam teaches that Jesus, although a great prophet, was only a creature, and therefore only mortal (Sura 43:59). He has no power to intercede with God for those who pray to Him (Sura 43:86). The Qur'an puts words in Jesus' mouth saying to Allah at the Day of Judgment that He did not tell any of his followers that He was God or that men should worship Him. *"Then God will say, 'Jesus, son of Mary, did you ever say to mankind: Worship me and my mother as gods besides God?' 'Glory be to you,' he will answer, 'I could never have claimed what I have no right to. If I had ever said so, you would have surely known it. You know what is in my mind, but I know not what is in yours.*

You alone know what is hidden. I told them only what you bade me. I said: "Serve God, my Lord and your Lord"' (Sura 5:116-117). Although this statement has absolutely no factual basis whatsoever, Muslims simply accept this as a legitimate prophecy because they believe that Allah is the author of the Qur'an.

Mariolatry or praying to Mary was practiced in Muhammad's time. The world of the Eastern Mediterranean had included many goddesses in their worship. Aphrodite of Greece, Astarte of the Near East, and Isis of Egypt, which some historians have said might have become the dominant religion of the Roman Empire if not for the power of Christianity. It was easy to see why Mary who was called "Mother of God" by the Council of Ephesus in 431 became almost divine in the minds of many in the Christian church. This is probably why the Qur'an incorrectly identifies the Trinity as God the Father, God the Mother, and God the Son. Why was Allah so limited in his understanding of Christian teaching? Nowhere in the New Testament or the early church was Mary accorded this kind of status or veneration. She certainly was never considered part of the Godhead.

Even though Jesus' disciples had testified to Jesus' claim, *"I and my Father are One,"* (John 10:30), the Qur'an makes a special point to deny that Jesus had any knowledge of the thoughts of God. Jesus prayer to the Father recorded in John 17 shows the intimacy, which He had with God the Father. As a Christian one can only conclude that Islam is a deception of Satan.

The central teaching of the New Testament is that *Jesus is the Son of God.* In fact the Apostle John wrote his entire biography of Jesus to declare this as fact, *"But these are written that you may believe that Jesus is the Christ, the Son of God, and that by believing you may have life in his name"* (20:31). The annunciation to Mary by the angel Gabriel, who is supposed to be Muhammad's teacher, said concerning her child, *"The Holy One to be born will be called the Son of God"* (Luke 1:35). Jesus answer to the Jews who wanted to kill him was, *"Why then do you accuse me of blasphemy because I said, 'I am God's Son?'"* (John 10:36).

The book of Hebrews in the New Testament was written, as were all the records in the New Testament, over 500 years before a single word of the Qur'an had been recorded. It begins with a statement about who is Jesus the Christ. This is a summary of the testimony of the eyewitnesses, the disciples, the apostles and the early church.

Muhammad and the Qur'an have defamed all these godly people as liars. I am sure that neither Muhammad nor any of his early followers ever read a word of the New Testament. They were easily deceived by the god of this world who sought to establish a new monotheism to compete with God's grace. Satan has energetically opposed God's plan to reconcile the world to Himself by means of the life, death and resurrection of His Son Jesus Christ. Here in the introduction to the book of Hebrews is the early church's witness to the Christ, which certainly takes precedence over anything composed hundreds of miles away, in a foreign world, hundreds of years removed from the events about which it claims authority to speak.

"In the past God spoke to our forefathers through the prophets at many times and in various ways, but in these last days he has spoken to us by His Son, whom he appointed heir of all things, and through whom he made the universe. The Son is the radiance of God's glory and the exact representation of his being, sustaining all things by his powerful word. After he had provided purification for sins, he sat down at the right hand of the Majesty in heaven. So he became as much superior to the angels as the name he has inherited is superior to theirs" (Hebrews 1-1-7).

The Qur'an's Strange Account of the Virgin Birth

There are two rather extensive passages in the Qur'an in Suras 3 and 19, which tell of (1) The announcement to Mary that she would have a child without a father and (2) the events that took place in the immediate aftermath as Mary faced her friends and relatives with the new baby.

"The angels said to Mary: 'God bids you rejoice in a Word from Him. His name is the Messiah, Jesus son of Mary. He shall be noble in this world and in the world to come, and shall be one of those who are favored. He shall preach to men in his cradle and in the prime of manhood, and shall lead a righteous life. 'Lord,' she said, 'how can I bear a child when no man has touched me?' He replied: 'Even thus. God creates whom He will. When He decrees a thing He need only say: "Be," and it is. He will instruct him in the Scriptures and in wisdom, in the Torah and in the Gospel, and send him forth as an apostle to the Israelites'" (Sura 3:45-48).

Sura 19 gives more detail. *"And you shall recount in the Book the story of Mary: how she left her people and betook herself to a solitary place to the east. We sent to her our spirit in the semblance of a full-grown man.* (Sura 3 says it was an angel or angels.) *And when she saw him she said: 'May the Merciful defend me from you! If you fear the Lord, leave me and go your way.' 'I am but your Lord's emissary,' he replied, 'and have come to give you a holy son.' 'How shall I bear a child,' she answered, 'when I have neither been touched by any man nor ever been unchaste?' 'Thus did your Lord speak,' he replied, "That is easy enough for me. He shall be a sign to mankind and a blessing from ourself. Our decree shall come to pass.' Thereupon she conceived him, and retired to a far-off place. And when she felt the throes of childbirth she lay down by the trunk of a palm-tree, crying: 'Oh, would that I had died before this and passed into oblivion!'* (Note that there is no mention of Joseph, Bethlehem, the inn, the stable, the manger, the shepherds or the wise men as recorded in the Gospels.) *But a voice from below cried out to her: 'Do not despair. Your Lord has provided a brook that runs at your feet, and if you shake the trunk of the palm-tree it will drop fresh ripe dates in your lap. Therefore eat and drink and rejoice."*

Later on carrying the child in her arms, she came to her people, who said to her: *'Mary, this is indeed a strange thing! Sister of Aaron, your father was never a whoremonger, nor was your*

mother a harlot.' She made a sign to them, pointing to the child.
(Mary's friends and relatives naturally were aghast that she
had had a child out of wedlock. So Mary pointed to the child
to make her defense. They were asked to listen to the baby
Jesus who was only a few months old.) *But they replied: 'How
can we speak with a babe in the cradle?'"* (Sura 19:16-29).

Compared to the Bible account, the Qur'an story is like a
fable or fairy tale. What the Qur'an claims happened next
can only be called weird. Jesus addresses Mary's people from
the cradle in order to back up Mary's story of his birth.

*"Whereupon he spoke and said: 'I am the servant of God. He has
given me the Book and ordained me a prophet. His blessing is upon
me wherever I go, and He has exhorted me to be steadfast in prayer
and to give alms as long as I shall live. He has exhorted me to honor
my mother and has purged me of vanity and wickedness. Blessed was
I on the day I was born, and blessed I shall be on the day of my death
and on the day I shall be raised to life'"* (Sura 19:30-33).

There are two other inconsistencies with the Biblical
history.

1. The Qur'an calls Mary a sister of Aaron who was of
   the tribe of Levi. Is this a subtle denial that Jesus was
   of the tribe of Judah descended from King David and
   an heir to the throne of Israel?

2. As a baby Jesus says that he was to be blessed on the
   day of his death and on the day he would be raised.
   Elsewhere in the Qur'an the death and resurrection
   of Jesus are said to have never happened. God supposedly took Jesus alive into Heaven.

In Sura 3 Jesus gives a further spectacular sign as a young
child, which probably comes out of the apocryphal literature
of the second or third century. When Jesus was less than 12
years old, the Qur'an describes a miracle he performed for his
young friends.

"*He will* say: '*I bring you a sign from your Lord. From clay I will make for you the likeness of a bird. I shall breathe into it and, by God's leave, it shall become a living bird. . I bring you a sign from your Lord: therefore fear God and obey me. God is my Lord and your Lord: therefore serve Him. That is a straight path*'" (Sura 3:49-51). This is another bizarre story, a fairy tale or fable, which discredits Jesus' origin and his character as portrayed in the New Testament.

Jesus performed miracles as a ministry to men by the power of the Holy Spirit, which descended upon him in the form of a dove at his baptism. There is no record in the historical accounts of the biographies of Christ we call the Four Gospels that Jesus ever performed any miracles before this formal initiation to his ministry at the time of his baptism by John the Baptist. The Qur'an has concocted a myth, a fantasy, an invention, or an outright fabrication.

Other References to Jesus in the Qur'an

The Qur'an used the authority of Jesus to support Muhammad's conflict with the Jews of Medina. The infidel Jews are said to have been cursed by both King David and Jesus, the son of Mary (Sura 5:78). So Muhammad's rejection and severe punishment of the three Jewish clans of Medina was backed up and justified by the curses of both their most illustrious ancient king and also their most famous rabbi.

It is also claimed in the Qur'an that Jesus prophesied Muhammad's coming as a prophet. Jesus is quoted as saying to his disciples, "*I am sent forth to you from God to confirm the Torah already revealed, and to give news of an apostle that will come after me whose name is Ahmad.*" Since this statement, of course, is not found in the Bible, Muslims have claimed that the coming of Muhammad 500 years after the time of Jesus was prophesied in Jesus' promise to send the "Paraclete."

This identification of Muhammad with the "Paraclete" is another pure fiction and hardly worth refuting. *Paracletos* in the Greek means, "One called alongside to help." The New Testament is very clear that this was fulfilled at Pentecost in the revelation of the Holy Spirit ten days after Jesus ascension to His Father. The Holy Spirit entering as a "violent rushing wind" and in the form of cloven tongues of fire anointed each of the 120 disciples who were praying together in one place. The New Testament declares the Holy Spirit to be the third person of the Triune God (Acts 2:1-4).

Jesus specifically tied the term "Paraclete," which is translated Counselor, to the coming of the Spirit of Truth immediately after He had returned to His Father (John 15:26-16:16). The Holy Spirit's task was to guide the disciples "into all truth." This is the Spirit who is said to testify of Jesus to the disciples who would themselves then testify or be witnesses to Jesus (15:26-27).

The Holy Spirit, who would empower the disciples in their ministry, is specifically identified with "the Paraclete." How could Muhammad who was not even born until 500 years later counsel, help, and guide Jesus' own disciples in their future witnessing and ministry of preaching and teaching for Him? This is another example of the utter nonsense and confusion in the Qur'an. It seems that Islam is "grasping at straws" to find an identity or continuity for Muhammad with past revelations of God in the Bible no matter how absurd.

No Christian, or even Jew for that matter, would recognize either the person of God or His Son Jesus as depicted in the Qur'an. The irony is that with all its contradictions and errors, the Qur'an, which is supposed to be the words of Allah, claims for itself final authority. In the context of telling about Jesus, the Qur'an states: *"And to you we have revealed the Book with the truth. (The Qur'an) It confirms the Scriptures, which came before it and stands as a guardian over them. Therefore give judgment among men according to God's revelations, and do not yield to their whims or swerve from the truth made known to you."* It is obvious that the Qur'an does not confirm but rather contradicts the

Scriptures. Instead of being a guardian over them, it denies or blasphemes the Bible's most important and precious teachings. We can only conclude that it is a lying, false, impious, ungodly, and idolatrous document. It shows every indication and in every part that Satan is its author. His goal is not the fulfillment of Judeo-Christian faith but rather its destruction. It is another deception concocted by the one the Bible calls "The Deceiver."

Islam—The Great Antichrist System

Muhammad dogmatically denied that Jesus was the Son of God. He said that anyone who believed this was an idolater and worthy of death and hell. The Bible has some final words for Muhammad and his followers:

"Dear children, this is the last hour; and as you have heard that the antichrist is coming, even now many antichrists have come. This is how we know it is the last hour" (I John 2:18). I believe that this is a prophetic statement by the Apostle John warning us that we could know we were in the last hour, not just the last day, when a host of antichrist powers manifested themselves on the earth. Islam is the greatest antichrist system of all time.

"Who is a liar? It is the man who denies that Jesus is the Anointed One. Such a man is the antichrist. He denies the Father and the Son. No one who denies the Son has the Father; whoever acknowledges the Son has the Father" (I John 2:22-23). John implies throughout his writing that the identification "Anointed One, Messiah or Christ" is equal to "the Son of God" as he uses these titles interchangeably. This passage indicates that Muhammad could not have had any kind of relationship with the Creator God who is called our Father. His revelations could not have come from the true God as he claimed. They are completely contradicted by the New Testament and by Jesus' revelations to his disciples over 500 years earlier.

"We know that we live in him and he in us, because he has given us of his Spirit. And we have seen and testify that the Father has sent his Son to be the Savior of the world. If anyone acknowledges that

Jesus is the Son of God, God lives in him and he in God. And so we know and rely on the love God has for us" (1 John 4:13-16). This confirms to us that the true God could not have inspired Muhammad nor could Muhammad have been close to the "God of Abraham, Isaac, and Jacob" who is our Father.

"Who is he that overcomes the world? Only He who believes that Jesus is the Son of God. He is a liar who does not believe the testimony that God has given about His Son. . He who does not have the Son of God does not have life" (1 John 5:5, 12). This means that we can only conclude that Muhammad was a liar and did not have God's life in him.

"Dear friends, do not believe every spirit (or angel), but test the spirits to see whether they are from God. Because many false prophets have gone out into the world. This is how you can recognize the Spirit of God: Every spirit that acknowledges that Jesus Christ has come in the flesh is from God, but every spirit that does not acknowledge Jesus is not from God. This is the spirit of the antichrist, which you have heard is coming and even now is already in the world" (1 John 4:1-3).

We have here a clear teaching by the Apostle John that leads us to a final conclusion that Muhammad was a false prophet and that Islam is an antichrist system. All of this may have implications for prophecies concerning the last days when an individual called "The Antichrist" or "the man of sin" will be revealed.

Epilogue

The enemy who is Satan has always wanted to replace God on His throne. He wants to be worshiped. He is called the ruler of the darkness of this world, the ruler of this world, the ruler of the nations, and the ruler of the kingdom of the air. It seems that Satan was God's designated custodian of the Earth until man was created with the purpose that some among Adam's descendants would "inherit the Earth."

Jesus is that descendant in the flesh and has earned the right to sit on God's throne. Satan sought to short circuit Christ's inheritance at the beginning of His ministry by offering Him a quick and easy way to inherit the Earth. Remember the last of the three temptations in Matthew 4:8-10 when the Devil took Jesus to a high mountain and showed him all the kingdoms of the world and said to Him, *"All these I will give you, it you will fall down and worship me."* Jesus answered Satan with a rebuke casting him out by quoting God's commandment. He said, *"It is written, 'You shall worship the Lord your God and him only shall you serve.'"*

"The reason the Son of God (Jesus) *appeared was to destroy the devil's work"* (1 John 3:8b). Is it any wonder that Satan's religion of Islam denies the crucifixion, the resurrection and that Jesus is the Son of God and the Savior of the world? These truths are at the very heart of the Gospel, which Satan hates and refuses to acknowledge because at the cross Satan's true character and rebellious hatred against the Creator God was exposed for all the universe to behold. The Devil's work and dominion over death was destroyed. A new race of beings, a priesthood of believers, has been chosen to ultimately replace Satan and his angels as the true inheritors and rulers of the Earth. *"And having disarmed the powers and authorities, he made a public spectacle of them, triumphing over them by the cross"* (Colossians 2:15).

Satan always has wanted to receive worship through idolatry. The Apostle Paul says that behind every idol there is a demon or emissary of Satan (1 Corinthians 10:19-20). There have been throughout all of human history a multitude of false religions, which Satan controlled or influenced as a substitute for the worship of the true God. None, however, were successful as a world dominating religion until Islam.

The revelation and knowledge of Jesus Christ who is called God's secret or mystery (Colossians 1:25-27) was beginning to sweep the Earth in the first several hundred years of the Church. Then Islam was revealed to Muhammad over 500 years after the coming of Jesus and blocked the Christian expansion trying to wipe it out and take its place.

But the message of the Gospel was eventually set free and has spread to every nation. Militant Islam seeks again to hinder and usurp this expansion. We have entered a new phase of conflict with Satan, which will continue until Jesus comes again.

This new monotheism is Satan's substitute for Judeo-Christianity and seeks to take over the Earth. It is an attempt to copy aspects of both Judaism and Christianity, while at the same time cutting the real meaning and heart out of each and substituting a reasonable deception and fraud. Satan's name is Deceiver. If we seriously and carefully compare God's revelation given to the prophets of Israel and through Jesus and his disciples as found in the Bible with the Qur'an and the teachings of Muhammad and Islam, there is no other conclusion to make than that this religious charade is a very clever invention of Satan, the imposter.

Islam provides no Savior, no grace, no salvation from sin, no lasting forgiveness, no real love and no intimate fellowship with God. At its heart it offers sensual or lust-of-the-flesh satisfactions which are in the category of Satan's appeal to Eve's flesh in the Garden of Eden. Islam's promised Paradise, for example, which can be achieved by dying for Allah, is a well-watered garden filled with tasty food and drink and an unending heavenly orgy of sex. There is no mention of the spiritual heavenly joy of experiencing the eternal presence of God and His glory. A Muslim can never have a close personal relationship with God or "know" God as his Heavenly Father in this life or in the life to come. One can only have this relationship with Jesus Christ who said, "*I am the Way, the Truth, and the Life. No one comes to the Father except through me*" (John 14:6). It is too bad that Muhammad did not know this statement of Jesus.

The god Allah is a caricature of the true God and will in these last days be manifested as the image and power of Satan. The Antichrist will be Allah or Satan incarnate. It is now through Allah, masquerading as the true God, that

Satan is fulfilling his lifetime desire to be worshiped. When He returns to the Earth, Jesus, who is Jehovah incarnate, will destroy the Antichrist, who will be the incarnation of Allah, who is Satan.

Christianity and Islam cannot both be right. Islam is replete with contradictions of the revelations of the prophets and of Christ Jesus and his apostles. Today it is fundamentalist Islam's confirmed commitment, furthermore, to destroy first the Jews and then Christians, who are called "The Crusaders."

This is Satan's final effort to thwart the will of Almighty God. (1) Eliminating the Jews nullifies God's promises of a restored Israel, and (2) Eliminating Christians will frustrate the second coming of Jesus Christ for his chosen ones. Some militant Muslims very frankly put it this way, "First we will wipe out the Saturday people and then we will eliminate the Sunday people." It reminds us that another of Satan's names is "the Destroyer." He will not succeed.

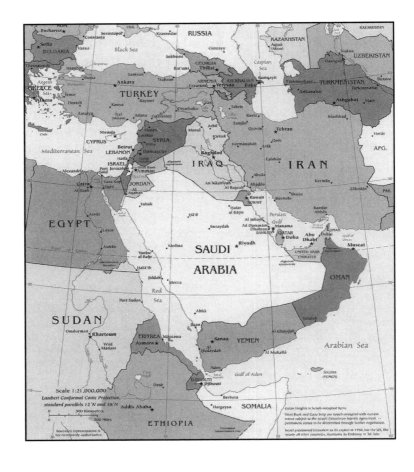

Chapter 7

DANGEROUS TIMES
AND GOD'S SOLUTION

Origin of the Conflict

Islam has been in conflict with Christianity almost since the time of its birth in the 8th century. This clash of cultures and civilizations is continuing with a vengeance. These "last days" are predicted to be "dangerous times" (2 Timothy 3:1). Is there any answer to this enduring conflict?

When Muhammad received his first revelations he identified Allah with the God of the Jews and Christians. He thought they would become his allies because he was leading his Arab people out of idolatry and paganism into the light of the worship of the one true god.

When the Jews rejected Muhammad's new vision and regarded him as less than a true spokesman for God, he became angry and lashed out enlisting the political and military power at his disposal as leader of the town of Medina. He banished some of the Jews and murdered the rest, in effect stealing their property.

Muhammad's first contact with Christians probably was during his trade caravan trips to Syria, when he was a teenager. He was impressed with the monks who were devoted in full-time service to God. Some must have been kind and generous to him because his memories of them were positive. The Qur'an speaks of their compassion and says that they showed love to Muslims and were good people (Suras 5:82 and 57:27).

Later on Muhammad's concept of Christianity was conditioned by the teachings of his wife Khadijah's cousin Waraqa. He was probably an Ebionite Christian. In the

Hadith of Al Bukhari, Waraqa is said to have had a copy of the Gospel of the Hebrews, which was very likely a portion of Matthew's Gospel in Aramaic. This incomplete biography of Jesus was the only Christian writing accepted by the Ebionites. If this is true, Waraqa believed Jesus to be a prophet and a teacher, a man sent by God whose ordination was confirmed by miracles and his sinless life. Jesus, however, was definitely not the Savior of the world nor had he been crucified or resurrected for anybody's sins.

Muhammad's attitude toward Jesus and his beliefs about him seem similar to the Ebionites. Anything more than their belief about Jesus had to be heresy, idolatry and the sin of *shirk* or the creating of competition with Allah. Christians were damned if they believed that Jesus was God or the Son of God. This teaching could not be accepted because God was *One* and indivisible.

Jews and Christians had both been given revelations by God, and these had been compiled in a book or earlier revelation—*al kitab* in Arabic. Muhammad probably never ever saw, much less read, a manuscript of either the Old or New Testaments. Waraqa certainly told Muhammad about the brief account he had read of Jesus. This, however, was an incomplete revelation. He was doubtless familiar with the scrolls of the Torah in Hebrew. Maybe there were even some codices of one or more of the Gospels in Greek or Syriac. Muhammad, nevertheless, could not himself have read any Jewish or Christian Scriptures even if they had been in Arabic, because he was illiterate.

Muhammad came to believe strongly in the precedence of his own revelations over any others in the past. These oracles, which came out of his mouth when he was in either an unconscious or semi-conscious state, were written down by his followers. He only learned them himself, as those who recorded what he had said read the revelations back to him. He must have memorized these recitations and later discovered that they contradicted what was being taught by orthodox

Christians.

He came to believe therefore that Jews and Christians had both strayed from the truth of the ancient monotheism, especially the Christians. He was so offended by their corruption of what he thought was the genuine truth that he vehemently forbade any Jews or Christians from anymore desecrating the land of Arabia with their presence. His deathbed wish was that any Jews or Christians who lived in Arabia be banished from the sacred ground of Allah's new kingdom.

Muhammad did not order that Jews and Christians be killed as he did the idolaters who refused to worship Allah. He probably thought that they were well enough informed to eventually see the light and become Muslims, or "submitters" to Allah. But he believed that they had misinterpreted the revelation that had been given to them. How could it be any other way since the Qur'an was surely God's revelation, and it contradicted both the Jewish and Christian teachings, as he understood them? Or he simply felt that when they did not immediately accept him as a true prophet and follow his directives, they were surely not abiding by the will of Allah, who was the true god. This set the tone for years to come in Muslim lands.

The Conquests

During Muhammad's lifetime all of the Middle East was part of the Eastern Roman Empire, which was called the Byzantine Empire. Also the lands in North Africa bordering the Mediterranean Sea beginning with Egypt and extending through Libya, Tunisia, and Algeria to Morocco were all Christian. These included the original bishoprics of St. Augustine and St. Cyprian and other famous church leaders. Lands under the control of the Western Roman Empire from Spain through Italy to the Byzantine Empire in Greece and what is now Turkey were also all largely Christian.

The Mediterranean that had been a Roman lake and then a Christian lake was soon to become a Muslim lake.

Muhammad's armies quickly conquered all these lands including Spain. But they were unable to conquer the rest of the Western Roman Empire or the heartlands of the Byzantine or Eastern Roman Empire. They did threaten to take France (Gaul) but were stopped at Tours in 732. Later they took the islands of the Mediterranean and southern Italy, and finally most of the Byzantine Empire including the Balkans. In 1453 the Ottoman Turks, who had converted to Islam, captured Constantinople, the last remaining Christian Patriarchate besides Rome. They advanced into Europe but were stopped twice at the gates of Vienna, or all of Europe would have become Muslim. The last confrontation was in 1683 when King John III of Poland defeated the Grand Vizier Kara Mustafa's Turkish army just over 300 years ago.

In lands that Islam conquered, Christians and Jews were allowed to live as second-class citizens or *dhimmi* subject not only to taxes but also to much humiliation and restriction. This was a sharp goad that motivated nominal Christians to become Muslims. Other Christians-in-name-only, when they heard that they could escape being taxed if they turned to Islam, also converted. Those who remained Christians or Jews were allowed to pay an annual tribute, which became a very important source of support for the Muslim political administrations. In fact, cooperating Christians were often impressed into helping administrate the lands taken over by the Muslim armies, who spoke only Arabic. Eventually the Arabic language of the conquerors became the language of all of these lands just as English became a major language in Nigeria, India, Egypt and other British colonies, and the French language was used in many African nations like Algeria and in spheres of French influence like Syria and Indo-China (Viet Nam).

Christians who resisted Islam were slaughtered just like the pagans. Literally hundreds of thousands lost their lives, and their wealth was confiscated. Allah in the Qur'an had promised his followers booty as a temporal reward.

We have already seen the vast extent of the conquests of Islam all the way from Morocco on the northwest coast of Africa to the southern Philippines in the South China Sea. This is all part of an area across all of the Old World called the 10/40 window—10 degrees to 40 degrees north latitude. From a Christian point of view, it is the least evangelized area on Earth. This is primarily because of the presence of Islam.

Trying to convert Muslims is against the law in most Islamic nations and may be punished by imprisonment or death. We have already seen that converts from Islam to Christianity or any other religion are always in danger of being killed by their families, friends, or countrymen. This fear of reprisal has kept the Muslim populace in line, and assured that Islam retains an overwhelming majority in most countries where they reside.

We have seen that one of the principal reasons for the success of the Muslim fighters is that Muslims believed that, if they died fighting for Allah, they would go immediately to Paradise where they would enjoy endless, sensual delights. They were therefore willing and even eager to fight to the death. Other armies were not so dedicated and they succumbed to the Muslims' fearless ferocity. Even today Osama-bin-Laden has said, "We will win because we want to die, and you want to live."

Islam's Continuing Offensive

After the years of their initial expansion, Arab Muslims saw that the two greatest infidel areas nearest to them, which they needed to control, were Europe to the northwest and Africa to the south.

Now, once again Islam is aggressively on the march, subduing infidels. This is especially true in sub-Saharan Africa, e.g., the southern Sudan and north central Nigeria, where they have been killing or enslaving millions of pagans and Christians.

Today, the radical Islamists do not seem as careful to make the distinction. Christians especially are being attacked and imprisoned or killed in almost all Muslim countries just like the pagans. There is no tolerance, no peace, and no religious freedom.

Churches, including home meetings, are invaded and congregations attacked with guns or jailed as in Pakistan, Indonesia, Nigeria, Egypt, and Saudi Arabia. Missionaries are captured and killed, such as the Burnhams in the Philippines.

The Voice of the Martyrs, Inc., on their website (www.persecution.com), where you may register for free, keeps a running tab on the persecution of Christians going on all over the world. They find that most Christian persecution today is in Muslim nations.

And they have become ruthless. You can look up almost any Islamic nation and find scores of news articles detailing these Islamist attacks. Here are a few headlines:

"Pakistani Pastor Killed;" "Pakistani Christians Injured in Church Attack;" "We will make your church red with blood;" "16 killed in attack on Pakistani church." (Only 4 of 45 articles in the last 5 years.)

"Indonesian Pastor Murdered During Church Service;" "Christians murdered in Ambon;" "Christians Flee as Jihad Strikes North Maluku Town;" "Christians Killed, 11 Injured in Indonesian Attack." (Only 4 of 25 articles.)

"Church Attacked in Upper Egypt;" "Christian Converts Persecuted in Egypt;" "Christians Held by Egyptian Police." (Only 3 of 10 articles.)

"Persecution and Prison in Saudi Arabia;" "U.S. Ally Saudi Arabia: No Friend to Christians." (2 of 10 articles.)

"Muslims Target Christians in Nigeria;" "Nigerian Pastor Killed in Escalation of Islamic Violence." (2 of 6 articles.)

"Philippine Prayer Rally Bombed;" "Hmong Believers Face Torture for Having Bibles."(2 of 7 articles.)

"Sudanese Christians Killed;" "Samaritan's Hospital

Bombed in Sudan;" "Massive Military Buildup in South Sudan—2002: Intense year of Persecution against Christians." (2 of 33 articles.) And we could go on and on.

Eurabia: The Euro-Arab Axis

Europe presents a totally different explosive threat. This hub of the Roman Catholic faith and the home of the Reformation has often been called post-Christian in its ideas and practices. The new European Union, e.g., just wrote a ponderous constitution which hardly makes mention of Europe's roots in Christianity that go back over 1600 years. European intellectuals and the elite are ashamed and scornful of their Christian past. This has created a barren wasteland for the potential planting of a vigorous Islam.

European leaders woke up one day and realized that they were not reproducing themselves. They were not making enough babies, and birthrates were not high enough to sustain even a constant population level. It takes 2.1 children per family to stay even. Europe's average is 1.4, Russia is 1.3, but Islamic nations were reproducing at a four or five times higher rate—Saudi Arabia is almost 6.0 and Yemen is almost 8.0. America is 2.07 or just about even.

When you have a population declining in numbers, the median age naturally increases and in the long run Europe was not going to be able to support its retirees and elders. Short workweeks, long vacations, and early retirement were the products of socialism and the welfare state.

A solution was to increase immigration levels and bring in guest workers that would provide the economic base to sustain the rosy status quo on which Europeans had come to depend. Former German Chancellor Helmut Schmidt had begun a program of bringing Turkish workers into Germany in the 1960's. After all, Turkey was part of NATO and a candidate to join the European Union. Algerians, Moroccans and Tunisians were brought to France, Pakistanis and Egyptians to Britain, and Libyans and Somalis were admitted to Italy.

Millions of Muslim immigrants were scattered among most of the nations of Western Europe.

In the multicultural environment of Europe, no one thought that a population of moral, hardworking Muslims could ever present a problem. Europeans had colonized Muslim countries and were familiar with the culture. Europe had many languages already. What problem was one more? Also all European nations had some differences in their cultural roots. Another cultural system could certainly be accommodated. Besides Europe needed to increase its proletarian base—workers who would do all the dirty and tedious jobs that affluent Europeans no longer wanted to be bothered with.

Europeans didn't consider two things: (1) European culture had been rooted in a foundation of Christian faith and values for over 1500 years. This was still true in spite of the great inroads of secular fundamentalism including humanism, atheism, agnosticism, and the anti-Christian bias of the Enlightenment and the French Revolution, which had planted the seeds for the development of Marxist socialism. (2) At heart Muslims were anti-secular, anti-Western culture, and anti-Christian. Europeans failed to take seriously the fact that less than 400 years ago Islam had tried for the third or fourth time to conquer Europe.

Now, Islam has become a 5th column embraced into the bosom of an ignorant, arrogant European elite who had come to question and even despise their own Western culture. They hated where they had come from and who they were. Liberals don't think that we deserve to survive. They said to themselves, "Let someone else try. We have failed." Modern pagan man is ashamed of his culture. Why? Because he himself has ruined and rejected the values upon which it was originally constructed. He is ashamed of what he sees, and he thinks that the failure is inherent in Western civilization, whereas the failure is in himself and is intrinsic to his own nature. He does not realize that he is responsible for perverting what he had been given. Europe's insightful political philosopher Alexis de Toqueville's observation suggests the danger here. He said, "Some peoples may let the torch (of their civilization) be snatched from their hands, but others stamp it out themselves."

A Christian society did not generate WWI and WWII. These conflicts erupted from the pagan ideas of the Enlightenment and the French Revolution, which produced first Napoleon and ultimately Hitler and Communism. Lenin himself said that the Communist revolution had originated in the French Revolution 125 years earlier.

The American Founding Fathers created an entirely different kind of revolution. They recognized that *"only a virtuous people are capable of freedom."* Only moral and disciplined men can produce a half way decent society. It was an essentially Christian idea based on the Bible's teaching. The venerable Benjamin Franklin, who gave us that maxim above, was confronted by some woman as he left the hall where a constitution for the United States had been hammered out in the summer of 1787. She asked him, "Sir, what kind of government have you given us?" He replied, "A republic, madam, if you can keep it!"

Contemporary liberals on both sides of the Atlantic are today ashamed of their culture. Why? Because they have ruined the values upon which it was built. They have rejected God and the teachings of His Word. Liberals scorn the very thing that made Western culture flower and succeed. A rejection or perversion of Biblical values will ultimately produce a miserable society. Calling good, "evil" and evil, "good" yields confusion and brings destruction. Western liberals hate Western civilization because they see its warts and blemishes, and that it is full of what the Bible calls sin, but it is their own doing! As Proverbs 19:3 explains it, *"A man's own folly ruins his life, yet his heart rages against the Lord."*

What have liberal pagans done? They have turned the Christian concept of a responsible freedom into a license to do as you please. In America the ACLU represents those who would let it all hang out and proclaims, "Anything goes!" Among many other licenses, it permits open sex in public, freedom for all kinds of pornography including child porn on the Internet, unrestricted abortion, euthanasia, the redefinition of family and marriage, legalized sodomy and drugs, minimal punishments which victimize the real victims—and these are just the bottom of the barrel. It is no wonder liberals are ashamed and want to hide their faces from what they have made.

Islam wants the world, and Europe is next on its list. The liberals, the humanists, the pagans, the secular fundamentalists, the atheists, and the hedonists may give it to them by default. They have no will to preserve what they are ashamed of. They think that the problem is intrinsic in the values of Western civilization. They don't see that it is in themselves and in their own perversion of what they inherited. Not only have they perverted the concept of freedom but also the idea of an unending multiplicity of human wants disguised as rights and the concept of an unrestrained personal privacy. We should be reminded that Jesus said, *"Men loved darkness rather than light because their deeds were evil"* (John 3:19).

Islam is the greatest threat Europe and the world has faced, more dangerous than the Nazis and more dangerous than Communism. And at this very time cultural tolerance in Europe has turned to a hatred, even a loathing, of their own history and culture.

Europe has been on the brink of committing long-term cultural suicide. Muslims would much rather Islamicize Europe than be Europeanized, and they have said so.

Multiculturalism has allowed them to retain their language, their culture, their dress, their sedition, their contempt for the West and Christianity, and their intolerant religion. The destructive rioting of Muslim youth in France is a spontaneous expression of Muslim contempt for all that is Western.

Probably as many as 50% of European Muslims are fundamentalists including homegrown 2nd generation youths trained in madrassas and harangued by radical imams every Friday in the mosques. With the rise and popularity of the ideal of Holy Jihad, they pose a great danger. Europe finds itself even more vulnerable than the United States. Actually Muslims, without firing a shot, may look forward to taking over Europe within 50 to 100 years because of the disparity in birthrates alone. Muslims are producing four times as many children and keeping them in the fold.

The only hope is that Europe is beginning to realize the danger. An interesting and provocative voice has been Oriana Fallaci, the Italian journalist for the newspaper *Corriere della Sera*, who has been stridently irreverent and politically incorrect in her letters, which were edited into an outrageous book, and published in many European languages where she was a hot best seller in many countries. (*The Rage and the Pride*, New York: Rizzoli International, 2001) She expresses her rock-hard conviction that Islam is a blight on this world, a serious threat to a superior Western culture, which does not realize the danger to its existence. "Troy will burn, Troy will burn," she shouts like Cassandra of Homer's Iliad. "They say, 'There goes that crazy woman again.' But Troy will burn because they have no passion, and they conduct this war with fear. If you go on being deaf and blind, you will be dead." (Quoted in the National Weekly Edition, *Washington Times*, 12/23-29, p. 12.)

With warnings like this and their own experiences with terrorists, Europe is beginning to look at its too tolerant laws, its loose immigration policies, and its benign responses to the Islamic threat as it belatedly tries to defend its future. America may learn some things here from Europe's awakening.

Christians and Muslims—Jesus and Muhammad

Muslims look at the immorality in the West and think

themselves superior. They want to be ruled by their own shari'ah law, and Canada and some European states might give them the freedom to do it. This would mean creating little legal, sovereign principalities within these nations that are enemies of the culture and the religious, social and political systems that surround them. But the Islamists are not much better. They are sinners, too.

But Muslims are arrogant, first, because they do not believe that they have a nature to sin. In many cases they do not even recognize what sin is. Their Perfect Model Muhammad was a robber, a murderer, a fornicator, a pedophile, a wife beater, a truce breaker, a liar, and one who had his enemies assassinated.

We not only reflect the character of our heroes, we will reflect the character of our god, and Allah cannot be trusted completely. He is distant, capricious and changeable; he is not a loving father but a demanding taskmaster; he is cold without unconditional love; he hates the sinner and the corrupt, and predestines everything with seeming legalistic arbitrariness countenancing violence and the killing of all those who will not submit to him.

Jesus said that we are not to judge because judgment belongs to God, but we can be "fruit inspectors." He said, "*By their fruit you will know them*" (Matthew 7:16). Man is a mental being and the fruit he produces—the product of his life—is really what is born in his mind—his ideas. As the popular saying goes, "Ideas have consequences." A similar principle is found in Proverbs, "*As a man thinks in his heart, so is he.*" Physically we may be what we eat, but mentally and spiritually we are what we think. The ideas of Christianity and Islam have produced two different sets of values, two different cultures, two different civilizations, and two different kinds of fruit.

Even in the material realm, the fruit of Islam is lacking. All of the Arab nations put together, more than 250 million people, do not produce any more than a single small nation in Europe like Finland. Their GNP altogether is no larger that the economy of one small nation. Without the oil, all Arab nations would still be in the Third World with no wealth or power. They produce very little fruit economically except what they have been given as a gift out of the ground, and even then they would not have been able to develop the oil fields without the help of the Crusader nations. Jesus said, *"Watch out for false prophets. They come to you in sheep's clothing but inwardly they are ferocious wolves. By their fruit you will recognize them. . Likewise every good tree bears good fruit, but a bad tree bears bad fruit"* (Matthew 7:15-17).

In many ways the fruit of Islam is bitter and bad. Muslims do not want to be reminded that they cannot control their sinful nature, which they do not believe they have in the first place, so they cover all their women's bodies to avoid lust, fornication, and adultery. They treat overt sins ruthlessly, cutting off fingers, hands, tongues, and even heads. They love suicide. They say that they want to die. Liberal pagans are the same. They want to destroy the culture, commit a suicide of their civilization, and plunge into hedonism to mask their pain and failure. What can we say? Satan is the Destroyer.

Islamists and leftist/liberals have much in common. They have a veneer of righteousness and believe that their system is the most moral. But they are supported by hatred and lying. Both liberals and Islamists play fast and loose with the truth. In fact, they accept no truth except that which advances their cause.

Contrasting and Comparing: What May We Conclude?

The ideas and ideals of Western civilization have been rooted in the deep soil of almost 2,000 years of Christian teaching and the example of Jesus and those who have followed Him. The ideas and ideals of Islamic civilization have been rooted in almost 1400 years of Qur'anic teaching and the example of Muhammad and his followers.

When we contrast the leaders—Jesus and Muhammad—there is absolutely no contest. We have noted some of the characteristics of Muhammad and his teaching, "Kill your enemies." We know of the purity of Jesus' character and his opposite teaching, *"Love your enemies, and pray for those who persecute you, that you may be sons of your Father"* (Matthew 5:43-48).

When Jesus was reviled and humiliated, he turned the other cheek, did not open his mouth, and committed himself to his Father. *"He committed no sin, and no deceit was found in his mouth. When they hurled their insults at him, he did not retaliate; when he suffered, he made no threats. Instead he entrusted himself to him who judges justly"* (1 Peter 2:22, 23). When Muhammad was rejected and humiliated, he ordered the assassination of his assailant.

What are the highest values in Christian faith? Love, sacrifice, humility, and compassion for others, which includes longsuffering. What are the highest values in Islam? The highest is fighting for Allah especially if you die in the process. As far as an ordinary Muslim is concerned, his highest value is doubtless going to Paradise and enjoying all the sensual delights promised to him. Although virtues are of importance in Islam, you never hear that love or patience, longsuffering or goodness, or faithfulness or truthfulness are of the highest value. Prayer and good works in keeping the Five Pillars are most important. Prayer and good works are very important in Christianity also, but they are a means to an end, not the end in itself. The Bible teaches us that all the qualities of love are the top priority in a Christian's life because this mirrors the character of God (1 Corinthians 13:4-7).

Christianity is more concerned with character because of the imparting of the new nature of God when a man is born again, as Jesus taught Nicodemus. It is the concept of becoming like God or becoming godly. Jesus said, *"Be perfect* (mature or complete) *as your heavenly Father is perfect"* (Matthew 5:48). A highest value in Christian faith is revealing the nature and character of the Lord Jesus in our personal lives and in our intimate personal fellowship and walk with God. It is called the "mystical union" of Christ and the believer. We are to be a fragrant perfume of the Lord Jesus. Islam has no concept of this because Allah cannot be known. There is no concept of fellowship with the divine as a life-changing experience.

We have already contrasted the means of salvation, including the fact that Muslims do not think they need to be saved by Allah, because they have been taught how to save themselves. Islam has no concept of a Savior and may even denigrate the idea as weakness. But Jesus said, *"For God so love the world that He gave His one and only Son, that whoever trusts in Him* (as Savior) *shall not perish but shall have eternal life"* (John 3:16).

What is the Islamists' highest goal? It is without doubt to be martyred in a physical battle for Allah in extending his sovereignty or the rule of his law on the Earth.

What is the Christian's highest goal? God tells us what His purpose is for us, and that ought to be our highest goal. *"For those God foreknew he also predestined to be conformed to the likeness of his Son"* (Romans 8:29). Now Jesus is *"in the express image of the Father"* (Hebrews 1:3). This means that to be conformed to the likeness of Christ is to be conformed to the likeness of God, and this is God's purpose for us. It ought to be our highest goal in this life and in the life to come.

God created us in His own likeness and image. We are told this in the story of the creation of man, of which the Qur'an makes no mention. This means that God wanted man eventually to be like Himself. He has never given up this purpose for us who know Him. We were created to be like God and to show His righteous character. *"God made him who had no sin* (Jesus) *to be sin for us, so that in him we might become the righteousness of God"* (2 Corinthians 5:21).

Islam has nothing to offer nor anything to compare with this. In fact, Islam would probably consider the idea of becoming like Allah sinful, maybe even the awful sin of *shirk*, because having an intimate relationship with Allah might demean or tarnish his character.

It is our prayer that Muslims everywhere will become acquainted with this great salvation available to them in the Lord Jesus Christ, which will make it possible for them by the power of the Spirit of God to be born again and live the pure life that they crave and to fulfill the purpose for which God made them.

APPENDIX ONE

A Glossary: Basic Terms and Definitions

Aisha—Muhammad's youngest wife. He married her when she was 9 years old and he was 52. She was his favorite wife and is a source of much information concerning her husband, which is a part of the oral tradition of Islam. She was 19 years old when Muhammad died at 62 years of age in 632.

Al Aqsa— "The farthest mosque" built on the edge of the Temple Mount in Jerusalem in 705 A.D. It is one of the three most sacred places and buildings in Islam.

Ali—Muhammad's cousin and son-in-law. The 4th Caliph but the first Caliph (imam) recognized by the Shiites. Ali was married to Fatima and their son Hussein died a martyr fighting the Sunnites. Sacred cities in the Shiite area in Iraq, such as Najaf and Karbala, are destinations for pilgrimages celebrating Ali and Hussein.

Allah—"The chief deity" recognized as the Moon god of the Arabs and many other peoples in the ancient Middle East. There are many commands in the Bible against moon god worship. In Islam he is a deistic type deity. He is unknowable, non-personal, unitarian, changeable, capricious, remote, only known indirectly through intermediaries, and offers salvation by works. He hates the sinner, the unbeliever and the corrupt person. His will is supreme and he is master not father. As creator he can do as he pleases and he predestines men to heaven or hell as he chooses. Even Muhammad said he had no assurance of going to Paradise.

Allahu Akbar— "Allah is the greatest," a common cry of Muslims. Sometimes translated simply "Allah is great," but the former translation is more accurate and tells us that originally Allah was the greatest of the gods of the Arab pantheon of many gods.

Al Lat, Al Manat, and Al Uzza—Three daughters of the Moon and the Sun gods who were themselves worshiped as goddesses by the Arabs before Muhammad. Considered daughters of Allah in his original role as the Mood god.

Al Mahdi—The seventh prophet whom Muhammad said would come at the end of the age. He will be a man guided and sent by Allah to restore the rule of justice before the end of the world. The seven prophets are Adam, Noah, Abraham, Moses, Jesus, Muhammad and al-Mahdi. Literally means "the rightly guided one."

Assassins—The name given to a special sect of Ismaili Shiites who were hired to assassinate a Seljuk Turkish leader

Ayat—A verse in the Qur'an, literally means "sign"

Ayatollah—A Shiite spiritual leader; title means "sign" or "shadow" of Allah. They are considered more holy, inspired or filled with the divine than ordinary imams.

Bismillah—"In the name of Allah" is the first phrase in the Qur'an and is usually used to introduce formal statements of all kinds either oral or written.

Burqa—A full veil and robe covering all but a woman's eyes. Used in Afghanistan by the Taliban. Also used in Pakistan. An extreme version covers the entire body and head leaving only a cloth screen through which to see.

Caliph (Khalif)—The political leader of the Muslim *ummah* who took Muhammad's place and "represents" him. There is no Caliph today, but it is the dream of Islamic fundamentalists to set up a Caliphate (Khalifa) with a new Caliph to rule over all Islamic states as one nation.

Chador—A veil or covering for women in Iran exposing only face, hands and feet. Usually black.

Dajjal—The Antichrist

Dar al Harb—Territory or House of Warfare—an area not yet submissive to Islam with which Muslims are always at potential war. Can be any non-Muslim nation. Literally means "House of Resistors."

Dar al Islam—The territory or House where the population is Islamic or in submission to Allah.

Dar al Kufr—A non-Muslim nation living in a temporary state of truce with the Ummah or Islamic community. Osama bin Laden offered Europe a truce or this kind of status if they would not participate with America in the war against Iraq. Truce is always only a temporary state of affairs in Islamic law. Truces are made to be abrogated or broken.

Dhimma and Dhimmi—A treaty—dhimma—given by Muhammad and Islamic authorities to Jews and Christians who submit to Islamic rule and pay an annual tax for their protection. They are called dhimmis and dhimmitude is their status—a second-class citizenship.

Emir (Amir or Wazir or Vizier)—A political leader whose authority is delegated by the Caliph for a certain time and/or a certain place.

Fatima—Daughter of Muhammad who was married to 'Ali the 4th Caliph of the Sunnis but the 1st Caliph recognized by the Shiites.

Fatwah—A legal or religious proclamation or sentence issued by a legal or religious authority.

Fez—Red Turkish hat worn by men over 100 years ago.

Fiqh—The study and application of Islamic law or Islamic jurisprudence.

Five Pillars of Faith—The disciplines ordained by Allah, which must be observed by every Muslim. These good works are the Muslim's means of salvation. They are:

(l) The Declaration of Faith (**Shahada**) "There is no god but Allah and Muhammad is his prophet." (Must be said before witnesses for conversion to Islam.)

(2) Prayer (**salat**) five times a day, prostrate on the ground facing Mecca.

(3) Almsgiving (**zakat**): A virtual tax of at least 2 1/2% of ones income given to the poor, to the mosque, or to charitable organizations. (Amounts to about 750 million dollar slush fund for Muslim groups in America.)

(4) Fasting during the month of Ramadan (**sawm**): Fast is only during the day when religious observances and prayers should be included. Eating and drinking permitted after sundown. Ramadan was the ninth month and sacred to Muhammad because it is when he first received his revelations in a mountain cave north of Mecca.

(5) Pilgrimage to Mecca (**hajj**): Once in a Muslim's lifetime he is required, unless physically impossible, to visit the Ka'aba at Mecca and perform all the proper rituals. Considered the highlight in a Muslim's life.

Hadith—The sayings of Muhammad apart from the Qur'an which included his opinions, his teachings, his warnings, his prophecies, his understanding of the Qur'an, and the application of all of this in his own life. His wife Aisha said, "Muhammad's life is the Qur'an."

Halal—That which is lawful or permitted. Like **kosher** in Hebrew.

Haram—That which is unlawful and forbidden

Hejaz—The region of Eastern Arabia where Mecca and Medina are located.

Hijra (Hejira)—Muhammad's flight for his life from Mecca to Medina in 622, which marks the beginning of the Islamic calendar and is considered the time of the formation of the religion. Muhammad became not only a prophet but also the political leader of Medina. He died in 632 and is buried there.

Hjab—A Muslim woman's head and hair covering. May extend as a robe as well. (See burqa and chador.)

Houris or Huris—The perpetual virgins of Paradise, which will delight Muslim men for eternity. Each man who has been faithful to Allah, especially as a martyr in battle, is awarded over 70 of these virgins for his pleasure when he enters Paradise.

Imam—The prayer leader in a mosque. He gives the sermon at the Friday prayer service. It is the closest that Islam comes to a clerical office although the imam is neither a pastor, priest, nor bishop. Among the Shiites the Imams had both political and religious authority.

Injil—The Gospel of Jesus or just Gospel. Muhammad probably was familiar with only an Aramaic version of part of the Gospel of Matthew. The Qur'an does not have a New

Testament definition of Gospel. Allah apparently didn't know the meaning of the word.

Irtidad—Apostasy punishable by death. Muhammad commanded death for rejecting himself as Allah's prophet and the religion of Islam.

Islam—Means "submission" and a Muslim is one who submits to Allah. Root meaning of Islam is also "peace," but peace is only possible within the Islamic ummah. All outside the Islamic community are called "the house of war."

Islamic fundamentalist—Any Muslim who takes the Qur'an and Hadith literally and wants to practice everything that Muhammad taught as it was in 7th century Arabia and the first century of Islam.

Ismaili—A Shiite sect in Islam led today by the Agha Khan. Nazili Ismailis were hired to assassinate Sunnite Seljuk Turk leaders in the 12th and 13th centuries.

Jahiliyah—The age or era of ignorance or barbarism in Arabia before the revelation of Islam. Applied today by Islamic Fundamentalists to societies that no longer follow a strict submission to Allah and the shari'ah. Pagan.

Jibril—The angel Gabriel who is supposed to have been Allah's messenger to Muhammad.

Ji'had—Means "struggle" and describes the Muslim's fight with the world, the flesh and the devil. The most important aspect for mankind is the concept of holy jihad or holy war, which was commanded by Allah and Muhammad to enforce the teachings and the rule of Islam in the whole world. Liberal Muslims interpret this spiritually. The Qur'an and Hadith teach it literally. Muhammad said that holy jihad or fighting for Allah was more important than prayer.

Jinn—A race of spirits or demons—good and bad—who seem to live in a parallel universe to human beings. Not angels and more evil than good.

Jizya—A poll tax or annual tribute paid to the Islamic administrators as protection for those who are not Muslims, e.g., Jews and Christians in any given nation.

Ka'aba—The sacred, black cubed building which houses the black meteorite, which was considered sacred by Arabs from time immemorial. It originally housed 360 idols but was sanctified by Muhammad and became the domain of Allah, the one and only true god.

Kafir—An unbeliever or an infidel. One who does not accept Islam or the prophet.

Keffiya—Male head covering in Palestine, Jordan, and Saudi Arabia. The headdress of Arafat irreverently called a "table cloth" often in a checkered design.

Khalifa—The Caliphate or the collection of Muslim lands under one leadership, the Caliph, which means "representative" of Muhammad. Administers Islamic law.

Kutbah—Sermon in the mosque on Friday presented by the imam at the time of the noon prayer.

Kitab—Literally "book" referring to the Scriptures of the Jews and Christians, and the Qur'an.

Madrassah—A school, usually for the teaching youth the Qur'an and the Islamic way of life

Masjid—The Muslim place of communal prayer led by the Imam. In Spain these were called *Mesquita*, which translates, into the English **Mosque**. Literally, "place of bowing down."

Mecca and Medina—The two most sacred cities of Islam located in the Hijaz or eastern Arabia about 200 miles apart. Muhammad was born in Mecca and ruled in Medina.

Minaret—The tower of the Mosque from which the muezzin calls Muslims to prayer five times each day. In modern communities these are sometimes recorded messages broadcast on loud speakers.

Muezzin—The one who calls the faithful to communal prayer in the Mosque from the tower of the Minaret.

Mufti—A private scholar who is a legal specialist or jurisconsult who is called upon to give a ruling (fatwa) on a disputed question of law. He may be appointed by a ruler to perform this duty for a specific area, such as the Mufti of Jerusalem, where he may act like an Emir. An interpreter of the law or expert in jurisprudence.

Mujaheddin—the Holy Warriors who were trained in the Afghan-Soviet war where they were called the Arab-Afghans. Some of them now are a part of many militant terrorist groups especially al-Qaeda.

Mullah—An Islamic teacher, such as Mullah Omar who trained the Taliban

Muta—A temporary marriage by agreement for a few days to a year, often in exchange for money. In use today only among Shiite Muslims. To avoid fornication

Nasiqh—A teaching in the Qur'an, which abrogates, cancels out, or corrects a previous teaching. Indicates a kind of progressive revelation.

Qadi—A Muslim judge who administers Islamic law.

Qibla—The direction in which prayers are made. Used to be Jerusalem but Muhammad changed it to Mecca when the Jews rejected him.

Qur'an (Koran)—The "bible" of Islam, which means "recitations." These were the recorded utterances of the prophet Muhammad when supposedly under the influence of Allah, and are considered the very words of Allah himself.

Quraysh (Kureish)—The tribe of Mecca into which Muhammad was born. Khadijah was his wife. Aisha, daughter of Abu Bakr, was his child bride and favorite wife after Khadijah died in 619. All the early Caliphs came from this Meccan tribe.

Ramadan—The sacred lunar month for fasting and devotional exercises (one of the five pillars). This was the 9th month of the Arab year when Muhammad received his first revelations in the cave on Mt. Hira. Occurs usually in the fall of the year.

Rashidun—The first four Caliphs who include Abu Bakr, 'Omar, 'Othman, and 'Ali. The word means "rightly guided," which indicates a difference from the Ummayad and Abbasid Caliphs to follow who were familial or hereditary dynasties. Shi'ites in general reject the first three Caliphs and the Caliphate and accept only 'Ali whom they call the first Imam.

Razzia—Raiding the caravans of an enemy and stealing the merchandise. The word used to describe what Muhammad and his followers did in accosting the commercial trading caravans of the Meccan tribes in retaliation for their rejection of Muhammad. They used the booty to support themselves in their early years in Medina.

Salam and **As-salam alaykum**—Peace and the greeting "Peace be unto you."

Shahid—A martyr in the cause of Allah. Word used to describe suicide bombers in Israel and Iraq. They believe they go immediately to Paradise.

Shari'a—Islamic law drawn from the Qur'an and the Hadith as understood and taught by the religious leaders and judges and accepted by the community. It does not include constitutional, administrative or even criminal law but rather covers personal behavior, such as marriage, divorce, bequests, inheritance and economic practice. It can extend even to manners or the customs of the community. It lays down the rules for human behavior, which will be the most pleasing to Allah. Literally means "pathway to water."

Sheikh or **Shaykh**—"Honorable old man." A tribal head man among the Bedouins. A title of respect for an important spiritual leader, theologian, or mystic.

Shiites—A minority sect of Islam which rejects the first three Caliphs and believes that the proper rule must come directly from Muhammad through his cousin 'Ali. They were ruled by Imams who were considered religious as well as political leaders. Iran and the 60% of Iraq nearest to Iran is the major Shiite area today. The religious leaders today are called Ayatollahs, which means, "shadow of Allah" as it is believed that they speak with the authority of Allah on earth.

Shirk—The very serious sin of ascribing partners to God like a son, a consort or another god.

Shura—A consulting body, such as the Shura Council called by Osama to declare war on America.

Sufi—A Muslim sect considered the most spiritual among Muslims, which sought a mystical experience with Allah. They wore wool or "suf"; hence the name Sufi.

Sultan—The holder of military power who exercised the governmental authority under the Caliph. When the Caliphate came to an end with the Mongol invasion of 1258, the Islamic world was divided into states many of whom were ruled by leaders called Sultans who held the political power and *'Ulamas* who had the authority in matters of religion.

Sura—One of 114 chapters in the Qur'an.

Suq or **Souq**—A stall or store in an Arab market place or bazaar where goods are sold.

Taliban—Students of the Qur'an who became holy warriors and sought to impose strict Islamic law on Afghan society under the leadership of Mullah Omar who led one of their schools in Kandahar. Many were trained in the madrassas of Pakistan. Literally means "student."

Taurat—The Torah or writings of Moses

Tawhid—The indivisible oneness of Allah. Devout Muslims try to order their lives and institutions in oneness with the sovereignty of Allah.

'Ulama—These men are scholars learned in the Qur'an, the Hadith and Shari'a who were interpreters of these sources of Islam and considered the moral conscience of the community. They were considered the spiritual successors to the prophet

Muhammad, as the Caliph was his political successor. Usually include the imams, muftis, and qadis.

Ummah— The Islamic community locally and worldwide.

Wahhabi—The strict conservative Islamic sect in Saudi Arabia, which is the primary influence on radical, extremist, or militant Islamists today.

Wudu—The washing ritual, which precedes the handling of the Qur'an

Yathrib—The original name of Medina where Muhammad fled in 622.

Zamzam—Hagar's well or spring in Mecca where she was supposed to have fled with Ishmael and saved his life. A site visited during the Hajj or pilgrimage to Mecca.

APPENDIX TWO

LETTERS TO AN IMAM

In the summer of 2003 I was asked by a minister friend of mine who had a national radio broadcast to answer some letters he had received from a Muslim imam. This Islamic teacher had responded to things my friend had said about Islam on his program. Some of what he had heard had made him very upset accusing my friend of hatred of Islam, saying that Jesus was defeated by the prophet Muhammad, and challenging him to a public debate.

I decided to accept the offer of corresponding with this person. Since Islam is a very legalistic religion with little emphasis on the love of God and no concept of the grace of God, I decided to share with this Muslim teacher the message of John's first epistle, which has often been characterized as God's love letter to His children.

Our correspondence continued for several months and my eight letters to him totaled well over 100 pages. I have included only the first two of these. I will address him as Hamid, although that is not his real name.

I found Hamid to be steeped in knowledge of the liberal historical criticism of the Bible, which unbelievers have used to attack Jesus, the Apostle Paul, and even the God of the Bible whom Hamid called "a demon," and the authority, authenticity, and accuracy of the Scriptures. You can get some idea of his objections and his arguments and how he responded to my words from my second letter.

Hamid's allegiance to Muhammad, whom he called the Perfect Model, amounted to a reverent adulation bordering on worship. His hatred and bitterness toward everything Christian was beyond my understanding.

I learned that there were no arguments, evidences, or apologetics that moved his heart or affected his thinking. He seemed incapable of a rational response. It became obvious to me that only the power of the Holy Spirit of God would be able to penetrate the prison and sever the chains that held him in bondage.

Even though I answered at length most of his arguments and misconceptions of the message of the Bible and Christian faith, he kept coming back with the same words and the same diatribes and the same confused misunderstandings and misinterpretations. Frankly, it was discouraging and frustrating.

Then I remembered the first missionary to the Muslims in the later Middle Ages Dr. Raymond Lull (1232-1315) from the island of Majorca. It was his deep conviction that he would be able through rational argument to convince Muslims of the superiority of Christian philosophy and doctrine. There is no record, however, that he ever made a single convert. On his last visit to Tunisia in 1315, furthermore, when he was over 80 years of age, he stood up in the center of the town square and began preaching. The people attacked him, took him outside the city walls, and stoned him to death for opposing Muhammad, Allah, and the Qur'an.

Missionaries to Muslim peoples have found that the only approach that may break the barriers and be accepted is a loving concern and the message Jesus gave that a man can be "born again." Sincere Muslims who want to live a good life but know they can never be good enough may eagerly accept the idea of receiving a new heart and a new life that will give them the inner power to live righteous lives.

This message has opened many a sincere Muslim's heart. Since it comes directly from the teaching of the prophet Jesus whom they respect, they may be open to receive this truth.

Argument will never open their hearts or minds.

In these eight letters, only two of which are recorded here, I attempted to teach Hamid everything I knew about my Christian faith from the beginning of the Bible to the end. I can only hope that the Holy Spirit may use it to bear some fruit.

LETTER #1

July 24, 2003

Dear Hamid,

I have been introduced to some of your writings concerning your religion of Islam. I am impressed that you are a strong advocate of your faith and that is good. But I have a problem. The Christianity that you picture in your writings is not one that I recognize. I wonder if you have misunderstood the Bible, which the Qur'an calls the "earlier revelation," and which was said to have been handed down by Allah. Those who are the "people of the earlier revelation" are to be respected by Muslims.

Sura 5:82 says that the closest ones to the believing Muslim are the people who say, "We are the followers of Christ." According to Sura 57:27 God put into the hearts of the followers of Jesus "compassion and kindness." The book in the Bible that best shows this is a letter written by the beloved disciple John to the Christians of his day. It is called I John and comes near the very end of the books of the Bible.

John is pictured as a favorite disciple of Jesus. He was the youngest of Jesus' twelve disciples being perhaps only 18 years of age when Jesus called him. We have very early copies of this letter and there is no doubt on the part of the scholars that this is John's writing, and it has not been corrupted. It is exactly as he wrote it. We are told in the Gospels that Jesus trusted John so much that he gave his mother Mary into his care when he left this earth.

John begins his letter by saying that he was one of those who heard, saw, looked at and even touched Jesus whom he calls "the word of God" because He brought God's word to the world. As the Qur'an states, God gave the Gospel to Jesus and he came to the earth to confirm God's word or communication to us. John says that he was an eyewitness to all of this. He is simply explaining things as he saw and understood them from the teachings of Jesus. He is not making these things up. Jesus would not have entrusted his mother to a dishonorable man.

John writes, *"We proclaim to you what we have seen and heard, so that you also may have fellowship with us. And our fellowship is with the Father and with his Son, Jesus the Messiah. We write this to make our joy complete.*" (1:3,4) John has no hesitation in identifying Jesus as "the Son of God."

Then John begins to review the message that Jesus taught. He writes, "*This is the message we have heard from him and declare to you. God is light; in Him there is no darkness at all. If we claim to have fellowship with Him yet walk in the darkness, we lie and do not live by the truth. But if we walk in the light, as He is in the light, we have fellowship with one another, and the blood of Jesus, His Son, purifies us from all sin*" (1:5-7). All the prophecies of the Old Testament promise that God will send a Savior. Why? Because man cannot "save" himself.

John continues, "*The man who says, 'I know Him,' but does not do what he commands is a liar, and the truth is not in Him. But if anyone obeys His word, God's love is truly made complete in him. This is how we know we are in Him: Whoever claims to live in Him must walk as Jesus did*" (2:4-6). (This means to walk in love and compassion just as Sura 57:27 says that true Christians do.)

John then warns his readers not to love the world or anything that is in the world, meaning "*the cravings of sinful man, the lust of his eyes, and the boasting of what he has and does.*" These things are not of God. "*The world and its desires pass away, but the man who does the will of God lives forever*" (2:15-17).

Then John begins to teach as a prophet. He says that we know that we are in the "last hour" (not just "the last day" but the end of the last day—the "last hour" of the "last day") because many antichrists have come. The meaning of this is antimessiah. (The word Christ is the Greek form of the Hebrew word Messiah. The word means, "Anointed one" or one whom God has anointed for a special ministry. The term "antichrist" means in the Greek language of the New Testament, one who is either against God's "anointed one" or one who tries to take his place—that is, either "against Christ" or "instead of Christ.") John is saying therefore that near the end of the last days there will be many who will be against Christ (2:18). We also know that there is one who will "take the place" of Christ.

Jesus Himself said that in the end times his followers would be hated by all nations because of Him; and there has been greater persecution and martyrdoms of Jesus' disciples in the last 100 years than in all of the previous 1900 years. (See Matthew 24:9.)

Then John enlarges on what he has taught, *"But you* (Jesus' disciples) *have an anointing from the Holy One, and all of you know the truth. I do not write to you because you do not know the truth, but because you do know it and because no lie comes from the truth. Who is the liar? It is the man who denies that Jesus is the Christ. Such a man is the antichrist—he denies the Father and the Son. No one who denies the Son has the Father; whoever acknowledges the Son has the Father also"* (2:20-23). Who therefore are the "antichrists" today, i.e., in this "last hour"?

John's letter is known as the letter of love. He tells us that the very nature of God is love. As the Apostle Paul wrote to the Romans, *"But God showed His love to us, in that while we were still sinners* (that is, before we even turned to God in repentance) *Christ died for us"* (Romans 5:12). The God of the Bible loves the sinner...in contrast to Allah who hates the sinner.

So next we have one of the most beautiful passages in the Bible, *"How great is the love the Father has lavished on us, that we should be called children of God. And that is what we are! The reason the world does not know us is that it did not know him. Dear friends, now we are children of God, and what we will be has not yet been made known, but we know that when he appears, we shall be like him, for we shall see him as he is. Everyone who has this hope in him purifies himself, just as he is pure"* (3:1-3). Jesus promised to return to rescue all his disciples from off the earth. They would ascend into the heavens to meet him just as He had ascended.

John continues to teach. *"Dear children, do not let anyone lead you astray. He who does what is right is righteous, just as He is righteous. He who does what is sinful is of the devil, because the devil has been sinning from the beginning. The reason the Son of God appeared was to destroy the devil's work. . This is how we know who the children of God are and who the children of the devil are: Anyone who does not do what is right is not a child of God; nor is anyone who does not love his brother"* (3:7-10). John is trying to tell us that those who commit evil deeds are "children of the devil."

John tells us to love one another. *"Anyone who does not love remains in death. . Anyone who hates his brother is a murderer, and you know that no murderer has eternal life in him"* (3:14-15). There are many murderers in the world today and many who have taken thousands of innocent lives even in the sacrifice of their own. Some have thought to wake up in Paradise, but obviously they have awakened in Hell. John tells us in this earlier revelation of God inspired by God's Spirit that these murderers who have been filled with hatred are "children of the devil."

Jesus said, *"If you love me, keep my commandments."* (Enclosed are the 49 commands given by Jesus to his disciples who in turn were to teach them to others) Jesus said that his two most important commands were (1) to believe on Him and (2) to love.

John explains what he learned from Jesus. *"And this is his command: to believe in the name of His Son, Jesus the Messiah, and to love one another as He commanded us. Those who obey his commands live in him and he in them. And this is how we know that he lives in us: We know it by the Spirit he gave us."* But John warns us to be careful to recognize the Spirit that comes from God, because Satan sends his angels and his spirits also. (In fact the Bible or what Muhammad called "the earlier revelation of God" teaches us that Satan masquerades as an "angel of light." The Apostle Paul writes in his second letter to the Corinthians (11:14-15), *"For Satan himself masquerades as an angel of light. It is not surprising then that his servants masquerade as servants of righteousness. Their end will be what their actions deserve."* Namely, hellfire!) So what does John say we should do? How can we know the truth?

He writes, *"Dear friends, do not believe every spirit, but test the spirits to see whether they are from God, because many false prophets have gone out into the world. This is how you can recognize the Spirit of God: Every spirit that acknowledges that Jesus the Messiah* (as God's Son) *has come in the flesh is from God, but every spirit that does not acknowledge Jesus* (as the Son of God) *is not from God. This is the spirit of the antichrist, which you have heard is coming and even now is already in the world...We are from God, and whoever knows God listens to us, but whoever is not from God does not listen to us. This is how we recognize the Spirit of truth and the spirit of false-hood"* (3:4-6).

Finally, a classic passage on love: *"Dear friends, let us love one another, for love comes from God. Everyone who loves has been born of God and knows God. Whoever does not love does not know God, because God is love. This is how God showed His love among us: He sent His one and only Son into the world that we might live through him. This is love: not that we loved God, but that He loved us and sent His Son as an atoning sacrifice for our sins. Dear friends, since God so loved us, we also ought to love one another. No one has ever seen God; but if we love one another, God lives in us and his love is made complete in us"* (4:7-12).

John concludes, *"We have seen and testify that the Father has sent his Son to be the Savior of the world. If anyone acknowledges that Jesus is the Son of God, God lives in him and he in God. And so we know and rely on the love God has for us. . . We love God because He first loved us. . . Who is it that overcomes the world? Only he who believes that Jesus is the Son of God. . Anyone who believes in the Son of God has this testimony in his heart. Anyone who does not believe God has made him out to be a liar, because he has not believed the tes-timony God has given about his Son. And this is the testimony: God has given us eternal life, and this life is in His Son. He who has the Son has life; he who does not have the Son of God does not have life. We know that we are children of God, and that the whole world is under the control of the evil one* [Satan]. *We know also that the Son of God has come and has given us understanding, so that we may know Him who is true. And we are in Him who is true—even His Son Jesus*

Christ. He is the true God and eternal life."

And so, Hamid, the "earlier revelation" is very clear. God loves us and would not deceive us. We have responded to His love, and Jesus is our Lord and Savior. Satan, however, is a liar from the beginning. Jesus called him "the father of lies." Is it not possible that he is the "angel" who deceived Muhammad?

Allah has the character that Satan, the son of the morning, would have if he were God. Even Muhammad in the hadith says that he thought he was being deceived by demons, but his wife Aisha dissuaded him of this idea saying that such a good man as he would not be deceived. Unfortunately Satan won, and God the Father permitted the deception of Islam as a testing for the entire world. Satan wanted a religion, which he could use to replace and substitute for the faith revealed by Jesus. So he lied and lied and lied especially about Jesus. But God permitted Satan to engineer the death of Jesus on the cross, so that Satan could be unmasked before all the angels in the universe as a hater, a liar, a murderer, and a deceiver. And then God raised Jesus from the grave as a testimony that He was truly His Son and that his death was an atoning sacrifice for the sins of the world. All who receive Jesus as Savior and Lord are given eternal life. Those who publicly reject him are judged with eternal death. You can take your pick, Hamid. The choice is yours! Pray to the God of Heaven and ask Him on the basis of His love to reveal His truth to you.

Very sincerely in Christian love,

Rev. James M. Murk, Ph.D..

LETTER #2

July 28, 2003

Dear Hamid,

I was amazed at your prompt response. Thank you for your letter and the booklet on Muhammad. Did I send you the chapter I wrote on Muhammad?

Let me answer your questions one by one: You are mistaken about Jesus being a prophet sent only to the "house of Israel." That was His first responsibility when He came, but when most of the Jews rejected Him, his message was to be sent to the entire world. Note the Great Commission in Matthew 28:18: *"Then Jesus came to them and said, 'All authority in heaven and on earth has been given to me. Therefore go, and make disciples* (learners) *of all nations, baptizing them in the name of the Father and of the Son and of the Holy Spirit* (the Trinity) *and teaching them to obey everything I have commanded you. And surely I will be with you always to the very end of the age.'"*

Jesus also said, *"I am the good shepherd. I know my sheep and my sheep know me—Just as the Father knows me and I know the Father—and I lay down my life for the sheep.*

I have other sheep that are not of this sheep pen (other than Israel or the Jews). *They too will listen to my voice, and there shall be one flock and one shepherd"* (John 10:15-16).

Jesus revealed this same teaching to the Pharisees. After telling them of the parable of the tenants who rejected the servants of the landowner (referring to the prophets that had been sent to Israel) and then killed the landowner's son (referring to Himself as the Son of the landowner), Jesus said, *"the stone that the builders rejected has become the keystone or capstone."* This prophecy from Psalm 118:22 Jesus obviously applied to Himself. (Some Islamic teachers have said that this prophecy refers to Muhammad, but obviously the teaching of Jesus contradicts this.)

Then Jesus continued saying to the Pharisees, *"Therefore I tell you that the kingdom of God will be taken away from you and given to a people who will produce its fruit"* (Matthew 21:33-43). In the context of the teaching of the Scriptures, this can only refer to the Gentiles who would receive the Gospel by default because of its rejection by the majority of the Jews. To apply it to Islam is more than 600 years too late. The Gospel had already been preached to the Gentiles for those 600 years and the entire Roman Empire had been transformed. In Acts of the Apostles it says that they *"turned the world upside down* (Acts 17:6)."

The reason that we know that he was speaking here of the Gentiles in the rest of the nations is because of the revelation that came to Peter in Acts 10 when he was told to accept and minister to the household of Cornelius, the centurion, whose whole family were born again (saved) and blessed by the Holy Spirit.

Then the Apostle Paul was sent specifically to represent Jesus the Messiah (meaning Anointed One) or the Christ (the Greek word for Messiah) to the Gentile world. He claimed that his revelation and commission as a missionary to the Gentiles came directly from Jesus on the road to Damascus (Acts chapter 9).

Also the prophets specifically mention that the "servant of the Lord," who represents the Messiah in the Old Testament, was to reach out to the Gentile world. Isaiah (42:5-7) prophesied of this quoting God's words, *"This is what God, the Lord, says—He who created the heavens and stretched them out, who spread out the earth and all that comes out of it, who gives breath to its people, and life to those who walk on it. 'I, the Lord, have called you* (my servant the Messiah) *in righteousness; I will take hold of your hand, I will keep you and make you to be a covenant for the people* (that is, the Jews), *and a light for the Gentiles* (the rest of the world), *to open eyes that are blind, to free captives from prison* (This is what "to redeem" or "to save" means.) *and to release from the dungeon those who sit in darkness."* (Jesus did this when he descended into Hades and "took captivity captive."—Ephesians 4:8)

After his death, burial, and resurrection, Jesus took to Heaven with Him all those—from out of what is called Abraham's bosom (Luke 16) or the "paradise" side of Sheol or Hades—who were willing to receive him as Savior and Lord. The Bible teaches, "He descended into Hell" and "preached to the spirits in prison." Then he "led captivity captive" with him to the presence of His Father (Ephesians 4:7-10).

Many passages in the Old Testament teach that God was going to spread His Gospel to the Gentiles, which Christianity has accomplished throughout the whole world. Another message in Isaiah's prophecy is very clear: Speaking of the Lord's servant the Messiah, God says, *"I also make you a light for the Gentiles, that you may bring my salvation to the ends of the earth"* (Isaiah 49:6).

This is why Jesus lived in Galilee and not Jerusalem. Matthew says in his Gospel: *"He went and lived in Capernaum which was by the lake* (Sea of Galilee) *in the area of Zebulon and Naphtali* (the traditional territory of two tribes of Israel)—*to fulfill what was said through the prophet Isaiah: 'Land of Zebulon and land of Naphtali, the way to the sea, along the Jordan, Galilee of the Gentiles—the people living in darkness have seen a great light; on those living in the land of the shadow of death a light has dawned'"* (Matthew 4:13-16).

Jesus identified Himself as *"the light of the world"* (John 8:12 and 12:46). He was called to minister, first of all, to the "the lost sheep of Israel" but he worked primarily in the geographical area that included many Gentiles in order to lay the foundation of what was to come—the sharing of the Gospel with the whole world.

Finally this fact was even prophesied at His birth in the Temple by the "righteous and devout man" named Simeon. God had told him that he would see the Savior of Israel. When Mary and Joseph brought the infant Jesus to the Temple, Simeon took the baby in his arms, praised God, and said, *"Sovereign Lord, as you have promised you now dismiss your servant in peace. For my eyes have seen your salvation, which you have prepared in the sight of all people, a light for revelation to the Gentiles and for glory to your people Israel"* (Luke 2:25-32).

So you see, Hamid, you are very mistaken when you suggest that Jesus was sent only to the Jews. When a majority of the House of Israel rejected Him, his message was designated to go the rest of the world. There is a lot more to explain here about Israel's hardness of heart and how God will finally save only a remnant when they see Him coming again in the clouds. They will "look on him whom they pierced" and many will be saved at his second coming. Two thirds of the Jews in Israel today will be destroyed by Muslim armies (Ezekiel 38-39), but Yahweh will defeat Allah in this great battle and the one third of the Jews who are left will turn to their Messiah. (The prophet Zechariah 12:10-14 and Revelation 7:1-8 explain it.) It is going to happen as soon as the next confederacy of Muslim nations attacks Israel to take Jerusalem and obliterate the Jews.

Muhammad told his followers that in the end times the Muslims would totally annihilate the Jews, which is what the militant Islamists today are hoping for. (Note my enclosure on Islam's hatred of the Jews.) But this will not be fulfilled because Muhammad was deceived in his prophecies. According to "the earlier revelation," Yahweh still has a purpose for his people Israel, but that is another story.

I

You asked to know what Jesus preached and taught. Enclosed is a list of 49 of His commandments distilled from his teachings. You will note that he commanded forgiveness not just 7 times but 70 time 7 times (#32 in the list). To us this means an unlimited number of times. He taught us to love our enemies and to do good to them who persecute us and promised us great reward in Heaven for doing so (Matthew 5:43-48). He set the example in this by saying on the cross even concerning those who were killing him, "*Father, forgive them, they know not what they do*" (Luke 23:34).

If you check the Hadith, either Al Bokhari or Al Muslim, you will find that Muhammad suggested that his followers assassinate those who had insulted him. He also said *"No umma* (a Muslim) *should be killed for killing a Kafir* (an infidel). *Whoever changes his Islamic religion, kill him"* (Hadith 9:50, 57). Look these teachings up for yourself. They are in great contrast to the spirit and attitude of Jesus. In fact, these are the commands and the example that the wicked, evil, radical and militant Islamists are following today in their Holy Jihad against Jews, Christians, and the West. Do you support these kinds of teachings?

Eight of the ten nations today who are killing and persecuting Christians the most are Islamic including Indonesia, Pakistan, Saudi Arabia, Egypt, and the Sudan. 2,000,000 pagans and Christians have been murdered or enslaved in the southern Sudan alone in order that the mullahs might make that an Islamic state where everyone obeys the "shar'i-ah." In northern Nigeria thousands of Christians have been killed by Muslims and hundreds of churches burned with no provocation. Even though they are in the minority, Muslims want to force Nigeria to become a Muslim state. This goes on in many Muslim lands today. Islamists are not just trying to kill all the Jews; they are also out to kill all the Christians they can. What kind of religion is that? Is this not the face of evil?

Christians have been accused of killing unbelievers, even Muslims, such as during the Crusades. The difference is this. The New Testament teaches Christians not to kill, not to behave this way; so those who do so are disobeying the teachings and commandments. However, Muslims believe that they are obeying both the commands of the Qur'an and the teachings and example of Muhammad. (Note my enclosed list of commands from the Qur'an and the Hadith.) (To the reader: These can be found in Chapter 5: Holy Jihad.)

This example of Muhammad includes his treacherous breaking of the truce of Hudaybiyyah. It was cited by Arafat as the reason the Palestinians would never keep the Oslo Accords which one mullah called "a Trojan horse," which means a sham or a fraud. Jesus would never have done a thing like that; nor would he have taken up arms against his brothers.

The contrast between Jesus and Muhammad is dramatic. Muhammad's breaking of the truce is overlooked by Muslims, and Muhammad is praised for being so gracious to the Quraysh when he conquered Mecca (as long as they became Muslims); but when they rejected Islam after Muhammad's death, Abu Bakr raised an army and in what is known as the War against the Apostates and murdered thousands of Arabs who had returned to paganism.

The Bible says of Jesus, *"To this you were called, because Christ suffered for you, leaving you an example that you should follow in His steps. He committed no sin, and no deceit was found in his mouth* (A prophecy from Isaiah 53:9). *When they hurled their insults at Him, He did not retaliate. When He suffered, He made no threats. Instead He entrusted Himself to Him who judges justly. He Himself bore our sins in His body on the tree* (the cross), *so that we might die to sins, and live for righteousness, by His wounds you have been healed"* (I Peter 2:21-24). I will let you be the judge, Hamid, as to who was the more righteous person with the more godly example and teaching—Jesus or Muhammad.

II

You ask about prophecies concerning Jesus. The prophecies about Jesus in the Old Testament abound. There are over 200 or maybe more. Let me share just a few: (I frankly do not care about prophecies in pagan writings to which you refer because they are written by Satan.)

Prophecy concerning His virgin birth: Isaiah 7:14 reads, *"The Lord Himself will give you a sign. Behold the virgin will be with child and will give birth to a son, and will call him Immanuel."* This is quoted by Matthew (1:22-23) who reminds us that "Immanuel" means "God with us," indicating that Jesus was God in the flesh.

Prophecy concerning His coming to Galilee, His being

the Light of the world, and His Sonship, and even His place as "the mighty God": were given by God to Isaiah. The prophet continues, *"In the past He* (God) *humbled the land of Zebulon, and the land of Naphtali, but in the future He will honor Galilee of the Gentiles by the way of the sea, along the Jordan. The people who walk in darkness have seen a great light, on those living in the land of the shadow of death, a light has dawned. . For to us a child is born* (Jesus), *to us a Son is given.* (God's only begotten Son). . *And He will be called Wonderful Counselor, the Mighty God, the Everlasting Father, the Prince of Peace. Of the increase of His government and peace there will be no end. He will reign on David's throne and over his kingdom, establishing and upholding it with justice and righteousness from that time on and forever. The zeal of the Lord Almighty will accomplish this"* (Isaiah 9:1-7).

Jesus came as a child and as the Son of God. In the future after His second coming He will rule the entire earth as a son of David, as a Jew and not an Arab—a son of Isaac, not Ishmael. God had made a covenant with David that his throne would last forever. This is why the Muslims will never defeat all the Jews because a remnant must remain when eternity is ushered in. God does not break His promises. All of Heaven declares that He, Jesus, is the *"only man worthy to receive honor, and glory, dominion and power." "Worthy is the lamb who was slain, to receive power and wealth and wisdom and strength, and honor and glory and praise"* (Philippians 2:5-11; Revelation 4:11, 5:12).

Prophecy concerning the crucifixion: One prophecy is found in Psalm 22 where the Psalmist pictures the crowd around one whose hands and feet have been pierced, all his bones are out of joint, his heart has turned to wax, and melted away within him (Doctors say that this is what would produce the blood and water which came from His side when it was pierced.) They divided his garments and cast lots for his clothing, etc., etc. Read the Psalm for yourself.

The fullest prophecy is found in Isaiah 53—*"He was pierced for our transgressions, he was crushed* (or bruised) *for our iniquities. . . by His wounds we are healed. All we like sheep have gone astray, we have turned everyone to his own way, but God has laid on Him* (Jesus) *the iniquity of us all."* Read the whole chapter. It is a perfect picture of all that Jesus did, written over 700 years before He lived and died and was resurrected for our salvation.

There are scores of other prophecies. Read the Gospel of Matthew. He quotes many of these prophecies in the text of his biography of Jesus, because he was writing to the Jews and wanted them to see Jesus as their Messiah predicted in the Old Testament Scriptures.

III

You wrote in your letter "Christianity's foundation lies on sin, "For all have sinned." Here, Hamid, you have realized one of the major theological differences between Islam and Christianity. The Bible teaches that man is a sinner and that he is born into sin. His nature is sinful and he cannot help himself. He can never be good enough no matter how hard he tries. This is why he cannot work for his salvation or ever be good enough to go to Paradise. If his works were to be weighed at the judgment, the evil works would always outweigh the good works. Man can never be righteous enough to go to Paradise. The Bible says that he is *"born in sin." "In sin did my mother conceive me."* (King David's lament in Psalm 51:5) and *"The heart is deceitful above all things and desperately wicked. Who can understand this?"* (Jeremiah 17:9 and read in particular Romans chapter 3.)

Islam does not teach that man is a sinner, only that man is weak and he sins; but if he really tries, he can be good and Allah will reward him with Paradise if his good works outweigh his bad works on Allah's scales at the judgment. This never works out in practice. Ask yourself honestly. Have you, Hamid, done more good works, had more good thoughts, and been a good person, more than you have done wrong works, had wrong thoughts and been an unrighteous person? I think I know your answer! No man, if he is honest can say that he is worthy of going to Paradise. Even Muhammad, as good a man as people said he was, did not claim that he was sure that Allah would reward him with Paradise.

There is no room or time to explain this all to you so I am enclosing a section of my writings on *"Islam, A Works Religion."* (To the Reader: Note this in Chapter 6.   Islam and Christianity) The Bible says that we are saved, *"By grace through faith and not by ourselves, it is the gift of God, not of works lest any man should boast. For we are His workmanship created in Christ Jesus in order that we might do good works"* (Ephesians 2:8-9).

The good works are not in order to gain salvation but God gives us the strength to do good works after we have His life in us. Also, *"Not by works of righteousness which we have done, but according to His mercy, He saved us"* (Titus 3:5). This is why Jesus came and died, as was prophesied in Isaiah 53, for example, so that our sins might be forgiven and that we might live righteous lives for him. And as long as we continue to *"walk in the light as He is in the light, the blood of His Son Jesus Christ keeps on cleansing us from all sin"* (I John 1:7). This is what brings peace, and love and goodness into a real Christian's life. *"The fruit of the Spirit is love, joy, peace, longsuffering, gentleness, goodness, faithfulness, meekness, and self-control"* (Galatians 5:22-23).

I should mention here that all who call themselves Christians are not true Christians, but only those who have been born again and have God's life in them. America is a very wicked nation. I am ashamed of the liberals and the leftists and the libertines in our country. We are definitely not a Christian country, but there are many Christians who live in America. Fortunately we have in George W. Bush a President who is a genuine, born again Christian who meets with God in prayer and study of the Word of God every day. He will make mistakes, but God is with him.

This is true in Muslim nations also. All who live in these nations are not good Muslims. Saddam Hussein is one extreme example. He and his sons, e.g., imported many cases of hard liquor into Iraq—the Jack Daniels brand to be exact. His sons Uday and Qusay had hundreds of pornographic videos and were guilty of many adulteries and extremely carnal and wicked behavior. Together all three of them were guilty of hundreds of thousands of murders and the torture of many thousands. Also thousands of Iraqis of the notorious Baath political party, which Saddam modeled after the Nazis, were just as evil.

No one in history who claimed to be a good Christian, as Saddam claimed to be a good Sunni Muslim, however, has ever acted as these Muslims. You may cite Hitler, but he was far from a Christian and had rejected his Catholicism and accepted teachings of the occult. He was a precursor of Antichrist and wanted to set himself up as the one to be worshiped in Germany. Today Hitler is a hero to the Jew-haters in the Middle East.

IV

You wonder if Jesus had not died on the cross if there could be an atonement. If Jesus did not die on the cross and was not resurrected from the dead, all our faith and belief is vain. The death of Jesus on the cross as a sacrifice for the sins of all mankind is the very central doctrine of the Christian faith and the second is as necessary; namely, His resurrection from the dead which proved He was the Son of God and the Savior. As the Apostle Paul teaches, that if these are not true, *"We are still in our sins. . ."* This victory that Jesus won over sin and death is the very meaning of the word Gospel or "good news."

The Apostle defines the Gospel as the message of the death, burial and resurrection of Jesus Christ for our sins in order that we might be born again and have the new life of God within us, which the Bible calls eternal life. Eternal life is not something we will get, but it is something we are given by God right now when we receive Christ as our Savior and our Lord. It is His own very life within us. *"Therefore if any man be in Christ, he is a new creation. Old things are passed away; behold all things are become new"* (2 Corinthians 5:17). Only those who are a part of this new creation are true Christians.

Please read how the Apostle Paul explains this in his letter to the Corinthian church—I Corinthians chapter 15. *"If Christ has not been raised, your faith is futile, you are still in your sins."* Note Paul's definition of "the Gospel" in verses 1 through 7.

The Qur'an has much to say about the Gospel, but does not seem to know what the word Gospel means. The Gospel is the message of salvation that is in Jesus because of His death, burial and resurrection for us. It is pictured in baptism, which means "immersion" not sprinkling or pouring, in the Greek language. Baptism is a picture of having died and then being buried and then being raised up again "to a new life." The Qur'an speaks blithely about the Gospel, but denies what the Gospel teaches. This does not make any sense.

Jesus said that He was baptized, "To fulfill all righteousness." It was, first of all, an example for his disciples to follow. Principally, however, it was a prophecy of what was going to happen to Him in order for Him to be the Savior of the world—His death, burial and resurrection. God the Father was pleased with this. Remember what happened at His baptism. Matthew describes it. *"As soon as Jesus was baptized, he went up out of the water. At that moment heaven was opened, and he saw the Spirit of God descending like a dove and lighting on him. And a voice from heaven said, "This is my Son, whom I love; with him I am well pleased"'* (Matthew 3:16-17).

V

You ask me to show you from the Gospels how Jesus is my Savior and did He save anyone while he was on Earth. You quote the meaning of his name, *"You shall call his name Jesus* (which means "Jehovah our salvation") *for He shall save*

His people from their sins" (Matthew 1:21). The Qur'an makes reference to Jesus at least 97 times. Does it accept the meaning of his name "Jehovah our salvation?" How can Jehovah be our salvation, as Jesus' name proclaims, and Allah be our Lord, or Rabb, at the same time?

The Bible teaches that He—Jesus and Jehovah—is the only One worthy to receive honor, and glory, and praise. Allah is a usurper of this honor. Remember Satan is an angel of light. He is not the fire-breathing dragon as he is often pictured. After all, God created him, and he has a multitude of wonderful qualities, which he will seek to pass on to "his children."

Satan's main sin is trying to set himself up as God, as a rival to the true Creator of the universe, which the Bible names as Yahweh (meaning "I am that I am"). He is more often simply called "The God of Abraham, Isaac, and Jacob." God himself said that it was by this name He would be known to the world. (Read Exodus 3 about the burning bush and Yahweh's appearance to Moses.) The Qur'an, of course, gives us no record of this.

Jesus came to offer salvation to his own people the sons of Israel. He was first of all sent to the House of Israel, but as we have seen this call expanded to the whole Gentile world, and Jesus sent His disciples out to offer this salvation, which was to be found in his life, death, and resurrection, to all men everywhere. This is the Gospel or the "good news."

Many Jews did accept Jesus and God's salvation through Him. Many rejected him, but those like Simon Peter said, "*Lord, to whom shall we go? You have the words of eternal life. We believe and know that you are the Holy One of God*" (John 6:68).

All of Jesus' disciples were Jews. The Apostle Paul was a Jew of the tribe of Benjamin born in Tarsus, where he was also a Roman citizen. Jews wrote the entire Bible including the entire New Testament. They recorded the words with which God inspired them. The Jews are called in Scripture, the custodians of the oracles of God (Romans 3:2). Jesus Himself said that salvation came to the world through the

Jews (John 4:22). All of Islam hates this very idea. So how can Islam be a revelation from the true God? This is why the Jews have been the object of so much hatred motivated by Satan. Satan wants to destroy them just like he tried to destroy Jesus. The principal means Satan is using today to destroy the Jews is Islam. In years past he tried to use Hitler, Stalin, and many others all of whom were obviously Satan's tools— Satan's people, the "devil's children." So now he is using Muslims. Whose children therefore are they?

Even the Catholic Church on occasion tried to destroy the Jews because they believe and teach that the Catholic Church has replaced the Jews. This is similar to the teaching of Islam, which believes that God has now chosen Ishmael over Isaac. This is called "replacement theology." Much of the Catholic Church today, especially in the hierarchy, however, is not truly Christian. The bureaucracy is a human creation. It is idolatrous and can be evil. There are children of God in the Roman Catholic Church, but there are also many of the "devil's children" who have found a home there.

The Bible is clear that they who practice immorality do not belong to God. I think that God will use Islam to destroy the Catholic Church and its idolatry throughout Europe. Thank God, there has been an opening among the Catholic people today especially in North and South America where through the a movement of the Holy Spirit, many Roman Catholics are finding Jesus as their personal Savior. Much of the organized church and hierarchy, however, is apostate, and someday God will destroy it.

You say that Jehovah has many sons, and this is true. This is why God is called over and over again in the Bible, our *Ab* or Father. Allah is never called *Ab*. All who receive Jesus are called "sons or children of God." This is because, through the born again experience, (Read John 3, especially Jesus' words in 3:16.) we are given Jesus' resurrection life inside of us. It is a new spirit called the "new creation" (2 Corinthians 5:17). In reality it is a part of God. It is God's very own nature. This is why we are commanded to be "godly," which means godlike or like God, in our thoughts and actions.

If we follow the commands of Jesus, and imitate Him, we will be learning to be godly here on Earth. But this process will continue throughout eternity, and God's children will take the place of Satan and all his cohorts—many millions of those we call demons—or principalities, powers, thrones and dominions. We will rule in their place with Jesus in the universe as God's representatives. We will be given new bodies to go with our new life or spirit, which will be like the body Jesus had after the resurrection when He appeared to His disciples so many times. (Read I Corinthians 15 about these many appearance—proofs of His resurrection.)

You too, Hamid, can have this life in you, if you are willing to tell God in prayer that you want to receive Jesus as your own personal Savior and Lord. The Bible says, *"That if you will confess Jesus as Lord, and believe in your heart God has raised Him from the dead, you shall be saved"* (Romans 10:9). Also John's Gospel says, *"He Jesus came unto his own* (creation), *and his own* (people—the Jews) *received Him not. But to as many as received him God gives the right to become children of God, who are born not of blood, nor of the will of man, but of God"* (John 1:11-13).

You too, Hamid, can be born of God. Just put it to the test. Pray and ask the true God with sincerity to show you the truth of the Gospel. I guarantee that scales will drop from your eyes and you will understand things by the Holy Spirit's power that you never understood before. It will be a long journey, but it begins and ends with eternal life.

One final word about the Bible: You seem to think that there are many Bibles that differ from each other in important beliefs. This is not true. Just as there is one Qur'an written in Arabic and many translations, which are a little different because no languages are entirely equivalent—so there is one Bible written in Hebrew in the Old Testament and Koine Greek in the New Testament, but there are many translations. Since languages do not have exactly equivalent words or phrases it is helpful to have several translations and check them against each other if we do not know the original Arabic, Hebrew or Greek. I have three translations of the Qur'an in English and many translations of the Bible in English. But I can also research the original languages to see which translation seems to be the most accurate. For the Bible in English I usually use the New International Version or the New American Standard. My three translations of the Qur'an include one by a Pakistani scholar Ahmed Ali, another by an Iraqi professor N. J. Dawood, and the third by a British scholar and student of Islam George Sale.

Sincerely,

Rev. James M. Murk Ph.D.

Some of Hamid's Objections and Claims Trying to Show the Superiority of Muhammmad over Jesus, and Islam over Christianity

1. Jesus was a prophet sent only to the lost sheep of the House of Israel, but Muhammad was the first prophet sent to the whole world.

2. Jesus never forgave anybody, but Muhammad was forgiving to his adversaries.

3. There are no prophecies about Jesus in the Old Testament. The prophecies that are there, such as Isaiah 9, are about Muhammad.

4. The foundation of Christianity is sin. The Bible says, "All have sinned" and teaches that men are born in sin.

5. How could Jesus save anyone when he cried asking God why He had forsaken him? Obviously Jesus was a sinner.

6. There are many Bibles, which contradict each other.

You may note my answers in this second letter and also my final appeal for Hamid to receive Jesus and at least seek God in prayer and ask Him to reveal the truth of the Gospel.

APPENDIX THREE

Signs of the "end of the age" or the "last days"

We have found that the Apostle John in his first letter (I John) prophesied that many antichrists would arise in the "last hour." He did not just say in the "last days," which may be a considerable period of time, but he specified "in the last hour," which presumably is at the very end of the period called "the last days."

Islam is the most powerful and pervasive system of antichrist that has ever existed. Muhammad and the Qur'an are very dogmatic that the creator god Allah does not, nor could he ever, have a son. Anyone therefore who believes that Jesus is the Son of God is an infidel and in grave danger of hellfire. The Apostle John, on the other hand, states boldly that any "spirit" that denies that Jesus is the Anointed One of God and God's Son is a deceiver and a liar. There is no compromise or middle ground here at all. I believe that the resurgence of the antichrist system of Islam at this very time is another of the many signs recorded by the Spirit of God in the Scriptures that we are on the brink of the "end of the age." (For other "signs" see especially Jesus' Olivet Discourse in Matthew 24, Mark 13, and Luke 21.)

Ishmael was the first son of Abraham and, without the miraculous birth of Isaac to Sarah in her old age, he would have stood to inherit his father's goods as well as the promise which God had given to Abraham that he would give to him the land, which we now call Palestine and more; namely, the Promised Land.

It seems that to this day, Ishmael has not given up his claim to the land promised to his father Abraham. The patriarchal record, the Taurat (Torah), or part of what Muhammad identified as the "earlier revelation" of Allah, states that the promise given to Abraham was handed down to his son and grandson— Isaac and Jacob, also called Israel (Prince with God). The descendants of Ishmael, however, claim that same promise and

239

the inheritance of Abraham for themselves. They are joined by other descendants of Abraham; namely, Abraham's grandson Esau (Edom), his other sons by Keturah, and the sons of Lot, his extended family. These include the Edomites, Midianites, Ammonites and Moabites. It is amazing that we are coming down to the wire in human history, and the physical and spiritual sons of Abraham are at this moment taking center stage in world events. We will look into all the details of this in our second book, Part 2 of *Islam Rising*.

Muhammad declared that Allah had inspired and sent six Major Prophets. They were Adam, Noah, Abraham, Moses, Jesus, and Muhammad. Then at the end of the age Allah would send a seventh and final prophet called Al Mahdi. All of these prophets are regarded by Islam as Muslims, or those who are in submission to Allah as the one true god.

Islam teaches that Abraham received the promises of Allah and started everything. Through Moses the Taurat was revealed with Allah's commands. The Qur'an teaches that Jesus came to confirm the Torah and reveal the Gospel. (We have noted that neither the Qur'an nor Allah, however, seem to know the Biblical definition of the Gospel.) Muslims say that the prophet Jesus was sent only to the "lost sheep of the house of Israel." He was not a prophet for the entire world. This was the role of Muhammad who restored everything that had been lost or corrupted and declared the truth of the ancient monotheism to the whole world. Just as the Qur'an supercedes all earlier revelations, Muhammad is the most important prophet among all who preceded him.

The seventh prophet—Al Mahdi or "the guided one"--will be revealed at the "end of the age." He will teach the world and establish the justice of Allah on the Earth. An important question here might be asked, "Who is the one guiding Al Mahdi?" Here are some words of Muhammad from the Hadith concerning this seventh prophet:

> *"The Mahdi will be of my family, of the descendants of Fatimah .*
> *. . He will   have a broad forehead, a prominent nose. He will fill*
> *the earth with equity and justice as it was filled with oppression*

and tyranny, and he will rule for seven years" (The Sahih [hadith collection] of Abu Dawud)

It is believed from Muhammad's teachings that the Mahdi will rule the Arab world from Damascus, Syria as the Caliph or representative of Muhammad for seven years. He is to defeat the "Romans" in the last days, which would include today at least the Europeans if not also the Americans, and be very powerful in the world. Muhammad continued:

> *"Listen to the good news about the Mahdi. He will rise at the time when people will be faced with severe conflict and the earth will be hit by a violent earthquake. He will fill the earth with justice and equity as it is now filled with injustice a tyranny. He will fill the hearts of his followers with devotion and will spread justice everywhere. The world will not come to an end until a man from the descendants of Husayn* (Muhammad's grandson) *takes charge of the affairs of the world."* (Collection of Biha al-Anwar)

Who do you suppose is the candidate put forward today as the fulfillment of this prophecy? Millions of Muslims have come to believe that Osama bin Laden is Al Mahdi. Here are several signs or confirmations, which are alleged by Islamic teachers, specifically Wahhabi clerics in Saudi Arabia.

In the 1890's it was prophesied by Islamic teachers that the next time that there were eclipses of both the moon and the sun during the month of Ramadan in Muslim lands, Al Mahdi would be revealed. Eclipses happened this year of 2005 on October 2 and October 17, which was within the period of the lunar month of Ramadan. Al Mahdi would be a direct descendant of the prophet Muhammad in the line of his daughter Fatima and her son Husayn. He would be tall, with a high forehead, a prominent nose, a long pointed beard like Muhammad's, and a mole on his face designating his prophetic office. He would also come out of a cave where he had been living. Osama bin Laden is said to fulfill all these requirements. There would also be a major earthquake just before the Mahdi is revealed. (There was just a 7.7 earthquake near the region where Osama is supposedly hiding.)

Osama may have accepted this role because he now signs his name Osama bin Muhammad bin Laden indicating that he is Muhammad's direct descendant, which is a requirement for the Mahdi. We know that 95% of the men of Saudi Arabia, including a number of Saudi clerics, and a great majority of Muslims all over the world are sympathetic with Osama's purposes, pronouncements, and directives. More and more are believing that Osama may very well be the promised seventh prophet. Since there have been many false Messiahs and false Mahdis in history, however, this hope of Saudi clerics is very tentative.

Who is Al Mahdi as far as the Bible is concerned? Prophecies specify that there will be a false prophet and the Antichrist—two cooperating leaders at the end of the age.

The false prophet seems to be a forerunner of Antichrist as John the Baptist was the forerunner to Christ's ministry. The false prophet therefore identifies the Antichrist and assures his authenticity before the world. Does Osama bin Laden have any role to play here? It is possible, but unlikely. Many Saudi clerics are favoring him to be the Mahdi because he fits so many of the qualifications for this seventh prophet. There have, however, been many false Mahdi's in the past just as there have been false Messiahs. Muhammad's words seem to indicate that Al Mahdi will be a ruler of all the Arabs for seven years and will defeat other nations. In this scenario the seventh prophet sounds more like the Antichrist. All of this may be only meaningless conjecture, but maybe we will know more by the time our sequel, *Islam Rising: Part II: The Never Ending Jihad Against the Jews and Israel*, is released.

A SELECTED BIBLIOGRAPHY

Abdul-Haqq, A. Akbar. *Sharing Your Faith with a Muslim.* Minneapolis: Bethany Fellowship, Inc., 1980

Ankerberg, John and John Weldon. *The Facts on Islam: Answers to the Most Frequently Asked Questions.* Eugene, Oregon: Harvest House Publishers, 1991 (Revised 1998)

Armstrong, Karen. *Islam: A Short History.* New York: The Modern Library, 2000 (An apologetic for Islam)

Blankley, Tony. *The West's Last Chance: Will we win the Clash of Civilizations?* Washington DC: Regnery Publishing Inc., 2005

Braswell, George W. Jr. *Islam, Its Prophet, Peoples, Politics, and Power.* Nashville: Broadman and Holman, 1996

Campbell, Dr. William. *The Qur'an and the Bible in the Light of History and Science.* Upper Darby, Pennsylvania: Arab World Ministries—Middle East Resources, 1986

Caner, Ergun Mehmet and Emir Fethi. *Unveiling Islam: An Insider's Look at Muslim Life and Beliefs.* Grand Rapids, MI: Kregel Publications, 2002

Esposito, John L. *What Everyone Needs to Know About Islam.* New York: Oxford University Press, 2002 (An apologetic for Islam)

Fallaci, Oriana. *The Rage and the Pride.* New York: Rizzoli International Publications, 2001

Fregosi, Paul. *Jihad in the West: Muslim Conquests from the 7th to the 21st Centuries.* Amherst, NJ: Prometheus Books, 1998

Fromkin, David. *A Peace to End All Peace—The Fall of the Ottoman Empire and the Creation of the Modern Middle East.* New York: Avon Books, 1989

Geisler, Norman L. and Abdul Saleeb. *Answering Islam: The Crescent in the Light of the Cross.* Grand Rapids, MI: Baker Books, 1993

Gibb, Kramers, Levi-Provencal, and Schact, (eds). *The Encyclopedia of Islam.* London: Luzac, 1960

Gilchrist, John. *Facing the Muslim Challenge: A Handbook of Christian-Muslim Apologetics.* Capetown, South Africa: Life Challenge Africa, 1999

Grant, George. *The Blood of the Moon.* Nashville: Thomas Nelson and Sons, 2001

Hahn, Ernest. *Jesus in Islam*. Hyderabad, India: Henry Martyn
    Institute, 1987

Haddad, Yvonne and Wadi Z. Haddad. *Christian-Muslim
    Encounters*. Gainesville: University Press of Florida, 1995

Hadith by Sahih al Bokhari…

www.usc.edu/dept/MSA/fundamentals/hadithsunnah/bukhari

Hitti, Phillip K. *Islam: A Way of Life*. Chicago: Henry Regnery
    Co., 1970

Holt, P.M., Anne Lambton and Bernard Lewis, (eds). *The
    Cambridge History of Islam*. NY: Cambridge University
    Press, 1970

Huntington, Samuel P. *The Clash of Civilizations and the
    Remaking of World Order*. NY: Touchstone Press, 1997

Hourani, Albert. *A History of the Arab Peoples*. New York:
    Warner Books, 1991

Latourette, Kenneth Scott. *A History of Christianity*. NY:
    Harper and Row, 1953, 1975

Lippman, Thomas. *Understanding Islam: An Introduction to the
    Moslem World*. NY: Mentor Books, 1982

Maqsood, Ruqaiyyah. *Islam*. Lincolnwood, IL:
    NTC/Contemporary Publishing (Teach Yourself Books),
    1994. (A detailed apologetic type presentation of Islam,
    simple and in great detail.)

McCurry, Don. *Healing the Broken Family of Abraham: A New
    Life for Muslims*. Colorado Springs: Don McCurry,
    Ministries to Muslims, 2001

Miller, William M. *A Christian Response to Islam*. Phillipsburg,
    NJ, 1980

Morey, Robert A. *The Islamic Invasion: Confronting the World's
    Fastest Growing Religion*. Las Vegas, NV: Christian Scholars
    Press, 1992

Nazir-Ali, Michael. *Islam: A Christian Perspective*. Philadelphia:
    Westminster Press, 1983

Oussani, Gabriel and Hillaire Belloc. *Moslems: Their Beliefs,
    Practices, and Politics*. Ridgefield, CT: Roger A McCaffrey
    Publishing, n.d. (Reprints from 1907 and 1936)

Pryce-Jones, David. *The Closed Circle: An Interpretation of the
    Arabs*. London: Paladin, 1990

Rutz, James H. *Megashift: Igniting Spiritual Power*. Colorado

Springs: Empowerment Press, 2005

Qutb, Sayyid. *Milestones*. Boll Ridge, IN: American Trust Publications, 1988.

Safa, Reza. *Inside Islam*. Orlando, FL: Creation House, 1996

Schaff, Philip. *History of the Christian Church—Vol. II: Ante-Nicene Christianity and Vol. IV: Mediaeval Christianity*. Grand Rapids, MI: Wm. B. Eerdmans Publishing Company, 1950-52 (Reprints)

Schmidt, Alvin J. *The Great Divide: The Failure of Islam and the Triumph of the West*. Boston: Regina Orthodox Press, 2004

Spencer. Robert. *Islam Unveiled*. San Francisco: Encounter Books, 2002

_____ *Onward Muslim Soldiers: How Jihad Still Threatens America and the West*. Washington D.C., Henry Regnery, 2003

_____ (ed.) *The Myth of Islamic Tolerance: How Islamic Law Treats Non-Muslims*. Amherst, NY: Prometheus Books, 2005

_____ The *Politically Incorrect Guide to Islam and the Crusades*. Washington D.C.: Regnery Publishing Inc., 2005

Trifkovic, Serge. *The Sword of the Prophet*. Boston: Regina Orthodox Press, 2002

Warraq, Ibn. *Why I am Not a Muslim*. Amherst: NY: Prometheus Books, 2005

Watt, W. Montgomery. *Islam and Christianity Today*. London: Routledge and Kegan Paul, 1983

_____ *Muhammad: Prophet and Statesman*. Oxford: Oxford University Press, 1974

Ye'or, Bat. *Eurabia: The Euro-Arab Axis*. Madison, NJ: Fairleigh Dickinson University Press, 2005

_____ *Islam and Dhimmitude: Where Civilizations Collide*. Translated from the French by Kochan and Littman. Madison, NJ: Fairleigh Dickinson University Press, 2002

_____ *The Decline of Eastern Christianity Under Islam*. London: Associated University Presses, 1996

Zacharias, Ravi. *Light in the Shadow of Jihad—The Struggle For Truth*. Sisters, OR: Multnomah Publishers Inc., 2002

Zwemer, Samuel M. *Islam: A Challenge to Faith*. London: Darf,

1985 (reprint)

_____ *The Moslem Doctrine of God.* NY: American Tract Society, 1905

Some Translations of the Qur'an (Koran):

Ali, Ahmed. *Al-Qur'an—a Contemporary Translation.* Princeton, NJ: Princeton University Press, 1986. (Originally published in Karachi, Pakistan in 1984 by Akrash Publishing) (This translation has the Arabic as an interlinear with the English.)

Dawood, N.J. *The Koran: Translated with Notes.* London, England: Penguin Books, 1956 (This is the most readable translation and has a very helpful index.)

Sale, George. *The Koran: Commonly Called the Alcoran of Mohammed.* Fifth Edition. Philadelphia: J.B. Lippincott & Company, 1870 (This translation has extensive commentary and notes but is harder to use because the text is not divided into verses.)

INDEX

ABOUT THE AUTHOR

Dr. Jim Murk was trained as an academician. He was a senior in high school at age 15, and by the age of 19 he entered graduate school at the University of Chicago by examination where he earned a Master's degree in the history of the Middle Ages, Renaissance, and Reformation. After two years in Bible College and Seminary, he earned another Master's degree from the University of Minnesota in Cultural Anthropology as a missions project, and another Master's in Theology from Bob Jones University where he was also chairman of the history department. His Ph.D. from Louisiana Baptist University bridges all of his major fields of study.

He also taught linguistics for the Wycliffe Bible Translators' Summer Institute of Linguistics, served briefly in Mexico, and then joined the staff of the Navigators. He and his wife Donna opened the Navigator home and ministered with the Missionary Internship Training Program in the Chicago area. He was next invited on the faculty at Wheaton College where he taught for 8 years and was briefly the chairman of the Anthropology Department.

He received a Danforth Teachers Grant and was candidate for the Ph.D. at the University of Chicago.

While teaching Dr. Murk won the national championship of the *Ted Mack Original Amateur Hour* on CBSTV in 1963 as a lyric tenor, which opened a call to a national and international ministry in music evangelism, preaching and teaching. He felt called out of the academic world and has been pursuing this public ministry with his wife and family members for 40 years having over 6,000 meetings in all 50 states and 25 foreign mission fields.

Dr. Murk had studied Islam at the University of Minnesota Graduate School of Anthropology and developed a course called The Islamic Culture Sphere for the Summer Institute of Missions and anthropology majors at Wheaton

College. Now since the recent resurgence of a militant Islam in the world, he has been conducting seminars around the country on "What Christians Need to Know About Islam!" This book is Part One of a two-part publication. Part Two, soon to be released, is called *Islam Rising: The Never Ending Jihad Against Jews and Israel.* This study will also cover Islam in America and Islam in Biblical prophecy.

Dr. Murk and his wife Donna are the parents of five children, all of whom are serving the Lord. They have 15 grandchildren, all being brought up as the Scriptures command "in the nurture and admonition of the Lord," many of whom are serving with their parents in ministry in many parts of the world.

Contact:

Jim Murk,
Murk Family Ministries, Inc.
P.O. Box 341
Chippewa Falls, WI 54729